JUVENILE CRIMES AGAINST THE ELDERLY

JUVENILE CRIMES AGAINST THE ELDERLY

By

FRANK P. MORELLO

Professor
Department of Political Science
Winona State University
Winona, Minnesota

CHARLES   C   THOMAS   •   PUBLISHER
Springfield   •   Illinois   •   U.S.A.

Published and Distributed Throughout the World by

CHARLES C THOMAS • PUBLISHER
2600 South First Street
Springfield, Illinois, 62717, U.S.A.

With THOMAS BOOKS *careful attention is given to all details of manufacturing and
design. It is the Publisher's desire to present books that are satisfactory as to their physical
qualities and artistic possibilities and appropriate for their particular use.* THOMAS
BOOKS *will be true to those laws of quality that assure a good name and good will.*

Printed in the United States of America
CU-RX-1

Library of Congress Cataloging in Publication Data

Morello, Frank P.
  Juvenile crimes against the elderly.

  Bibliography: p.
  Includes index.
  1. Aged--Crimes against.   2. Juvenile delinquency.
I. Title.
HV6250.4.A34M67   363.2'3   81-21267
ISBN 0-398-04658-1   AACR2

To my wife Connie.
To my mother Rosalie.

To Mary Gross, the victim of a brutal and senseless crime.

PREFACE

MY first contact with the subject of crimes against the elderly occurred when I was a youngster of eleven or twelve years of age. During these early years, I lived with my parents about a mile or so from Brooklyn's Prospect Park. My brother, my two cousins, and I spent many summer days playing in the meadows and streams of this park. Here, also, I witnessed assaults against the elderly, although such incidents were infrequent occurrences. The policemen who were on foot patrol in the park were always on the alert for groups of young toughs and would chase them out of the picnic grounds and the meadows area.

In recalling such incidents, I remember that most assaults were confined either to purse snatching or to the stealing of a picnic lunch. Most of the time the offenders would work in pairs. One boy would distract the victim's attention while the other would snatch her purse. Sometimes they would work in groups of four or more members. They would "play" near their selected victim's picnic table, then, quite suddenly, one would be off with a picnic basket.

Today, the tactics have changed. The offender now waits for his victim to come out of a bank or some other place of business. He then follows his victim, usually a woman, to her apartment building and assaults her either in the vestibule or in the lobby. Other offenders will follow the victim into her apartment. These are called the "push-in" robbers. In most instances, the victim is tied to a chair. Many are beaten, and some die as a result of the beatings. In other words, the offender has moved off the street and into the building. He can commit his crime at his leisure and with little chance of being observed or being apprehended during the commission of the act.

The treatment of crimes against the elderly has been largely ignored by most authors of criminal justice texts. In an effort to correct this apparent deficiency in the availability of data on the subject, I decided to write this book to provide an in-depth treatment of juvenile crimes against the elderly. Although the central theme of the book will focus on the plight of the elderly in the areas of racial transition, one chapter will include a study of the typical youthful offender who frequents the city's high-crime areas. In addition, the book will include a chapter on the use of hypnosis as an investigative tool.

F.P.M.

ACKNOWLEDGMENTS

THIS book would not have been possible without the cooperation and support of the New York City Police Department, my family, and my associates. My cousin, Rosemary Carbonaro, whose work as a police decoy inspired this study, provided the basic data on decoy deployments and tactics. Milton Schwartz, assistant chief inspector, who as commanding officer of Patrol Borough Brooklyn South approved the project. Chief Schwartz also allowed me to accompany decoy teams on field operations. Lieutenant Raymond Coles, Sergeant Timothy Byrnes, and Sergeant Richard Fitzpatrick were constant sources of information and expert advice on administrative procedures and regulations, unit operations, and high-crime area strategies. Unit field personnel gave me the support and freedom necessary to observe criminal activities in high-crime areas and the effectiveness of police countermeasures.

The draft was edited for publication by Margaret Boddy, Professor Emeritus, Winona State University. Dr. Boddy provided valuable inputs and made a number of suggestions and criticisms that improved the form of the book. My secretary, Susan Phillips, did all the typing with her usual skill and self-confidence.

My mother, Rosalie, and my brother, Carl, with whom I lived during the study, and my sister, Angie Fisher, had the patience to put up with me and to suffer my moods during the summer of 1979. They know how greatly I appreciated their patience and support.

I am grateful to my sister-in-law, Catherine, and her husband, Joseph Celentano, and to my sister-in-law, Mary Saco, for their kindness to my wife, Connie, during my absence.

I thank my daughter, Cecelia, and her husband, Paul, my son, Peter, and his wife, Lone, and my daughter, Lucille, for putting up with me once again.

Finally, my appreciation to my wife, Connie, whose understanding, patience, and support has enabled me to continue and complete this book.

CONTENTS

JUVENILE CRIMES AGAINST THE ELDERLY

CHAPTER 1

PROLEGOMENON TO THE STUDY OF CRIMES AGAINST THE ELDERLY

T HE criminal justice system is a vast and complex institution intended to perform many social functions including, among others, the maintenance of public order, education, control of criminal behavior, punishment for the commission of crimes, restitution, rehabilitation, and the protection of the rights of both the victim and the offender.

Members of the law enforcement community, in particular, the police, the prosecutors, the courts, and the correctional authorities, are in a seemingly never-ending and increasingly difficult battle of controlling deviant social behavior. In its efforts to understand better and to cope with the many social problems that confront people in their everyday lives, the law enforcement community has closely coordinated its activities with a number of support groups including the legal profession, criminologists, psychologists, social welfare agencies, and the academic community.

The coordination of efforts between the law enforcement community and these various support groups has resulted in many studies, theories, and models on the causes of crimes, on deviant behavior, and on the effects of restitution, rehabilitation, and diversion, among others. Although most studies have contributed to a somewhat better understanding of deviant social behavior, none has provided a completely satisfactory framework for its control. The disturbing facts are that in areas where order has broken down (for example, during the recent riots in Miami) it is the criminal who is in control of the situation and not the police.

The police, because of pressure from community groups and the liberal elements in society, are restricted in their efforts to assume control of the situation and to take effective measures to prevent further deviant criminal behavior. Compounding the problem for the police and, and one might add, as well as for the community is the liberal attitude of the courts in the processing of criminals. More often than not, the criminal is returned to the streets in a matter of weeks; sometimes in a matter of days. This is particularly true of the juvenile felon who is diverted from entry into the juvenile justice system. Diversion has been described by Professor Robert Carter and Professor Malcolm Klein as: "a process which minimizes penetration of the offender into the criminal justice system or as an alternative to entry into the criminal justice system."[1]

The high incidence of juvenile crime has long been of major concern to the law enforcement community as well as to concerned members of the general public. Juvenile crimes have been committed against all segments of the community and have ranged from shoplifting and simple assault to robbery, aggravated assault, and murder. Of particular intensity and brutality, in recent years, have been crimes committed against the elderly, particularly against those too weak to ward off younger and much stronger assailants. The majority of crimes committed in the inner city no longer talk place on the streets or in the parks. The crimes now take place "off the streets," in vestibules or lobbies, in darkened hallways of buildings, or in the apartment of the victim. This sharp increase in off-street crimes has led New York City Police administrators to develop innovative procedures to combat the new menace to the elderly citizen. One of the many measures taken by police administrators has been the establishment of plainclothes street anti-crime units in four major boroughs of the city.

This study is centered on the problems of the elderly living in the South Brooklyn section of the borough of Brooklyn. For purposes of police jurisdiction, it is identified as Patrol Borough Brooklyn South (PBBS). The area containing close to a million people can be said to be a city within a city. It includes some of the finest residential neighborhoods in the city, as well as many parks and playgrounds, churches, public and private schools, movie theaters, hotels, an excellent library system, several colleges and law schools, a museum, a botanical garden, and a medical school. It also includes a large waterfront area for shipping, four beaches, the Coney Island recreational area, a marina with facilities for deep-sea fishing, a yacht basin, and one of the nation's oldest military bases, Fort Hamilton.

During the first half of the century the area was inhabited almost entirely by Caucasians of Scandinavian, German, Irish, Italian, and Jewish stock. Most neighborhoods were composed of people of the same stock. There was an economic separation, however, as the more affluent tended to live in the better neighborhoods. There were crimes, of course, but street crimes were a rarity, and when they did occur, they were committed mostly in the lower-income neighborhoods.

In later years, particularly during the early 1950s, the composition of some of the more affluent neighborhoods, for reasons which will be discussed subsequently, began to change. During these years, lower-income black and Hispanic families began to move into these once all white neighborhoods. In contrast, most of the lower- and middle-income white neighborhoods remained almost unchanged during the transitional years.

In the areas of racial transition many of the crimes against the elderly have been committed. It is in these areas that the author conducted the major portion of his studies during the summer of 1979. Many of the names of the victims and of the offenders have been changed in order that the rights of all the participants may be protected. The events reported in this book, however, and as related by the author, will be accurately described.

The facts reported in this book should not be construed as an indictment of any ethnic group involved in the study. It is a sad truism that had the study been conducted in Patrol Borough Brooklyn North, or in the borough of Queens, or in the borough of the Bronx, the names and ethnicity of the victims and of the offenders would be different, but the violence and the brutality of the crimes would remain the same.

THE CRIME AREA

The transformation of what were once peaceful residential areas with an extremely low incidence of street crime into the violent, crime-infested inner cities of today has been the subject of much study and discussion among students and observers of the criminal justice system. South Brooklyn is one of the many areas in medium and large cities throughout the nation undergoing racial transition. It is the subject of this study because its problem are typical of those that confront the citizens and police in similar areas.

The South Brooklyn area consists of a number of neighborhoods containing a mixture of medium and large apartment house complexes, three- to four-story brownstone multiple dwellings, and two-family and single-family residences. During the early part of the century, large numbers of residents from Manhattan's lower east side began to move across the East River to Brooklyn. The move continued into the 1930s. Many of the more affluent moved into the apartment house complexes.

The apartment house complexes, particularly the larger ones, were the latest in style and luxury, and it was a mark of wealth and status to reside there. The streets were lined with trees and were well kept. Many building complexes had elevators and doormen, and some had open courtyards that led to several entrances. The more elaborate had brick archways and footpaths leading to closed courtyards and were protected by special guards. Deliverymen, repairmen, cleaners, and the like were directed to rear entrances where they would be admitted by building superintendents who were always on duty. Peddlers, solicitors, and salesmen were turned away. The occupants of these dwellings lived in surroundings that afforded them a degree of security, privacy, and seclusion.

Most of the complexes were within walking distance of shopping areas, neighborhood grocery stores, delicatessens, synagogues, parks, community centers, and movie theaters.

The interiors of most of these structures reflected the old-world cultures and traditions and the newly achieved opulence of their occupants. Many of the buildings were divided into two wings, each requiring, in addition to the elevators, sets of stairways for the front and for the rear of the buildings. Many buildings had marble lobbies and stairways; others, particularly the larger ones, had large portraits or frescos adorning the walls, Oriental rugs, potted plants, and crystal chandeliers or other ornate lighting fixtures.

In later years, the very nature of these complex structures, with their front and rear entrances, elevators, dual stairways, fire escapes, and adjoining rooftops worked to the disadvantage of the elderly tenant and to the advantage of the youthful offender.

The scene has changed much since the early 1950s. The doormen are gone, as are the special guards. Building superintendents are no longer on duty at all times, and sometimes they are not to be found. Some of the buildings are still maintained in moderately clean and good condition, though many of the buildings are in disrepair. The rooftops are littered with rubbish. Empty beer cans and empty wine bottles are strewn over the entire area. Adolescents urinate in hallways and in elevators, and the stench remains even after the janitors have cleaned the buildings.

Anyone can enter a building from any of the entrances, day or night, prowl the halls, and sleep in basements or on rooftops, and no one would notice or even care. Drifters and wayward adolescents are a common sight in the area.

The change in these neighborhoods did not occur suddenly. During the early 1950s, the inevitable transformation of the composition of the family began. The children, now grown, went off to college or married. As a result, some of the occupants either moved to smaller apartments or left the area. As the original occupants moved out of the complexes more apartments became available. Because of the high rents and often because of restrictive covenants then in force, the landlords were unable to lease the increasing number of vacant apartments.

Changing economic conditions coupled with the Supreme Court's ban on restrictive covenants forced many landlords to lease the apartments to lower-income families. The subsequent influx of low-income families into the area resulted in an increased departure of its original residents. As has been the case in many areas of New York City, when the blacks or the Hispanics move in the whites move out.

During the early stages of transition the neighborhoods of the area remained relatively safe. The influx of minorities into the area was accompanied, however, by an increase in vandalism and other misdemeanors. Blacks and Hispanics, once considered outsiders, now blended in with the community. The fact that these youths now lived in the community made it difficult for the police to stop and question them as in the past. As a result, persons whom the police considered potential offenders were able to move about the neighborhood more freely.

With increasing frequency, juvenile and youthful offenders began to victimize the neighborhoods. The crimes they committed included but were not limited to vandalism, burglary, robbery, or assault and battery. For the obvious reason of age and the probable inability to resist, the elderly citizen was singled out by offenders as a prime target.

THE SENIOR CITIZEN IN THE INNER CITY

The elderly citizen in the crime area studied range in age from sixty-five to ninety-two, with the average age at approximately seventy-four years. About three quarters are female; many are widows. Most remained in the area after their spouse's death simply because the area was safe, and they were comfortable in their familiar surroundings. Some stayed after the area became dangerous to their personal safety because they had no other place to go. They either could not or would not live with their children. Others stayed because they refused to live in nursing homes. As one rather alert and independent eighty-three-year-old woman explained to the author: "As long as I have my mind and I can get around, I will go no place but here!"

The elderly are aware of the dangers on the streets and rarely leave their apartments during the evening hours without an escort. They do, however, go out during the daylight hours to the grocery or drugstore or to the bank in order to withdraw money. Often, after shopping, they may stop at a local coffee shop or dinette for a cup of coffee or for lunch. Most of these activities take place either prior to or shortly after the noon hour. Yet it is the daylight hours and not the evening hours that pose the greatest dangers to their safety.

In particular, it is the return walk to the apartment that is most dangerous to the senior citizen. In addition to the normal infirmities of age, many of the elderly are hampered by physical disabilities, sometimes severe. As a result, they are apt to walk slowly and with some difficulty; hence, they become easy prey for the much stronger and more agile youthful offender. As subsequent case studies will disclose, it does not matter whether the elderly victim takes precautions when on the street or when entering the building. The offender has his victim "marked" and will make his "hit" at the proper time. A study of crime statistics in this area has disclosed that he has been uncannily correct in timing more than 98 percent of his "hits."

The following incidents are typical of the dangers confronting the senior citizens in the crime area.

On Friday morning, June 3, 1979, Mrs. Clara Bader, a seventy-six-year-old widow, with impaired hearing, was sunning herself on her front lawn. At approximately 11:30 AM, Mrs. Bader went inside for a glass of water. While in the kitchen, she heard a noise in the rear of the house. She thought it came from her bedroom. Upon entering the bedroom, Mrs. Bader was confronted by a black male, approximately thirty years of age. The man seized an empty wine bottle that was sitting on a dresser, and, without saying a word, he hit Mrs. Bader on the head. Mrs. Bader was knocked unconscious. Upon recovering she called her tenant, who lived upstairs. The police were called, and a radio car responded. Mrs. Bader was taken to the hospital where she received six stitches and was then released.

The police found that some jewelry and an undetermined amount of money was stolen. On the same day that she was released from the hospital, Mrs. Bader left for Ohio to stay with her daughter for a few days.

On Tuesday, the author accompanied the senior citizen robbery unit (SCRU) investigators — Officers Salzano, Rainone, and Carbonaro — to Mrs. Bader's home in order to conduct an investigation of the crime.

Without Mrs. Bader's presence it was difficult to obtain much firsthand information of the incident.

Officer Salzano, the team leader, directed investigators Rainone and Carbonaro to conduct a search of the area in order to determine the direction the assailant came from and his point of entry into the home. In the meantime, the author accompanied Investigator Salzano on a house-to-house canvass of the area in an attempt to locate possible witnesses who could provide some clue to the identity of the assailant.

The house-to-house canvass proved fruitless. All of the neighbors questioned said they either were not at home or that they saw no suspicious persons in the area at the time of the attack. Investigators Rainone and Carbonaro were unable to uncover any evidence as to the direction of the assailant's route or his point of entry into the residence.

Investigators Salzano and Rainone spoke to Mrs. Bader and her tenant upon Mrs. Bader's return. Neither could supply additional information. The case remained open for six months. To this date, the assailant remains at large.

On Wednesday, June 6, 1979, the author accompanied investigators Herlihy and Carbonaro to a public housing project on

Nostrand Avenue in response to a citizen's complaint. The complainant, Mr. Irving Stein, is seventy-eight years old, blind in one eye, and partially deaf. Mr. Stein informed Investigators Herlihy and Carbonaro that he was assaulted at 10:15 AM, Thursday, May 31, 1979. At the time of the assault, Mr. Stein was in the basement laundry room of the building when he heard a noise in the room. He thought it was a handyman who works in the buildings. He called to the man, "Walter, is it you?" The assailant grabbed Mr. Stein from behind and said, "No, it isn't Walter!" Then he ordered Mr. Stein to fall to his knees and said, "Hand over your money." Mr. Stein gave him the money, seven dollars, and was not harmed. Mr. Stein, although he could not positively identify his assailant, was convinced that the man was an American black, well spoken and probably educated. The investigation is not being actively pursued, and the assailant is still at large.

An interesting sidelight in this case is that Mr. Stein is a rather tough and stubborn man. He informed Investigator Herlihy that he always carries a policeman's nightstick wrapped in black tape, which gives the appearance of an umbrella. He said that he intends to use it on anyone who attacks him. His "weapon" was not within reach at the time of the attack. Herlihy cautioned him to be very careful and not to use the stick. He said to Mr. Stein, "These kids are tough, and you could get yourself killed." Mr. Stein's reply was, "So what?"

In appreciation for its past services to the elderly, the senior citizen robbery unit was to receive an appreciation award from the Flatbush Inter-Agency For The Aging. The presentation was to take place on Tuesday, June 12, 1979, at the picnic grounds in Brooklyn's Prospect Park. In conjunction with the award ceremonies, the agency was to hold a picnic for a large group of elderly citizens.

On the morning of the award ceremonies the author was assigned to field activities with a unit decoy team. The team consisted of Officers William Lohse (director of the team), Eileen Thompson (decoy), Tom Meehan, Joe Dailey, and Jules Alper. The author accompanied Sergeant Richard Fitzpatrick to the park, and the team arrived at the picnic area at approximately 10:45 AM.

The director of the agency advised Sergeant Fitzpatrick that the award ceremonies would begin about noon. There were some 800 seniors in the area, and in the immediate area were approximately a dozen youths. Every so often, a pair or two would wander into the picnic area. These events are a favorite target area for youthful offenders, as they can come in from any direction, pick up a handbag, and make a quick escape. Sergeant Fitzpatrick instructed the team members to take up positions at various points on the periphery of the picnic grounds and to keep a watch for possible offenders. Officer Thompson, the decoy, mingled with the seniors. It was difficult to distinguish the thirty-three-year-old decoy from the elderly ladies in the area.

The seniors were having a good time. Many brought their own picnic baskets and others ate the substantial luncheon supplied by the agency. A band consisting of senior citizens played Jewish songs, and many of the women danced with each other. Approximately 80 percent of the group were women.

One thing that the author finds difficult to erase from his memory is the sadness of many of the women at the picnic. Although they laughed and talked and danced, there was something missing. Their faces indicated joy, but their eyes spoke the pain of a terrible loneliness.

The youths who had been "playing" near the picnic area soon realized that the dirty looking men in T-shirts and denims, who appeared to be dozing or just loafing around, were not merely drifters or park bums, but were members of PBBS' anti-crime unit. One by one, or in pairs, the youths slowly drifted out of the area.

After the award ceremonies, the decoy team and other members of the unit left the picnic grounds and proceeded to their assigned target for the day. The senior citizens were not left unprotected. Stationed in the immediate vicinity were members of the task forces' street crime unit.

BACKGROUND OF VIOLENCE

In New York City there is a call for police assistance about every five seconds. In 1978, the department answered seven million telephone calls for help, mainly through its 911 emergency police-call system. The calls for assistance involved among others, drownings, gas leaks, automobile accidents, injured children, heart attacks, family arguments, pregnant women in distress, stalled elevators, industrial accidents, boiler explosions, and bomb threats. In most instances, the police were able to respond within two minutes of the call. Two out of ten calls involved crime and violence.

In this last category, the police made an arrest every two minutes, for a total of 232,338 arrests. Included in these arrests were 1,203 for murder, 1,327 for rape, 1,633 for picking pockets, 15,910 for burglary, 10,099 for auto theft, 12,094 for felonious assaults, and 19,227 for robbery.

Assisting the police department in its continuing efforts to control crime in the inner city are the civilian patrols, or as they are commonly called, the *Auxiliaries*. They are not vigilance groups. The Auxiliaries, numbering approximately 25,000 volunteers, are composed of dedicated citizens who are concerned about crime in their neighborhoods. They are not uniformed and carry no weapons. They perform, however, an invaluable service to the community by acting as the eyes and ears of the police.

Operating either on foot or in their own automobiles, mostly in the evening and early morning hours, the Auxiliaries patrol the streets and the stairways and elevators in private and public housing complexes. Through the use of walkie-talkie devices they are able to communicate with other civilian patrols in the neighborhoods and to alert the police to criminal activities in the area. The main channel of police communication is the computerized 911 emergency police call number. This computerized system enables police units in the area (for example, radio patrol cars, or senior citizen robbery units, or anti-crime units) to respond to a call for assistance in a matter of minutes.[2]

As a point of interest to the student and observer of the criminal justice system, the American Civilian Patrol or Auxiliary, although it operates on a strictly local scale and although it does not have as broad a scope and authority, can be compared in purpose and function to its Soviet counterpart, The People's Patrol or *druzhiny*. Druzhiny is an old Slavic word referring to the band of comrades (*druzhinniki*), who advised the princes of Kievan Rus (862-1240 AD) and at the same time formed the nucleus of their armies. Various organizations performing auxiliary police functions existed during the 1920s and were often known as "Commissions of Social Order." By 1930, these were reformed into "Voluntary Societies for Aiding the Police." In January, 1930 there were 2,500 such societies in the Russian Republic alone.

Beginning in 1958, People's Patrols, with some millions of members, were formed throughout the country. The 1960 Russian Soviet Federated Socialist Republic statute on People's Patrols grants them broader functions than those exercised by the earlier organizations. The *druzhinniki* has the right to demand that a citizen stop violating public order and to demand that he produce identification papers or a driver's license; to take an offender to the headquarters of the patrol, to the police, or to the local soviet; to obtain transportation for the victim of an accident or a crime; and to freely enter clubs, stadiums, cinemas, and other public places, in order to maintain order. Disobeying a lawful order of a *druzhinniki*, insulting him, or resisting him have been made criminal offenses, and an attempt on his life (if accompanied by circumstances that aggravate the offense) has been made punishable by death.[3]

In contrast, the American Auxiliaries receive no national or even statewide recognition; its members are not recruited by the local law enforcement authorities; they are not reimbursed for mileage or for damage to their vehicles while on patrol; the equipment that the Auxiliaries use is purchased and maintained either from "out-of-pocket" monies or from funds donated by neighborhood organizations; and the city of New York does not provide its members hospital, medical, or compensation benefits in the event of injury or death.

In addition, in some neighborhoods, the police sometimes receive valuable assistance from groups known as the *block watchers*. These groups, composed of local citizens, care enough to take the time to sit at their windows several hours a day in order to keep a close watch on the activities in the streets. Upon spotting suspicious persons loitering near buildings or when noticing that "something is wrong," they phone a central number that puts them in contact with the police. A police unit, usually a radio patrol car, will respond to the citizen's call and check into the situation.

Yet, in spite of this moderate measure of assistance to the police by community-spirited citizens and in spite of continuing police efforts to control criminal activities, crime in the inner city continues to rise steadily across the nation. Although it is difficult to provide ready answers to this seemingly insoluble problem of urban America, it is clear that the youthful offender has been and continues to be one of the major contributors to this phenomenon.

Perhaps a partial answer to the crime problem in the area under study can be found in the values and attitudes of the people who live in the area. It is an accepted fact, generally, that not all citizens will cooperate with the police; the residents of this area are no exception. The added difficulty here is that many of the area's residents regard the police with suspicion and are, at times, openly hostile to them. This hostility is manifested in many ways. For example, when the police are investigating a crime and are searching for evidence or for possible witnesses, people respond to questions with a sullen silence. Rare is the instance when a resident will supply the needed information, much less volunteer it. The typical reply to a policeman's question is, "I didn't see nothing." This attitude prevails even when the crime was committed on the street in full view of passersby. This attitude may not always be engendered by a generalized hostility toward the police. It may also be conditioned by a sense of identity with the offender or by a fear of retaliation by the offender or by his friends.

A generalized hostility toward the police by the black community can be attributed, at least in part, to the black's perception of reality. To many blacks the policeman is considered to be a threat to the existence of this group. In support of his position the black leader often points to the instances of police brutality against the members of his race. He alludes to the fact that more than half of the persons arrested, convicted, and sent to prison are blacks. To the black man it seems that the police will use any pretense to beat up, shoot, or kill a member of his race. Given this attitude, it can be said that the black member of society reacts according to his images of a particular situation, and, because he characterizes a situation differently than others, he will deduce different conclusions from it and will behave differently. In other words, it is not the state of the situation that matters, it is what he believes it to be, and often his images of reality will be different from reality.

An incident that occurred during the summer of 1979, and in which the author participated, will illustrate the point.

On Thursday, June 14, 1979, the author accompanied a SCRU decoy team on a routine operation. The decoy for this operation was Officer Ellen Alwill, who's code name was Evil Ellen. The director of the operation was Officer Jules Alper. The backup team was composed of Officers Abe Hurtado and Bob Gibbons. The author was assigned to the command car with Officer Alper, and the backup team was assigned to the observation van.

The team moved into position at the intersection of Church Avenue and East Twenty-first Street. Officer Alwill selected a Chinese restaurant at that intersection as the base of her operations. Officer Alper parked the command car on Church Avenue, approximately 100 feet away from the restaurant. From this position he could observe the decoy as she moved from store to store on Church Avenue. The van was parked on Twenty-first Street, approximately sixty feet from the restaurant. From this position, the backup team could observe Officer Alwill if she chose to walk north on Church Avenue or to Twenty-first Street. All of the team members were able to communicate with the decoy by portable radios.

During the operation, after Officer Alwill made several "plays" on potential suspects, a gang of youths smashed the window of a jewelry store, which was located approximately fifty feet to the rear of the command car. Officer Alper immediately notified SCRU headquarters of the incident and requested instructions. In the meantime the youths, after seizing the jewelry in the window, ran past the command car. Several youths ran north on Church Avenue; some turned and ran east on Twenty-first Street.

Sergeant Byrnes, at SCRU headquarters, returned Officer Alper's call and ordered him to breakoff the decoy operation and to assist other police units in the area. After providing for the safety of the decoy, the team joined street crime unit members, who were already on the scene in pursuit of the suspects. Officer Alper pursued the youths who had proceeded north on Church Avenue. Having had them in sight during the short wait for clearance from headquarters, he seized three of the youths in a pizza store. Displaying his shield and without using his weapon, Officer Alper ordered the youths to the rear of the store and frisked them. They were clean. That is, the youths probably had discarded the jewelry during the chase. Without the evidence required for a legal arrest, he released them.

While Officer Alper was frisking the youths, a small crowd gathered near the front entrance of the store. Someone from the crowd yelled, "Leave the kids alone, they didn't do anything!" Another said, "They're always picking on our kids!" The mood of the crowd was decidedly hostile. The situation could have become dangerous had Officer Alper displayed his weapon or used force.

The fact that the people in the crowd did not know that the youths had just participated in a crime, coupled with the generalized attitude of the black community towards the police, could have precipitated a riot. It was clear that most of the elements for violence were present in this situation.

Incidents such as these and robberies committed against the elderly occur frequently in the crime area. For reasons that shall be discussed presently, it is the elderly female who is the most vulnerable victim of the juvenile offender.

A substantial number of the elderly who live in the area are widows. Having few friends, most live alone. Some of these women live in comfortable, well-furnished apartments and have adequate incomes. Others live in less luxurious surroundings and have no source of income other than their social security benefits.

The less fortunate live in small, single occupancy rooms in buildings that at one time contained thirty or forty apartment units. The landlords converted each apartment unit, depending on the number of rooms in an apartment, into four or five single rooms. There are no water or bath or toilet facilities in any of the rooms. These facilities, once a part of the original apartment, are shared in common by the occupants of the unit. All of the entrances to the buildings as well as the entrances to the former apartment units are unlocked. The buildings are poorly maintained and dirty, and, in the opinion of the author, are nothing more than ordinary flophouses.

Under such conditions, the occupants, most of whom are elderly, are often subject to harassment, beatings, robbery, and sometimes rape by the many drifters, vagrants, and youths who frequent the buildings.

Perhaps the greatest dangers facing the senior citizen today are the crimes of assault and robbery. Once the elderly citizen leaves her apartment and ventures out of doors, she may, as has often occurred, become a potential target for a "hit" by the ever alert youthful offender. In the past, most of these crimes were limited to "on-the-street" robberies, which were sometimes accompanied by simple assaults. In most instances, the offender would encounter his potential victim coming out of the grocery store or any other place of business. He would then follow her for awhile, waiting for the proper opportunity to steal her purse. For a time, these "on-the-street" tactics worked. With the increase of uniformed police surveillance in the high-crime areas, however, many perpetrators were apprehended.

Today, the youthful offender commits these crimes "off the streets," that is, either in the vestibules, or in the lobbies of buildings, or in the apartment of the victim. The latter type, although it is an "off-the-street" robbery, has been officially designated as a "push-in" robbery. By following his victim to her apartment building and going indoors, the offender has minimized several of the dangers that were present in his earlier tactics. First, he is no longer in the area under uniformed police surveillance, and his chances of being observed or identified by anyone are minimal. Second, once in the victim's apartment, he can work, so to speak, at a slower pace. Besides money, he also has access to furs, jewelry, silverware, and whatever else he believes he could fence. And third, once in the building he is less apt to be apprehended, as he has several escape routes, such as rear entrances, basements, fire escapes, and rooftops.

At times, it appears that the youthful offenders follows an established pattern in selecting and robbing his victim. At other times, no patterns are discernible to the police. He does, however, follow one of several tactics once he has selected his target.

In the first instance, he may encounter his victim by chance. This is while on the street and with no intent of committing a robbery at that particular moment, he may spot an elderly person coming out of a supermarket or a bank. Many elderly people are not very cautious and have a habit of counting their money as they are leaving such places of business. This "flashing" of money, as it is called, is an open invitation to the ever alert youth. Upon spotting the money, he will slow his pace and, perhaps, take a few looks back at his target. Once he has determined that the woman has money and that she is alone, the hunt is on. He will follow her at a discreet distance, sometimes from across the street, other times from the same side of the street, usually at a distance of about 100 feet. He has no fear of losing his victim. The elderly, because of age and various infirmities, usually walk slow, and when laden with a shopping bag or a cart, their pace is even slower. As his victim nears the apartment building area, the offender will pick up his pace. At this time, he is normally on the other side of the street. As she turns into her building, he moves quickly across the street and follows her into the building.

The second tactic used by the youthful offender is the "stakeout." This offender normally positions himself at a discreet distance from a supermarket, or a pharmacy or a bank, and waits for a likely target. If he does not know where his victim lives, he will use approximately the same tactics as in the earlier case. In many instances, however, the youth knows where his intended victim lives and knows the route she takes to go home. The chances are that he may have followed her on some other occasion or that he may have missed a "hit" on her at an earlier time. Sometimes he will follow the same tactics; at other times, the offender will walk ahead of his target and will wait for her either in the vestibule or in the lobby of her apartment building.

In either case, the offender will usually feign reading names of the occupants of the building that are listed in the vestibule, or he may look into a mailbox pretending to look for mail. As soon as the woman becomes preoccupied in opening the door to the lobby, the youth will take the purse and leave. If the purse is out of reach, however, or if she catches him in the act of stealing it and resists, then he will assault and beat her in order to get the purse. At that time the offender may also take any jewelry that the victim may have on her person.

In the third offense, the "push-in" robbery, the street and vestibule tactics are similar to those used in the two robberies that were previously discussed. In this instance, however, the offender may enter into the building with the victim, or he may be waiting for her in the lobby. Sometimes he may get on the elevator with her. When she gets off at her floor, he will proceed to the next floor and will then use the stairway to reach her floor. At other times, the offender may lie in wait for his victim by a stairway. After she enters the elevator, he will proceed up the stairs and check each floor until she emerges. Even if he miscalculates and misses her the first time, he still has sufficient time to retrace his steps until he finds her. The victim, laden with a shopping bag or a cart, has another disadvantage: she must unlock her door, which usually has two locks. By the time she finally opens the door, the offender has his arm around her throat and is able to push her into the apartment with relative ease.

Once in the apartment, the assailant will remove the victim's glasses and will then push her into a bedroom where he will tie her to a chair or to a bedpost. The victim is blindfolded and gagged either with scarves or with panty hose. With the victim securely bound, the assailant leaves the room and begins a systematic ransacking of the apartment. During this time, he will rip out the telephone wire, pull the shades down, and turn on the radio or the television set. In the event that he cannot find any money or jewelry, or if he finds some and is not satisfied, he will return to the bedroom and will tell the victim to reveal where they are hidden. If the victim refuses to divulge the hiding place, he will proceed to choke and beat her until she tells him. Even if the victim loses consciousness, the assailant will wait until she awakens and begin the process over again.

Based upon interviews with victims, SCRU investigators have estimated that the push-in robber usually spends from one to three hours in the apartment. Some victims have been able to free themselves after a few hours; others have remained tied to a chair or bedpost for periods ranging up to fourteen hours. Some were found alive, while others have died as a result of their ordeals.

As a seventy-eight-year-old widow, Mrs. Julia Beckel, in relating her experience to SCRU Investigator Bobby Noblin, said: "He hit me on the head, and I fell to the floor unconscious. When I woke up he was still there. I said to myself, 'Oh God, he is going to kill me!' Then I said, 'God can't let me die because I have a sick son to take care of, (Mrs. Beckel has a 42-year-old son in a mental institution) and God didn't let me die." Mrs. Beckel was hit on the head with a blunt instrument. Her scalp was split in two places, which required twelve stitches to close the wounds.

Mrs. Gertrude Rapfogel, a seventy-three-year-old widow, told SCRU Investigator Noblin, investigating an assault on her in her apartment, that when she left the elevator she didn't see anyone in the hall. And when she got to her door, she looked in both directions before she unlocked the locks and saw no one. But just as soon as she opened the door, as Mrs. Rapfogel recalled, "He grabbed me by the throat and pushed me inside." The robber was able to ransack the apartment without detection by her neighbors.

A POLICE PROBLEM

Police administrators at all levels of supervision as well as borough precinct personnel were quickly aware of the new tactics in crime. Crime statistics disclosed that while in the business districts robberies against the elderly were decreasing, such crimes were increasing in the residential areas. Most disturbing to the police was the nature of the crimes. Not only were the elderly being robbed at an ever-increasing rate, they were also being beaten, sometimes severely, by their assailants.

As discussed earlier, during the initial phase of the police program to combat violent street crimes, the level of uniformed police patrol was increased in the high-crime areas. However, the increase in police patrols did not appreciably reduce the overall crime rate. The criminal merely moved out of the protected areas and moved into the relatively unprotected neighborhoods.

In analyzing the problem, and in a search for new methods of policing to combat street crime, police administrators began to develop innovative police crime control tactics to supplement the highly visible uniformed preventative patrols.

Commenting on the need for new methods of policing to combat street robberies and assaults a New York Police administrator said, in part:

> Patrolmen in uniform are expected to be highly visible and thus deter crime by their conspicuous presence. . . . But given the cost of personnel and the resources available to the city, it is inconceivable that enough uniformed patrolmen could be employed to completely cover the city in this way. . . . A patrolman in uniform, while a reassuring sight to many, is not the deterrent to crime that many people assume him to be. In a sense that he performs the functions of a scarecrow, which is to say that he can only be effective within the short range of his ability to effectively observe and respond to criminal activity. In this respect his presence can be reassuring to criminals as to the law-abiding. The potential felon knowing where a policeman is can safely deduce where he is not and guide himself accordingly. . . .[4]

The new method of preventing street crimes involved the use of plainclothes policemen in high-crime areas. The first of the plainclothes units developed by police administrators is the street crime unit (SCU). The unit, created in 1971, is composed of carefully selected and specially trained patrolmen and supervisors. Utilizing plainclothes surveillance and innovative decoy tactics, the unit attempts to apprehend suspects in the act of committing a crime.

A study of crime statistics during the period of 1971-1975 disclosed that the unit was, and continues to be, very effective in helping to reduce the crime rate in the city's high-crime areas. Crimes against the elderly, however, continued to increase during the same period. Hence, it was clear to police administrators that additional innovative methods had to be developed in order to provide better protection for the city's elderly citizens.

NOTES

1. Carter, Robert and Klein, Malcolm, Back On The Street (Englewood Cliffs, New Jersey: Prentice-Hall, 1976), p. 11.
2. Cited in New York Police Foundation Report (Ruder and Finn — The Inter-Public Group of Companies Inc., New York, 1976), pp. 1-4.
3. Berman, Harold J., Justice In The U.S.S.R. — An Interpretation Of Soviet Law (Cambridge, Mass.: Harvard University Press, 1963), pp. 286-288.
4. Halper, Andrew and Ku, Richard, An Exemplary Project — New York City Police Department, Street Crime Unit (Washington, D.C.: United States Government Printing Office, 1975), pp. 1-5.

CHAPTER 2

THE SENIOR CITIZEN ROBBERY UNIT

THE NEED FOR THE UNIT

During 1975 and 1976 juvenile assaults against the elderly continued with increasing frequency. The victims suffered not only financial loss and physical injury but also psychological damage.

Economically, the loss of ready cash created a hardship for the victims because most had no income other than social security or small pension benefits. Some of the more fortunate were able to draw from their meager savings in order to subsist until they received their next benefit checks. Others had to turn to public or private welfare agency assistance for funds. As one victim told a SCRU investigator during an interview, "He (the assailant) took everything — the rent money, the medicine money, the food money — he cleaned me out. I had nothing left. I had to wait until Monday to get some money from the welfare people."

It can be reasonably assumed, therefore, that the loss of money, the injuries suffered as a result of beatings, and the fear of being attacked on the street in broad daylight or in an elevator or even in one's own apartment had a psychological impact on a number of victims. It is difficult to determine the extent of this damage because of the lack of formal data on the subject. A study of police investigative reports, however, has disclosed that there were marked changes in the attitudes of a number of victims.

Investigators reported that the victims who had reported attacks to the police were initially willing to cooperate with them. They provided the police with important information about the details of the action and the identifying characteristics of the criminals, though the reports show an increasing unwillingness of such victims to continue their cooperation.

It is difficult to determine the time when the change began to take place or the cause of the change. All that is known by the police is that many victims who provided valuable information during the initial interviews could not remember details of the crimes or the characteristics of the criminals when the investigators returned for follow-up interviews. Some victims refused to admit the investigators into their apartments. Others refused to speak to the investigators when they were contacted by telephone.

In discussing this change in attitude with some victims, the investigators learned that they were concerned with their safety if they continued to cooperate with the police. They feared that either their assailants or their assailants' friends would return and inflict further harm on them. They were aware that once the police left they would be alone and unprotected. Hence, despite police assurances of protection, many refused to identify their assailants in police lineups or to testify against them in court.

This increasing reluctance of the elderly to cooperate was one of a number of perplexing problems that faced the people in attempting to deal with the situation. Of greater significance was the fact that most of the crimes committed against the elderly occurred in areas where the racial and economic makeup was changing. Adding to the difficulty of the police was the fact — discovered only after a number of offenders were apprehended — that most offenders lived either in or near the crime area. The criminal was now indistinguishable from the other members of the community. And thus, it became increasingly difficult for the police to identify a potential offender by focusing on the outsider — the one who did not belong in the community.

In response to this increasing threat to the safety of the elderly, police administrators decided to add a new anti-crime unit to Patrol Borough Brooklyn South's task force. The new unit was to be primarily concerned with crimes against the elderly. Directly responsible to the task force commander, the unit was to operate free from precinct control and independently from uniformed police patrols and street crime units.

Although the new unit was to be modeled along lines similar to those of the existing street crime unit, its personnel assignments, deployment procedures, and tactics were to be flexible and innovative. This was mandated by police administrators in order that unit members would be free to adapt and develop deployments and tactics designed to meet changing and unique situations in the field.

On November 1, 1976, the Office of the Police Commissioner issued Operations Order Number 96, Series 76 to all commands.

The order directed area commanders as follows:

SUBJECT: COORDINATED PROGRAM TO COMBAT CRIME AGAINST THE ELDERLY AND THE ESTABLISHMENT OF AREA SENIOR CITIZEN ANTI-CRIME UNITS.

1. A coordinated program to combat crime against the elderly was initiated effective 0800 hours, November 1, 1976. This program, previously in existence in some area commands, has been enlarged and extended citywide.

2. The program is intended to give greater emphasis to the prevention and investigation of crime against the elderly and encompasses the establishment of specific senior citizens anti-crime units in each area under the direction, supervision, and control of the area commander. Members assigned to these units will perform duty in plainclothes and/or uniform as circumstances dictate. Deployment will be based upon careful analysis of all pertinent data including crime trends.

3. In addressing the overall problem, members of each senior citizens anti-crime unit will establish close liaison with the New York City Department For The Aging and with the various public and private social and related agencies who may be able to assist the elderly crime victim or potential crime victim.

4. In addition to the deployment of the senior citizens anti-crime units, other resources of the department will be fully utilized in a cordinated manner to assist in the protection of the elderly. In this respect area commanders shall:
   a. Enlist the assistance of the crime prevention section in providing lectures, films, etc.
   b. When deemed advisable, request assistance from the commanding officer, street crime unit in targeted areas, day or night.
   c. Increase visible uniform presence by deploying area task forces in high-hazard locations and by increasing auxiliary police patrols in such areas when possible.
   d. Coordinate efforts with detective area commands.
   e. Direct precinct commanders to:
      (1) Develop responsive and vertical patrol programs in areas of high-senior density, utilizing officers assigned to radio motor patrol cars, scooters, and foot patrol.

(2) Insure precinct investigation unit, uniform, and anti-crime personnel are kept informed of senior citizen crime problems and become actively involved in senior citizen prevention and apprehension efforts.

(3) Cause appropriate use of "stop and frisk" procedures and insure that each "stop" is properly documented.

(4) Fully utilize crime prevention and community affairs officers to assist in educational phases of the program and to identify locations where numbers of senior citizens congregate or frequent.

(5) Encourage increased citizen participation in the Block-watcher and Operation Identification programs.

(6) Insure intensive crime analysis is conducted to determine crime patterns, *modus operandi*, prone locations, etc. The known or approximate age of crime victims shall be recorded to assist in this analysis.

5. Area commanders will monitor activities of their respective senior citizens anti-crime units and other protective measures employed. All unusual occurrences and arrests related to the current situations desk and the deputy commissioner of public information.

6. Each area commander will submit an evaluation of the program to the chief of operations on the fifth day of December, 1976, January, 1977, and February, 1977, covering the previous month's activities including but not limited to:

   a. Average daily commitment of senior citizen anti-crime units

   b. Personnel by tour

   c. Areas of deployment

   d. Tactics employed

   e. Summary of other resources committed

   f. Programmatic adjustments

   g. Number and types of crimes committed against the elderly, (60 years or over) comparing current month to the same month of previous year

   h. Evaluation of results and recommendations

7. The report due February 5, 1977, shall include the overall evaluation of the program for the three (3) months of its existence as well as recommendations to assist in a determina-

tion as to continuation and level of effort to be applied.[1]

On the same day, the senior citizen robbery unit, PBBS was activated under the command of Lieutenant Frank Rahill. Sergeant Raymond Coles (now lieutenant and PBBS task force commander and Detective Sergeant Timothy P. Byrnes were the unit's first supervisors). Officer Rosemary Carbonaro was the unit's first decoy.

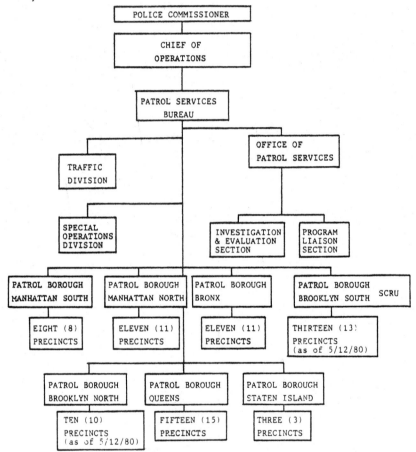

Figure 2-1. PARTIAL OVERVIEW OF NEW YORK CITY POLICE DEPARTMENT ORGANIZATION

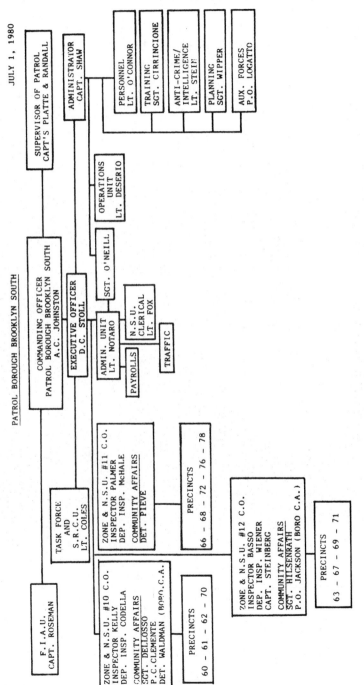

Figure 2-2. PATROL BOROUGH BROOKLYN SOUTH (PBBS) ORGANIZATION

ORGANIZATION AND ADMINISTRATION

The senior citizen robbery unit is a component of the area task force command of Patrol Borough Brooklyn South. The task force commander is directly responsible to the area's executive officer and, ultimately to the commanding officer, PBBS.

The three figures presented will serve to illustrate the organizational structures involved in SCRU activities. Figure 2-1 presents a partial overview of the New York City department organization within which Patrol Borough Brooklyn South is located. Figure 2-2 illustrates the structure of Patrol Borough Brooklyn South within which SCRU is located. Figure 2-3 diagrams the internal organization of SCRU.

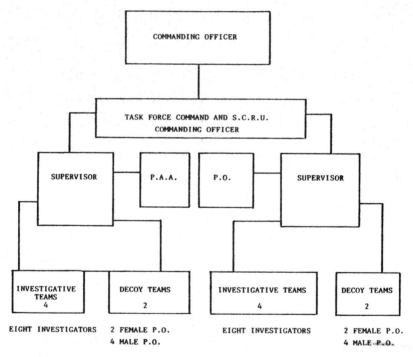

Figure 2-3. SENIOR CITIZEN ROBBERY UNIT (SCRU) ORGANIZATION

The southern district of Brooklyn, which has been designated Patrol Borough Brooklyn South, contains some 956.42 miles of streets, fourteen police precincts, and is approximately 52.31 square miles in size. This entire area has been assigned to SCRU jurisdiction for its prime function: the protection of the elderly citizen. As a result of this broad jurisdiction, unit members are free to cross precinct boundaries without prior notice to or approval from precinct commanders when in performance of their duties.

In order to facilitate team deployments throughout the area and to identify specific geographical locations as high-crime-rate areas, PBBS has been subdivided into the following zones:

Zone 1: Precincts 67, 70 and 71

Zone 2: Precincts 69 and 75

Zone 3: Precincts 60, 61, (SCRU headquarters), and 62

Zone 4: Precincts 66, 68, 72 (task force headquarters), 76, 78, and 84

Table 2-I below indicates present SCRU personnel strength by rank.

TABLE 2-I

SCRU PERSONNEL

	Field Squad	Administrative Staff	Total
Lieutenant	0*	1	1
Sergeant	0*	2	2
Detective Male	0**	0	0
Detective Female	0	0	0
Police Officer Male	20	1	21
Police Officer Female	8	0	8
Civilian	0	1	1
Total	28	5	33

*Except for special decoy team assignments or for special investigative projects administrative personnel do not normally accompany teams on field assignments.
**Prior to March, 1980, four detective investigators (crime prevention specialists) were assigned to SCRU.

Policy Considerations

In establishing short-range policy goals for SCRU, police administrators decided that the new unit was to operate with its own command structure. They were convinced that if SCRU was to cope effectively with the growing threat to the elderly it had to have a reasonable degree of autonomy. This meant that the new unit was to be free from the control of precinct and other external department commanders. Beyond these initial policy considerations police administrators were not prepared to go because SCRUs life span was established at three months. After that time the program was to be evaluated and a decision as to its continuation would be made.[2]

As a result of the temporary nature of the new unit such policy matters as recruitment and selection of personnel, size of decoy teams, and coordination of effort with other department personnel were left largely to the determination of field supervisors.

In February, 1977, police administrators, after evaluating the performance of the new unit, decided to extend its life span for an indefinite period. With this decision, PBBS planners began to develop long-range policy goals for the unit. By June, 1977, its communications and coordination with other departments units were greatly improved. The unit's operations were extended to "off-street" robberies. Finally, an investigative section was added to the unit, which doubled its personnel strength and increased its effectiveness. In November, 1979, the activities of this section were extended to the protection of the elderly against various kinds of confidence games.

The single purpose of the SCRU mission has given it a degree of flexibility and freedom of movement not usually accorded to other departmental units. This grant of freedom of movement raised some unanticipated jurisdictional problems during the early stages of operation. For example, when an arrest by a SCRU decoy team is effected in the area of a given precinct, does the precinct assume custody of the suspect and jurisdiction of the case, or does SCRU retain custody? In this regard, police administrators issued the following instructions to all commands: "In all arrests involving elderly citizens SCRU shall assume jurisdiction. It does not matter where the arrest takes place or which unit effects it."

"Conversely, when a suspect is apprehended by SCRU personnel acting in support of an uniformed police patrol unit or any other anti-crime unit, the suspect will be released to the custody of the unit that initiated the action or to the unit which has jurisdiction in the matter."[3]

Administrative policymakers have also decreed that SCRU teams engaged in decoy operations shall not respond to other street crimes that may occur in their presence without prior approval from the unit supervisor.

The author was present in two separate occasions when SCRU personnel became aware of criminal activity in the immediate area. In the first incident the team reported the crime and received permission to participate in the activity. In the second incident the team leader reported the criminal activity to street anti-crime personnel for them to take the necessary action.

To some observers this rule may seem to be rather restrictive and contrary to effective law enforcement procedures. To policemen engaged in street anti-crime activities, it is a good rule for a number of reasons. First, in most instances there may be plainclothes anti-crime personnel on the scene who are in position to intercept the suspect. Second, unannounced participation in the action by third parties could result in injury or death to passersby as well as to participating policemen. Third, by alerting all personnel who are in the immediate vicinity of the criminal activity, the cognizant unit will assume responsibility, and the danger of injury or death is minimized. Interpreting this rule strictly, uniformed police patrols and street anti-crime personnel will normally refrain from participating in crime situations that involve the elderly unless assistance is requested by SCRU personnel.

Personnel

The most important element of such a specialized unit as the senior citizen robbery unit is its personnel. The men and women in this type of unit are deployed in high-crime areas and are often involved in dangerous situations. Operating under high-stress conditions they must be able to react quickly and decisively to the unexpected and to use their ingenuity and imagination in bringing the situation under control. It is essential, therefore, that the officers assigned to the unit be of uniformly high caliber.

In discussing the quality of police officers assigned to plainclothes duty, a police administrator said:

> By its very nature, civilian clothes police work requires men (and women) of initiative and imagination — men (and women) who possess a high de-

gree of integrity and can function effectively in an area of corruption potential with a minimum of supervision.

These men (and women) spend their full time and energy actively engaged in outwitting the street criminal in his own element — the street. They function almost exclusively in high-hazard areas. . . . They focus their attention on crimes of violence without the identification factor furnished by a uniform and/or marked auto. . . . This requires, as well as personal courage, a high degree of resourcefulness and tenacity.[4]

Recruitment

Most of the officers in the senior citizen robbery unit have been selected by the task force commander and by the unit's supervisory sergeants; others are volunteers. There appears to be no problem in finding police officers who want to join the unit. At the present time there are approximately twenty applicants waiting for a vacancy.

The question posed to all police officers who want to join a specialized unit such as SCRU is, "Why do you want to join this unit?" The answers to this question are interesting and may provide some insights into the type of individuals who are attracted to plain-clothes police work. Some circumstances or reasons explaining the enthusiam for a unit assignment are:

Most persons who become police officers do so because they want to take an active role in fighting crime. In a specialized unit they are provided with the best opportunity for doing this, whereas much other police work is routine and consists largely of community service activities.

Assignment to the unit satisfies an officer's career advancement obligation to work in a "busy shop" (high-crime area).

In some specialized units, such as the street crime unit, the tour of duty schedule requires the officers to work 75 percent of their time at night, thus qualifying them for the advantage of night differential pay. In SCRU the tour of duty schedule requires the officers to work only day and afternoon tours with weekends off.

Specialized units are organized along less "military" lines than most police units. Lieutenants, sergeants, and team work together in the field, resulting in an easy flow of communication along the chain of command and a sharing of responsibilities.

The specialized unit provides an opportunity for non-conformists to express themselves in police work. They can wear beards and dress unconventionally.

Specialized units have great pride and self-esteem, and such units as well as their personnel are held in high regard by fellow officers.[5]

There are two other reasons for wanting to join a specialized unit, not mentioned by prospective applicants, but apparently operating:

> The specialized unit seeks and receives a good deal of publicity. The very fact of its existence must be publicized to help provide the desired deterrent effect on potential street criminals. Unit personnel share in this publicity and this also attracts prospective members.

> The work gives officers the opportunity to be "actors," it challenges their ability to blend into the street scene, and it provides an opportunity to test their street savvy.[6]

Commenting on the reasons why police officers volunteer for plainclothes duty, Lieutenant Coles considered the circumstances just discussed to be broad generalizations that could be applied to members of most specialized units, including SCRU. Insofar as these generalizations applied to SCRU, he was of the opinion that there were two or perhaps three significant factors that continue to induce police officers to seek plainclothes duty. The first — not necessarily in order of priority — is the challenge presented to the individual in this type of police activity. The element of danger and of the unknown has always attracted a certain type of individual. The second factor is the opportunity for career advancement. The officer working in high-crime areas has the advantage over other members of the force when promotion to detective rank is considered. The rank entitles an officer to the coveted gold shield and a $2,500-a-year salary increase. Finally, the plainclothes officer is afforded the opportunity to test his/her skills as an actor. This is particularly true of the SCRU decoy. The success of the operation depends on her ability to convince the potential offender that she is an elderly woman. The decoy is aware of this fact and will make elaborate preparations to achieve her goal. She derives much personal satisfaction from the knowledge that a criminal has been apprehended primarily as a result of her efforts.

Lieutenant Coles emphasized that although promotion to a higher rank is always possible for outstanding officers throughout the department, it is not used as an inducement for recruitment of prospective SCRU members. Promotion to the rank of sergeant, for example, may be attained only through passing the regularly scheduled competitive examination. On the other hand, promotion to the rank of detective may be achieved through extraordinary performance in the field. The New York City Police Department does not suffer from a lack of excellent officers; hence promotion to this rank is a highly selective process.[7]

Selection

As discussed earlier, the SCRU mission is different from that of other street anti-crime units in that it is concerned solely with crimes committed against the elderly. The selection process, therefore, will include a search for (those) officers who are, in the opinion of SCRU officials, particularly suited to work with the elderly as well as for those with street experience.

The selection procedure is both formal and informal. In its formal aspect the selection of personnel for the unit is based upon department guidelines that have been established for all street anti-crime units. For example, a candidate must be recommended by his commanding officer and have served on the police force for at least two years. Many of the successful candidates come from precincts that have high crime rates. Some have also worked in precinct anti-crime operations.[8]

After the candidate has been officially recommended, his/her personal record is reviewed by SCRU administrators. The candidate's name is run through the central personnel index to check for any complaints in the files of: (a) Internal Affairs Division, (b) Medical Unit, (c) Civilian Complaint Review Board, (d) Personnel Screening Unit, (e) Disciplinary Records Unit, (f) Public Morals Division, and (g) Organized Crime Control Bureau. Any substantiated complaints against the candidate filed with any of these units will disqualify him/her for duty with SCRU or any other street anti-crime unit.

The process is informal in the sense that the task force commander has the discretion to set aside the list of certified candidates and search for a suitable officer either within his own command or in other commands. In most instances, a telephone call to the prospective candidate's commanding officer will suffice for obtaining the desired officer's release. Formal requests through official channels are rare.

This informal procedure was initiated by Lieutenant (then Sergeant) Coles at the time SCRU was established in late 1976. Commenting on the selection of the unit's original personnel, he said:

It all started with a phone call. An assistant chief of the borough called me. He outlined the department's plans for the formation of a new unit — the senior citizen robbery unit. (Assistant) Chief Jules Saxon gave me the job of setting up the unit and picking the personnel. The first people we selected for the unit had worked for me or for Sergeant Byrnes at one time or another. Sergeant Byrnes and I had been involved in an auto larceny unit during the early part of 1976.

I made the telephone calls and picked up the people. The type of people we were looking for at the time were police officers who had some type of plainclothes street experience — specifically anti-crime experience.

We were able to pick up two men from the seventh precinct and two from the seventy-first precinct. We also picked up two detective investigators at that time. Detective Dattolico was the first one selected. His selection was based on personal knowledge and on recommendations by his lieutenant. Dectective Dattolico had specialized in a precinct level senior citizen program in the sixty-first. These five men, plus one other detective, formed the nucleus of the unit.

At a later date, the administration decided that in addition to street-type activities, the unit was to be involved in investigation of all other crimes against senior citizens. This meant that in addition to finding people who had street experience we now had to find people who had investigative experience. We picked up four more detectives; again the selection was based on personal knowledge and recommendations.

We then selected white-shield police officers from different precincts. These were men who had had some investigative experience or who we felt were capable of performing this type of work. During this period we were able to select anyone within PBBS that we wanted.

In the past two years the situation has changed because of personnel problems. Workload in PBBS has increased while the number of personnel has decreased. We have two avenues open to us for replacement personnel. If we have a man who wants to leave the unit and go to a particular precinct or command within PBBS, we can select a man from that precinct or command. It is a one-on-one situation. I can also take a man from the uniformed task force if need be, with or without a replacement.[9]

The second and most important part of the selection process is the personal interview. It is conducted by Lieutenant Coles or by one of the supervisory sergeants or by a combination of the three men. In addition to discussing the applicant's views on working with a partner of the opposite sex, his/her arrest activity, past street experience, attitudes toward departmental policies and use of firearms, he/she is given an oral examination.[10] In discussing this examination Lieutenant Coles said:

They are given hypothetical situations during the interviews. Their responses to the questions and situations are taken into account when we make our final determination as to whether we want them or not.

We give them problems to determine what their reactions would be in quick response situations.

We also try to determine if they can become part of the team. We try to keep individualists out of the senior citizen unit because it is a team operation. The men have to act as a group. This is extremely important because without the proper attitude and coordination of effort we could lose a decoy or a backup team member.[11]

This informal process supplemented by a personal history questionnaire has been a significant factor enabling SCRU administrators to select the quality personnel who make up this unit.

Training

The selection process employed by SCRU administrators is designed to identify and recruit police officers who possess an acceptable level of knowledge and experience in street anti-crime activities. Additional training is required, however, to instruct officers in the tactics and methods used by SCRU in plainclothes surveillance, investigation, and decoy work.

The senior citizen robbery unit does not have a specially assigned training officer because of its limited personnel strength. This function is normally performed by the supervisory sergeants. Specialized instruction is conducted by a departmental training officer as required.

The new member receives initial orientation training from the unit supervisor. The initial training is normally conducted within a two-day period. After this the trainee is assigned to field duty with an investigative team. Sometimes the new member is assigned from team to team on a rotating basis until the necessary field experience is acquired. At other times, the trainee teams up with an experienced investigator and remains with him after the training period is completed.

In decoy operations the new member is assigned to work with the team leader. After a few days of observing team deployments and tactics, the trainee will be assigned to backup team activities with an experienced partner. During the training period he/she may be assigned to other decoy teams. After the completion of the training period the new member will be given a regular team assignment.

The task of training the apprentice decoy is difficult, and much depends upon the natural skills and the learning ability of the individual. The new member may benefit somewhat from observing the activities of experienced decoys and from discussing tactics and techniques, but there can be no substitute for experience. In other words, the decoy must go into the field with her team in order to develop the sense of timing and to perfect the techniques that are vital to a successful operation.

All members of the New York City Police Department below the rank of captain are required to attend quarterly unit training sessions. In the SCRU these sessions consist of presentations by videotape cassettes and lectures, on tape or in person, as prescribed by the police academy.

As a supplement to unit training, SCRU supervisors periodically conduct lecture and discussion sessions on such subjects as psychology of crimes against senior citizens, juvenile crimes, public relations, aiding the elderly victim of a crime, fear of crime, and race relations.

The SCRU training program is one of a number of programs that have been established in all NYCPD commands. These programs offer a thoroughly informative series of videotapes and lectures that are intended to increase the officer's knowledge of department policies and of his specialized field.

Supervision

In the senior citizen robbery unit, supervisors and subordinate personnel work in an environment in which close cooperation and coordination between them are vital factors in accomplishing the unit's mission.

Operating under the team concept, supervisors and subordinates hold frequent and open discussions on subjects ranging from community relations and racial problems to decoy tactics and deployment strategies. This exchange of ideas has been instrumental in an extraordinary working relationship.

Commenting on this relationship Lieutenant Coles remarked: "We know our people and we trust them. We also know that when they go into the field they will go to work. Of course, some supervision is needed, and unannounced spot checks are conducted. So far, our policy of minimum supervision of field personnel has been justified."[12]

At this point, Sergeant Byrnes who was present during the interview discussed the necessity of allowing field teams to operate in this manner. In this regard, he said:

> Supervision isn't too much of a problem, particularly when you have selected your people with care.
>
> Another thing that we didn't discuss is the decoy operation. When our people are working on a suspect, the important thing is not to interfere in the operation. If we show up, the suspect could spot us and he'll take off. On the other hand, if our people know we are in the area it might inhibit their activities. They have enough to be concerned about in doing their job. Our policy is to observe activities at a distance and to maintain a low profile.[13]

Lieutenant Coles acknowledged that department regulations place the responsibility directly on all commands to exercise a sufficient degree of supervision over subordinate personnel to ensure effective implementation of departmental policies and goals. The degree of supervision, however, is left to the discretion of the individual commander.

Personnel Evaluation

Senior citizen robbery unit administrators continuously evaluate personnel under their command to ensure and maintain the high standards that have been established for the unit. Although these evaluations are informal and the results are maintained in the files, they are considered as part of the overall rating of the individual officer and will be included in the yearly formal evaluation report. The individual under evaluation is advised of his/her rating on a current basis. Hence, if an individual is not performing in accordance with the established standards, he/she will have the opportunity to correct the situation before the yearly formal evaluation period. Those officers who fail to measure up to unit standards are returned to patrol duty.

Among other factors, the following criteria are used by SCRU administrators for evaluation purposes: (a) integrity; (b) quality arrests (quality arrests are those that lead to a conviction in court); (c) absenteeism; (d) acceptance of responsibility; (e) maturity and stability; (f) willingness to contribute to team effort; (g) initiative and resourcefulness; (h) compliance with department procedures and guidelines and the directions of immediate superiors;

and (i) job knowledge.

The question of personnel evaluation was discussed at length with Lieutenant Coles and Sergeant Byrnes. The officers considered this to be a sensitive subject among supervisors and subordinate personnel. According to Lieutenant Coles, the most important factor underlying a personnel evaluation is its effect on an individual's career opportunities. Both agreed that there are many variables involved in the evaluation process that are difficult to assess under the formal departmental guidelines.

The following dialogue took place after the author inquired into the specific criteria used by SCRU supervisors when evaluating subordinate personnel:

SERGEANT BYRNES: "That's a touchy subject. You see we get an evaluation form which is universal in nature. It requires comments on the individual's performance and other factors. Paramount in our evaluation is the facts that our people, because they are in the unit, are considered to be the elite of the police force. Bearing in mind we have to preface our statements in the evaluation reports by stating, 'These officers function in a specialized unit. They were selected because of their special talents.' We then go on from that starting point and evaluate them. Now it would be unfair to compare, for evaluation purposes, one of our people with, let us say, a uniformed officer who writes traffic summonses everyday. But this is just what is being done.

"What I am saying is that the same criteria are used for evaluations for all police officers regardless of assignment. An above-average traffic cop cannot be compared to an average member of this unit."[14]

LIEUTENANT COLES: "We are locked into the official evaluation procedure of the department. As Sergeant Byrnes pointed out, criteria are used for all police officers. This, of course, is not a fair method of evaluation. We try to counteract this a bit by prefacing our reports with a statement that serves to remind reviewing personnel that these officers are operating in a specialized unit.

"The formal rating system is unfair in the sense that it does not take into account that the individual units and their qualities. We have men in our unit who have white shields who do more work and higher quality work than detective investigators in some of the homicide squads. But yet our evaluations, although they have weight, are not enough to move a person from a police officer (white shield) to detective rank gold shield).[15]

SERGEANT BYRNES: "So, we do have our problems with the rating system. But I believe, now, that the borough commander and all others who are involved in the overall supervision of the unit are aware of the quality of work that we do.

"Therefore, whenever he (the borough commander) needs qualified people for promotion he realizes that he must give our people some consideration. And this is something that the unit has earned by performance."[16]

LIEUTENANT COLES: "We have to keep on top of evaluations and promotions. We constantly remind higher echelons that we have quality people here who deserve serious consideration for promotion. We owe it to our people.

"It's possible that, in time, the present rating system will be changed for the better. Until that time, we have to live with it and, at the same time, do the best we can for our people."[17]

The opinions expressed by Lieutenant Coles and Sergeant Byrnes should not be construed as complaints against the department system. On the contrary, these men are experienced and dedicated police officers who are aware that they function in a large and complex public service organization with an intricate chain-of-command structure. To add to the complexities of command, the department is part of the large and multifaceted city civil service system. Under this type of corporate-like command structure, merit promotions, open competitive examinations, retirement benefits, rating systems, and the like are subject to review and approval by police administrators and by members of the Civil Service Commission. It follows that any proposed personnel policy change, such as a change in the rating system, is apt to involve a long and tedious process before it is approved.

Moreover, it appears (to the author at least) that top echelon police administrators prefer a general rating guideline rather than a specific one for the single reason that no specific guideline can be tailored to fit the needs or desires of every unit within the department.

Morale

Morale in the unit is, in general, high. There are, of course, as in any other comparable unit, public or private, the usual number of minor complaints about one thing or another. It would not be a normal situation if it were otherwise.

There are a number of reasons for high morale. In the first instance, there is nothing pretentious about the SCRU office or its personnel. Team members are not given to slogans or to histrionics. There is, however, a sense of professional pride in their work and in the unit's accomplishments. Second, they like their work. They are engaged in the type of work for which they joined the unit. Third, under the team concept members work together in dangerous situations and form close personal relationships. Fourth, there is an excellent relationship between supervisors and subordinate personnel. Ideas and concepts are discussed openly and are considered during the formulation of policy. Finally, the SCRU officers are aware that other police officers and members of the community esteem them highly.

The motivation and the commitment of SCRU personnel are perhaps best exemplified by the extensive role preparation done by the decoys and by the frequent discussion sessions held by team members on tactics, timing, and deployment.

To prepare for the role of an old lady, a female officer will spend much time in the field studying the mannerisms and habits of the elderly. This is often done on the officers off-duty hours. Some officers have purchased theatrical makeup, wigs, and clothes at their own expense.

Team members will frequently assess the day's operation candidly, pointing out possible errors in timing and coordination and to avoid repeating mistakes. New ideas in tactics and deployment procedures are also discussed at these sessions. Such dedication lies at the heart of the SCRUs success.

Equipment

The equipment needs of the senior citizen robbery unit are especially important because of the unit's unique field operations. The creation of new police commands will always require lockers, office furniture, typewriters, clerical supplies, and other ordinary materials. But street crime needs, unlike those of conventional units, require special equipment.

The covert aspect of the unit's field operations requires that none of the vehicles be recognizable as police automobiles. This presents no problem to SCRU administrators because of the availability of the "conversion" automobile. Conversion automobiles are unclaimed or confiscated vehicles being safeguarded by the department's property clerk. These vehicles are obtained and converted to police use by the motor transport division. By using vehicles not usually associated with the police department, SCRU personnel are able to operate in the target areas undetected by the streetwise criminal. Special observation vans, when required, are supplied by the task force command.

The department's property clerk's office has also furnished canes, crutches, wallets, pocketbooks, and similar items that support blending and decoy tactics. In addition, a quantity of other specialized equipment has been accumulated. Some of it has been loaned by persons in private industry and some contributed by SCRU members themselves. The special equipment locker is stocked with a varied collection of wigs, dresses, hard hats, telephone repairman's equipment, butcher's aprons, and the like.

The department also furnishes binoculars, cameras, tape recorders, armored vests, and fingerprint kits. Walkie talkies are provided by the task force command at the beginning of each day's operation.

Coordination of Activities With Other Departmental Units and Commands

The senior citizen robbery unit operates in the same high-crime areas as do the uniformed police patrols and the street crime units. At first glance, the idea of three separate anti-crime units operating in the sane area would suggest a conflict of jurisdiction and of functions. This is clearly not the case. Careful planning by police administrators has resulted in a well-coordinated and cooperative effort among the units.

With the territorial jurisdiction and functions of each unit clearly defined, the cause for conflict is eliminated. Thus, if a street crime unit or uniformed police patrol, acting in response to an elderly citizen's call for assistance, is first to arrive at the scene of the crime, it will assume temporary control of the situation until the arrival of a SCRU investigative team. Conversely, if a SCRU team captures a suspect while assisting a uniformed police patrol or a street crime unit, the suspect is remanded to the custody of the unit that initiated the action.

The SCRU also coordinates its activities with other departmental units on a regular basis. The following examples will serve to illustrate bases for this coordination.

On occasion an investigative team will discover evidence that leads its members to believe that a drug addict may have committed the assault on an elderly victim. The team will contact the narcotics squad and an exchange of information will take place. Sometimes the information may be of sufficient quality to allow the SCRU team to continue its investigation independently. At other times, the narcotics squad may be requested to take an active role in the search for the suspect. The exchange of information and the cooperation between the two groups may lead, as it often has, to the eventual arrest and conviction of the suspect.

The push-in robber, in addition to taking the victim's money, will ransack the apartment for anything that he can carry away. The criminal will steal such items as, jewelry, silverware, stamp collections, furs, portable radios, and television sets.

In a robbery/burglary situation SCRU investigators will often seek the assistance of the burglary squad. The squad has a citywide knowledge of known fences, registered informers, drops (places where criminals take stolen goods), and a sophisticated system of tracing such items. The information obtained from the squad will enable SCRU investigators to continue the search for the criminal for a longer period of time and to extend it beyond their normal jurisdictional limits. Unit investigators must obtain supervisory permission before they may extend their operations beyond PBBS boundaries.

The senior citizen robbery unit does not conduct murder investigations. Hence, when an elderly victim is murdered or dies as a result of an assault, the Homicide Detective Division is notified and the detective squad will assume control of that phase of the case. In major cases a unit investigator will be assigned to work with the detective squad in order to facilitate the exchange of information between commands. In all instances the SCRU team will continue its independent investigation of the robbery/burglary phase of the case. At all times during the investigation the two groups will maintain a direct line of communication until the case is either solved or terminated.

Objectives of the Senior Citizen Robbery Unit

The objectives that were established for the SCRU mission were at once realistic and attainable. They were realistic because they were not based upon theoretical models or upon existing street anti-crime units. They were attainable because police administrators did not establish quotas to be reached or maintained in arrest and conviction rates.

The objectives that were established for the unit were, and remain, as follows: (1) reduction of the crime rate in high-crime areas; (2) increase of arrests in high-crime areas; (3) attaining high-conviction rates through quality arrests; and (4) experiencing low-level line-of-duty injury rates to unit members.

Although the decoy teams experienced some anticipated difficulties in communication, i.e. timing and coordination during the formation stage, it soon became evident to police administrators that the unit would become another effective street anti-crime unit. A study of SCRU's performance during the first four years of its existence has disclosed that it has far exceeded the expectations of its founders.

Table 2-II represents a profile of persons arrested by SCRU personnel for robbery/grand larceny (person) in PBBS area.

Table 2-III represents a profile of the victim of robbery/grand larceny in which an arrest was made by PBBS-SCRU.

As of December 1980, more than half of the unit's decoys have been involved in extremely hazardous situations. Every decoy has been assaulted at least once in the line of duty. In most instances the injuries were minor in nature, and the officers were able to return to duty within a few days. Some required extended leave. In one instance, the decoy received injuries that required an operation to correct the damage sustained during a robbery. After being placed on limited duty for more than a year, the officer was retired on a disability pension.

During this same period four male officers received injuries in the line of duty. Most returned to duty within a few days. Three officers required hospitalization; one remains on limited duty.

This extremely low-level line-of-duty injury attests to the high

TABLE 2-II

PROFILE OF PERSONS ARRESTED FOR ROBBERY/GRAND LARCENY

Average Age of Offender	Sex	Race or Ethnicity	Arrest Record	Occupation	Drugs	Residence	Reason for Crime
17.4 years	95.4% males 4.6% females	86.1% blacks 9.3% Hispanic 4.6% white	90% had prior arrests	52.9% claimed to be students. 36.5% claimed to be unemployed. 10.6% claimed menial employment.	98% claimed no drug abuse.	65.3% lived within a few blocks of the crime.	The majority claimed that it was spontaneous.

TABLE 2-III

PROFILE OF VICTIMS INVOLVED IN ROBBERY/GRAND LARCENY

Approximate Age of Victim	Sex	Race or Ethnicity	Injuries (Physical)	Deaths
71.9 years	70.2% females 29.8% males	85.2% white 9.7% black 5.1% Hispanic	38.4%	0.008%

degree of cooperation and coordination maintained by team members. Although the decoy is afforded maximum protection at all times during an operation, she remains the most vulnerable member of the team.

NOTES

1. Operations Order Number 96, Commissioner, NYPD, November 1, 1976, p. 1.
2. Operations Order Number 96, p. 2.
3. Interview with Lieutenant Raymond Coles, Task Force Commander, Author's tapes, August 3, 1979.
4. Halper, Andrew and Ku, Richard, An Exemplary Project, New York City Police Department — Street Crime Unit (U.S. Government Printing Office, Washington, D.C., S.N. 027-000-00-238-9), p. 17.
5. Halper, A. and Ku, R., p. 18.
6. Halper, A. and Ku, R., p. 19.
7. Coles
8. Halper, A. and Ku, R., pp. 20-21.
9. Coles
10. Halper, A. and Ku, R., pp. 21-22.
11. Coles
12. Coles
13. Sergeant T. Byrnes, Coles Interview, August 3, 1979.
14. Byrnes
15. Coles
16. Byrnes
17. Coles

CHAPTER 3

UNIT DECOY TEAMS

THE single most important member of the senior citizen robbery unit is the decoy. The initial success of an operation rests on her ability to effect the proper contact with the potential suspect. In other words, the criminal must be convinced that the decoy is an elderly woman. In this respect, a potential suspect may study and follow his target for ten or fifteen minutes and sometimes longer before deciding to make a hit.

In addition to her disguise, the decoy's attitude is extremely important if the operation is to be a success. She must be willing to place herself in an almost defenseless position in potentially high-risk situations. For example, once the potential suspect begins his chase and moves closer to his target, all communication between the decoy and her backup team is discontinued. This procedure is followed during all operations because voice communications can be heard from distances of approximately fifteen feet, and the identity of the decoy could be exposed to the streetwise juvenile. From that moment on, the decoy is on her own. The high-risk situation occurs when she enters a building and is no longer in sight of the back-up team. It is at this time, for approximately ten to fifteen seconds, that she is exposed to serious injury or, perhaps, death. All of the unit's decoys have exposed themselves to this danger.

The following interview with the unit's first decoy, Officer Rosemary "Rip-off Rosie" Carbonaro, is typical of the attitude of the women who are willing to risk such dangers in the performance of their duties. Rosemary said, in part:

> . . . This unit was given the challenge of confronting the mugger, beating him at his own game, placing him under arrest, and removing him from the street. . . . Most people think that the role of a decoy is a passive one. The opposite is true. A decoy is a hunter, the police department's secret weapon. She goes on the prowl looking for the prowler, the decoy's victim. And who are the victim's of the decoy? Muggers, robbers, rapists, just to name a few. . . . In other words, the hunter becomes the hunted. . . .[1]

47

Composition of a Typical Decoy Team

The typical decoy team is normally composed of four to five members: a team leader, a decoy, and two or three backup members. The total number of team members depends upon the nature of a particular assignment or upon the availability of personnel on a given day. Inclusive of the decoy, no team is ever sent into the field with less than four members.

The team leader, who is also a participating member of the backup team, directs the activities of the team, although the decoy normally selects the locations for the days' activities, such as the bank or supermarket from which she will operate and the building that she will enter after contact is made. The team leader who has the final word will place himself and the other members of the backup team in positions strategically located so as to afford them (a) an unhampered visibility of the target area, (b) an opportunity to give the decoy maximum protection (i.e. she must always be in sight of at least one team member from the time she leaves an operational post to the time she enters an assigned building), and (c) to be in position to apprehend the offender by closing off all avenues of escape.

Crime Analysis

Under the direction of the task force commander of Patrol Borough Brooklyn South, senior citizen robbery unit supervisors work in close coordination with the department's crime analysis unit. The crime analysis unit is a component of the anti-crime section, which is, itself, a component of the Special Operations Division under the general supervision of the Field Services Bureau.[2]

The senior citizen robbery unit does not perform its own analysis. This function is carried out by the Administration and Crime Analysis Division of the citywide anti-crime section.

The Crime Analysis Division compiles, compares, and analyzes crime data from all available sources. Such sources include the SPRINT SYSTEM (daily crime reports current to within 72 hours) and precinct anti-crime reports prepared on a monthly basis. New York's precincts are ranked monthly according to the level of activity within certain categories of crime. These include robbery, grand larceny, grand larceny auto, assaults, street crime (the total of robbery, burglary, and grand larceny auto), and all crime (includes felonies, misdemeanors, and violations).[3]

Selection of the Target Area

Precinct rankings are submitted to the task force commander for review and deployment assignments. The Crime Analysis Division then details the criminal activity (only crimes against the elderly) occurring in those precincts to which SCRU teams will be deployed. The SCRU supervisor, in consultation with the task force commander, prepares detailed information from the present crime reports on crime patterns, including type of crime (e.g. on-street, push-in), time of crime, location of crime, description of perpetrators, age and sex of victim, and criminal *modus operandi*. The SCRU supervisor then provides unit members with informational folders in which this information is updated daily.

Patrol Preparations

Senior citizen robbery unit personnel work a forty-hour week, Monday through Friday. There are two tours of duty of eight-and-one-half-hour durations each. Weekend tours have been discontinued because crime statistics have disclosed that few or no crimes are committed against the elderly during this period. The hours of duty are as follows:

First Tour — 0930 to 1800 hours
Second Tour — 1600 to 2430 hours

The two-hour overlap in duty tours allows unit supervisors to coordinate their activities, exchange information, assign personnel to critical areas, and to conduct general or special meetings with all personnel. It also affords field personnel the opportunity to exchange information, to discuss deployment and tactics, and to discuss any unusual activity in the area.

Members of the unit assigned to the first tour usually arrive at the office from 0900 to 0930 hours. The routine here is similar to that of any large business organization. Keep in mind that the New York Police Department employs some 23,000 uniformed and plainclothes policemen, in addition to approximately 5,000 civilian personnel. Hence, the department can be compared, in terms of size, organization, and administration, to most major corporations. In this regard, policemen socialize as do many co-workers in like situations. They discuss families, friends, and sundry subjects over mid-morning coffee. However, the routine of the office differs considerably when police officers turn to their duties.

Prior to conducting field activities for the day, unit investigators are required to submit a daily activity report. The report, a summary of the previous day's activities, will include the following: (a) the exact location of the area under surveillance, (b) problems encountered, (c) unusual activity, (d) arrests made, if any, (e) progress of previously assigned cases, (f) response to civilian complaints, and (g) response to other emergency calls.

As required, investigators will consult with the unit supervisor and other investigative teams. During the consultations, area crime statistics and reports from evening tour investigative teams are reviewed. The investigators exchange information on area problems, suspects, and deployment and tactics. Acting on the basis of the available data, the supervisor will assign a team to a new high-crime area, or assign a new case to a team, or he may continue team activities as previously assigned.

The decoy team on assignment for the day is briefed by the supervisor and is advised of the latest activity in the target area. Area charts are studied to determine the specific location or locations from which the elderly were spotted by the suspect(s), the routes they travelled on the way to their apartments, and the building(s) in which they were assaulted and robbed. The team will operate in the area in which the most numerous and the most recent crimes have been committed.

Prior to going into the field, the team leader and the backup team members conduct a check on the vehicles and the equipment to be used for the day. Normally, both the team leader and the backup team will use unmarked squad cars. Sometimes the backup team will use an unmarked police observation van.

The vehicles that have been assigned to the unit are usually automobiles that have been impounded by the police for various reasons. For example, some have been stolen and recovered by the police but not reclaimed by the owners; others have been used in robberies and were confiscated by the police. These vehicles have been repaired, refurbished, and refitted for use in police activities.

Besides the officers personal weapons, the major items of equipment are walkie-talkie-type receiver-transmitters, which are limited in range. The team leader and the backup team also wear headbands. The headband is usually worn on the wrist until such time as contact is made with the suspect and is being pursed by team members. At the time of initial contact with the suspect, the headband is then placed around the forehead. The color of the headband is changed daily, and all precincts in the areas under SCRU jurisdiction are notified of the color in use for the day. The purpose of the headband is to allow SCRU team members in pursuit of a suspect to be recognized as plainclothes policemen by uniformed radio patrols and other street crime units that may be operating in the crime area.

While the other members of the team are checking out the necessary vehicles and equipment, the decoy is preparing her disguise. The disguise is of major importance to the success of the mission. The decoy must be able to convince the potential suspect, at close range, that she is indeed an elderly woman. This can create some difficulties because the decoy is usually a young woman. The average age of the decoy is twenty-eight years.

In addition to wearing clothes similar to those worn by elderly women, the decoy uses a wig and applies theatrical makeup to her face and hands. Under the outer garments she will carry a portable receiver-transmitter and her service revolver. The decoy is required to wear a bulletproof vest and her police shield. The receiver-transmitter is strapped to the decoy's body, and a microphone is taped to her left arm, just below the shoulder. With the microphone located in this position, the decoy, by turning her head slightly to the left, is able to communicate with her team without difficulty. A hearing plug is placed in the ear with its wires behind the ear and down the side of her neck. The wires are taped into position and are hidden from view by the wig.

Having studied the mannerisms of the elderly, the decoy will walk in slow, halting steps. This is a mannerism peculiar to the elderly. It gives the appearance of a person walking with some difficulty. To further heighten the effect of her disguise, the decoy will sometimes wear a theatrical hump, which gives her a stooped appearance, or she will use a walking cane.

The male members of the team usually dress in worn denims,

faded shirts, and sneakers, and generally maintain an unkempt appearance. After completing all preparations and receiving last-minute instructions, the team will proceed to the target area.

DEPLOYMENT AND TACTICS

Deployment

On the way to the target area, the team leader and the decoy will discuss and agree on the exact location she will use as a base for her operations. This choice is usually left to the discretion of the decoy. For example, the decoy may select a supermarket, and from this base she will work her way down the avenue, stop at a store to window-shop or to browse, and then move to the next store. If she does not encounter a potential suspect, she will repeat the procedure. The procedure may be repeated ten or fifteen times during the course of an operation at one location. In this type of an operation the backup vehicles may be deployed as follows. The command car will be parked approximately 50 feet north of the decoy on the opposite side of the street. The backup vehicle (sometimes a car or an observation van) will be parked approximately 100 feet south of the decoy.

At another time, the decoy may select a setting with a bank on one corner and a "safe" apartment building east of the bank and on the same side of the street. A "safe" apartment building is one with an unlocked street door and a locked vestibule door inside. In this type of an operation the backup vehicles may be deployed as follows: The command car will be parked approximately 50 feet west of the bank and diagonally across from it; the backup vehicle will be parked approximately 100 feet east of the entrance to the building.

The deployments described in the preceding examples have been developed to afford the team several advantages. First, the decoy is provided maximum security. Second, with a clear view of the area, the team leader is able to direct the activities of the decoy and to alert her to possible dangers. Third, the decoy is always in sight of at least one member of the team. Fourth, the suspect will find escaping difficult because the team can move in either direction. And last, this deployment makes it easy to use the "triangle method" of apprehending a suspect.

In the bank deployment situation the "triangle method" works as follows: With the vestibule door of the building locked, the suspect has no choice after robbing his victim but to return to the street. On the street he is confronted by three plainclothes policemen approaching him from the east, west, and south. Thus, all routes of escape are closed. Further, in the event that the suspect decides to double back into the building and force his way inside, the decoy, now armed, will be waiting for him.

In instances when a potential suspect focuses his attention on an elderly citizen instead of the decoy, the team leader automatically calls off the decoy operation, alerts SCRU headquarters, and calls for assistance. After providing for security of the decoy, the team uses the same deployment and tactics as in regular operations. In the event that the suspect enters the building proper, the team assisted by support personnel will secure all entrances to the building as well as the rooftops of adjacent buildings. The team will then conduct a floor-by-floor search for the suspect.

If the suspect is caught he is usually remanded to the custody of a support team, which then takes him to the area precinct for action on the arrest. This is the first step of the criminal justice process. As a matter of policy, the decoy team moves to a new location before resuming its activities.[4]

Tactics

Street crimes against the elderly are for the most part crimes of opportunity. The criminal may encounter the potential victim as she is leaving a supermarket or some other business establishment and may observe something that attracts his interest. For example, the woman may be counting her money, or she may have her purse or wallet in an open shopping bag. The ever alert criminal will follow his intended victim until such time as she is preoccupied or distracted, and, while she is in this state, he will steal her purse.

During the early phases of this type of street crime, the juvenile offender soon became aware of the fact that the elderly citizen was the easiest target for a robbery. Emboldened by his success in picking up a few easy dollars and safe in the knowledge that there was little likelihood of capture, he returned time and again to the scene of his crimes.

As time passed, the suspect became aware of the movements and the characteristic behaviors of the elderly. Through his observations of elderly persons, the streetwise juvenile became aware of several factors. First, he knew when the elderly received their pension checks or social security benefits. Second, he knew that the elderly left their apartments to go shopping or to the bank on certain days and during certain hours of the day. It was not by accident that most of the crimes against the elderly were committed during the hours of 10:00 AM to 4:00 PM, on Mondays, Tuesdays, and Fridays. Finally, the suspect apparently realized that his frequent appearances in places of business could arouse the suspicion of store employees and lead to his eventual identification and arrest. More likely than not, this is the reason why he changed his tactics and waited outside business establishments for his intended victim.

The suspect's tactics were successful for quite some time. Much of his success depended on timing and upon the inability of the victim to identify him. He had to be careful not to arouse the suspicions of his intended victim and not to take the purse until the proper moment. As a result of his ability to time his assault properly, the victim was seldom aware that she had been robbed until she tried to make her next purchase or until she had returned to her apartment.

After the police administrators increased the number of uniformed patrols in the crime areas and later supplemented them with the plainclothes street crime units, the number of some street crimes decreased. Crimes against the elderly, however, continued to increase. The police administrators decided, therefore, to organize the new anti-crime unit specifically to deal with crimes against the elderly. The new unit was to be composed of select personnel experienced in street crime control and specially trained in the problems of the elderly. Moreover, its members have to be sufficiently flexible to adapt themselves to the ever-changing conditions of the streets. This meant that they had to be able to develop and to implement innovative deployment procedures and tactics on a continuing basis. A major innovative feature of the new unit was to be the utilization of a female plainclothes officer as a decoy to combat crimes against the elderly.

As a result of this decision, the senior citizen robbery unit was established on November 1, 1976. The unit was placed under the command of Lieutenant Frank Rahill, task force commander, Patrol

Borough Brooklyn South. Its supervisors were Sergeant Raymond Coles and Sergeant Timothy Byrnes. The decoy team was composed of three males and one female plainclothes police officers. Collectively, the team had thirty years of street experience.

Officer William Lohse was designated as the team leader by the SCRU supervisors. The backup team consisted of Officer Louis Ippolito and Officer John McCafferty. The unit's first decoy was Officer Rosemary Carbonaro.

As the third backup officer, the team leader was to be responsible for (a) deployment of the backup team, (b) communicating with the decoy and directing her activities, (c) changing the location of the operation, (d) directing the activities of the backup team, and (e) terminating an operation. It was also agreed that the backup team was to utilize the triangle method of suspect apprehension.

In the beginning the team's decoy operations were not successful. After being in the field for a week the team had not yet made an arrest. After consulting with the unit's supervisor, the members of the team decided to suspend decoy operations for several days. The team, instead, went into the field and mingled with the crowds. It was a time for evaluating deployment and tactics, testing their disguises, and for observing the mannerisms of the elderly as they went about their daily activities. At the end of the surveillance period the team members concluded that deployment and tactics were good and that their disguises were effective. There was no ready explanation for the team's failure to make an arrest.

In recalling this problem, Officer Carbonaro told the author:

> There was one very important thing missing: the key to the rip-off. It was a very depressing and frustrating time for us. I decided to interview mugging victims in an effort to find a common denominator. And, finally, after several interviews it became clear. The key to the rip-off was money. Most of the victims were taken-off after having exhibited money while making a purchase, or paying a bill, or when cashing a check. I had to bring myself to the attention of a potential suspect by showing money.*
>
> . . . I took two dollar bills and wrapped them over several sheets of newspaper which I had cut to the size of a bill. With this new prop, we returned to the field. This time things were different. My "plays" were being noticed because as I made them I would go through the act of putting the roll of money in to my wallet and then placing the wallet in my

---

*Play money was later substituted for the dummy newspaper roll. For purposes of evidence all bills are initialed by the decoy.

pocketbook. A perfectly natural action, one that I observed countless people do in the most absentminded fashion. Finally, one of my plays caught
the eye of the right person. This individual spotted the money, followed
me for a while, and when I appeared preoccupied, he stole the wallet. As
the suspect moved away from me, the backup team moved in on him.
Three men, a postal clerk, a telephone repairman, and a hippie had him
surrounded. Then I heard the words I had been waiting for, "Police, don't
move!" We finally got our first collar. I was relieved and happy.[5]

In the following months, the new technique was used with con-
siderable success in South Brooklyn's high-crime areas. And as the
team coordinated its efforts with greater efficiency, the number of
street crimes declined correspondingly. These early successes, however, were short-lived, as the criminal, faced with the increasing
danger of arrest, changed his tactics. Although he continued to wait
for his intended victim outside of a supermarket, for example, he no
longer assaulted her in the street. The new tactic was to follow the
victim to her apartment building and to commit the robbery after
she went inside. Thus, by committing his crimes off the street, the
criminal greatly improved his chances of survival.

As "off-street" crimes increased, SCRU personnel addressed
themselves to the new problem. Members of the unit studied crime
reports and conducted follow-up interviews with victims to determine the criminal's *modus operandi*. As a result, Officer Carbonaro
suggested that the decoy team operations include the interior of
buildings. The decision posed for SCRU a new set of problems that
required the development of new deployment procedures and tactics. Heretofore, during an operation, the decoy had always been in
sight of at least one member of the team and was thus afforded maximum protection. The new tactics required the decoy to move into a
building. Once in the building, she was out of sight, and, for a short
period of time, she could expect no assistance from her backup team.

The major concern of the backup team was the increased
vulnerability of the decoy. It was apparent to the team that there was
no positive method of assuring her protection. The best that could be
hoped for was that the risks be minimized as much as possible. In
discussing the development of the tactics, Officer Carbonaro said, in
part:

    . . . And so began another phase of this work, and with it another set
    of problems. The decoy was now going inside. . . . How far inside the
    building should I go? The further into the building, the greater the risk to

my safety, and the longer it would take the backup team to get to me. I decided that to go beyond the vestibule of an apartment building would be a foolish risk. My team agreed that to go beyond this area would make it impossible for them to give me even reasonable protection. In making my decision, I considered another important fact. And that was: escape routes.

In a decoy operation you must seal off as many escapes routes as possible. If I went beyond the vestibule area, the suspect could escape from any number of exits. When the rip-off takes place in a vestibule and the door is locked, the only way out for the suspect is the way he came in, and that is to the street. He will run into the waiting arms of the backup team. This was the only way to go![6]

Officer Lohse added another precaution to the procedure. A member of the team was to approach the building immediately after the suspect entered. The officer was not to enter the building unless the decoy signalled for assistance. To do this, she was to depress the transmitter button twice in rapid succession.

It was this last procedure — the attempt to depress the transmitter button in a call for assistance — that almost proved fatal to Officer Carbonaro. The incident, as recalled to the author by Officer Carbonaro, follows:

> . . . it was just this movement that nearly got me killed one hot summer night. I was followed into a building by a very nervous nineteen-year-old who, as soon as he approached me, started pushing me around and yelled, "Where's the money? Where's the money?" He also threatened me and told me not to move. When I attempted to depress the transmitter button to give the prearranged signal for help, my antagonist caught the motion and he put a gun to my head.
>
> At this time one of the team members had arrived at the building's entrance. As he looked through a glass partition on the entrance door he could see that a gun was pointed at my head. This was an anxious moment for my teammate, as it occurred to him that any unexpected action might cause the perpetrator to pull the trigger, even reflexively. Finally, the young man took the wallet, and, when he turned to leave the vestibule, I hit him on the head with my cane. . . .[7]

CONTACT AND APPREHENSION OF THE SUSPECT

A significant factor in all decoy operations is the identification of a possible suspect by the team leader or by one of his assistants. The success of the operation depends on the ability of the backup team and, in particular, of the team leader to select the one youth who, in his opinion, is the person most likely to commit a robbery.

A study of the activities of decoy teams and of the mannerisms of potential suspects leads to the conclusion that the selection process is, in most instances, one of chance. That is, although the street-experienced officer will focus on youths who fit into a specific category such as mode of dress, peculiar hair style, or an identifiable mannerism, his chances of selecting the next person to undertake an attack on an elderly person are perhaps thirty or forty to one. Sometimes an arrest is made within fifteen or twenty minutes after the start of an operation. At other times the decoy team may work for hours or even days at various locations without making an arrest. However, the same study indicates that 95 percent of the youths arrested had one or more of the characteristics expected by the experienced officers.

Identification of a Possible Suspect

It is important to note that appearances are the basis for many of the decoy team's activities. The team leader usually decides on a possible suspect on the basis of the suspect's looks. For example, on June 7, 1979, the author accompanied a SCRU decoy team on a field operation. During the operation the team encountered approximately twenty youths. From this group, the team leader, Officer William Lohse, selected nine youths as subjects for the decoy's play.

At first, the author reasoned that the team leader was randomly selecting his subjects. After observing the team leader's techniques and after discussing the reasons why he selected one youth as the subject for a play and rejected another, however, the author decided that the selection process was based on a careful study of each youth. In other words, the team leader looked for some cue in the appearance of a youth that enabled him to make his selection.

The following dialogue that took place in the command car should prove of interest to the reader:

(First Suspect Approaching)

TEAM LEADER: (to the decoy) "Eileen, there's a kid coming up on your right. Red shirt, blue pants, get ready. (pause) Forget it, Eileen, go back."

AUTHOR: "Why did you send her back?"

TEAM LEADER: "He was coming too fast. He looked like a 'goer,' but I don't think he would have picked up the play."

(Second Suspect Approaching)

TEAM LEADER: "Eileen, on your right. Baseball cap, brown shirt, blue jeans. He is strolling. (pause) He went into the radio store. (pause) He is out now. (pause) He is looking across the street. He is coming your way now. (pause) Forget him, Eileen."

AUTHOR: "Why didn't you call Eileen out?"

TEAM LEADER: "He isn't looking for a hit."

AUTHOR: "Why do you say that?"

TEAM LEADER: "He isn't looking for old people today. He didn't look at the old lady who passed him before he went into the store. He probably wants some parts for his radio. He just walked into the radio store down the street. We'll let the anti-crime people take care of him."

(Third Suspect Approaching)

AUTHOR: "There is a fellow across the street who has been watching people coming out of the bank. The one standing near the mailbox."

TEAM LEADER: "I know. I have been watching him."

AUTHOR: "Do you think he is up to something?"

TEAM LEADER: "No. He looks clean. He is probably waiting for someone."

Later in the day, the team leader selected another youth as the subject for a play. The decoy was alerted. As the youth approached her location, she stepped out and made her play. The youth took the bait and robbed the decoy. He was arrested moments after the robbery.

The team leader having had years of street experience was familiar with the appearances and mannerisms of the youths in the crime area. He was able, therefore, to see each situation in a way which differed from that of the inexperienced civilian observer, who saw nothing suspicious in the appearance of most of the young men encountered that day.

In discussing this perceptive characteristic of the police, Jerome Skolnick observed: "The police tend to develop ways of looking at the world distinctive to themselves, cognitive lenses through which to see situations and events."[8]

Because the criminal blends with the community in areas of racial transition, the police rely heavily on this crude and sometimes troublesome technique. Commenting on the use of this technique as a method of identifying potential offenders, Howard Daudistel said:

> Were the policeman's task to see only what is out of the ordinary, it would be less difficult than it actually is. One can imagine that individuals who are 'up to no good' can use normal appearances to their advantage. And indeed, consequently, the policeman's task is complicated by the fact that those whose intentions might ordinarily cause alarm (were they to appear out of the ordinary) frequently are aware of the importance of their appearance and attempt to normalize it. . . .[9]

The play by the decoy has raised charges of entrapment by defense attorneys and by some jurists. New York Police administrators contend that the decoy does nothing out of the ordinary. She properly pretends to be an elderly citizen and awaits the coming of a thief. As a means of satisfying himself on the issue of entrapment, a Brooklyn trial judge recently observed a SCRU decoy team (without the team's knowledge) in operation. He came away convinced that the decoy's play did not constitute entrapment.

State law governs entrapment. The few decisions by the Supreme Court involving entrapment were decided on the basis of the Court's "supervisory power" over lower federal courts, e.g. United States v. Russell, 411 U.S. 423 (1973); Hampton v. United States, 425 U.S. 484 (1976). In each of these cases the justices were sharply divided on the definition of *entrapment*. The majority of justices focused on the defendants' predisposition to commit the crime — the "origin of intent" test. Under this test, a subjective determination is made of whether the original intent to commit the criminal act was the product of the creative activity of law enforcement officer(s) or of the defendant(s). It is not sufficient for the police merely to afford the defendant an opportunity to commit an offense; the defendant must lack a predisposition to commit the crime in order to be entrapped. Thus entrapment becomes a question of fact for the jury rather than a question of law for the court. The minority view (espoused by the dissenting justices in Russell and Hampton) is known as the "police conduct theory." Under this test, an objective determination is made of whether the police conduct in a particular case constitutes a proper use of governmental power, i.e. was the conduct of the police reprehensible? In this view, entrapment is a question of law to be decided by the court not the jury. Most states utilize the "defendants' predisposition" test, and only a few states use the "police conduct" theory.[10]

The Play by the Decoy

As we discussed earlier, the key to a successful operation is not the disguise effected by the decoy, although this is of paramount importance, but the *play*. The play is the displaying or flashing of money by the decoy in the presence of a potential offender. How well she accomplishes this function could spell the difference between success or failure of a particular operation.

Moreover, it is precisely at the moment when the decoy displays the money to the suspect that the defense has charged the police with entrapment. Hence, the decoy's actions must appear normal. She cannot, in other words, lure the subject into committing the crime. As Professor Hazel Kerper observed:

> Entrapment is designed to protect only those defendants who had no basic disposition to commit the crime, but were simply caught up in a government attempt to 'manufacture' a crime. . . . If the idea of committing a crime was not affirmatively planted in the mind of the defendant by the government agent — that is, if the defendant thought of committing the crime on his own initiative — then the defendant obviously has a prior disposition to commit the crime. What the government had done is nothing more than to plant a trap for an unwary criminal.[11]

Mindful of the question of entrapment, SCRU personnel have placed much emphasis on the element of timing. It is the single most important technique in the decoy operation. If the timing is right, the chances that the play will succeed are extremely good. If the timing is off, the play will not go down. There are two phases to the timing technique.

In the first phase, timing is a matter of coordination between the team leader and the decoy. During this phase, the team leader plays a significant role in the operation. In addition to directing the activities of the entire team, he must advise the decoy of approaching suspects and guide her movements accordingly. For example, he will advise the decoy that a suspect is approaching from her right, and that he is about six feet tall, and is wearing a blue shirt, tan trousers, and white sneakers. He will also advise the decoy that the suspect is walking close to the building line. Most importantly, he must gauge with a high degree of accuracy how fast the suspect is walking. This information, which is also relayed to the decoy, will enable the team leader to command the decoy to move out on the street at the precise moment that the oncoming suspect will cross her path. Timing is extremely important here. If the team leader's timing is good, there will be an encounter between the decoy and the suspect; if it is not good, the decoy may exit either too early or too late, and the play will not "go down."

The information relayed to the decoy will allow her to make several determinations. First, she can visually identify the suspect if there are other people near him when he arrives at her location. Second, aware of the direction from which he is approaching and that he is walking close to the building line, the decoy will make a right turn at a slight angle. This movement will avoid a collision and will keep him between her and the building. By contrast, if the suspect is walking in the middle of the sidewalk, the decoy will turn right at a wider angle. This movement will allow her to keep to his left or to cross his path and move to his right. Either way, an encounter with the suspect is certain to occur.

In the second phase of the timing technique, which is the third determination that she will be able to make from information received in the first phase, the decoy will be able to exit from her base at the speed required for the encounter. In other words, having information as to the rate of speed that the suspect is moving, the decoy can coordinate her movements with the exit command of the team leader. Finally, the decoy must determine, with a high level of accuracy, the proper moment to display the money to the oncoming suspect. If she moves too slowly toward the suspect and if the money is not prominently displayed, the timing will not be right and the play will not go down.

Confrontation and Chase by the Backup Team

Once the suspect has focused on his intended victim, the backup team will move into position and monitor the movements of the decoy and the suspect. As the suspect closes in on the decoy, at a signal from the team leader the two members in the second vehicle will approach the suspect on foot from different directions. At the moment the robbery occurs, the backup team, with headbands in place and with police shields prominently displayed, will form the triangle around the suspect.

The suspect will be cautioned in a loud and clear but controlled voice, "Police! Don't move." This is a critical moment for all concerned. The suspect, taken by surprise, may simply surrender to the police. He may decide, however, to break and run. If he does, a miscalculation by any team member may result in an unnecessary injury or death to the suspect, a policeman, or to an innocent bystander. Under such circumstances, the team will adhere to specific departmental guidelines that limit the use of firearms.

The position of the New York City Police Department regarding the use of firearms is specified in *Department Patrol Guide 104.1,* which states: "The following guidelines have been developed not to restrict an officer from properly performing his duty, but rather to make it incumbent upon him to use good judgment before using his firearm. The guidelines have been prepared to reduce shooting incidents and consequently protect life and property. Department policy concerning the use of firearms is as follows":

1. a. Reasonable means, minimum force (with exceptions as listed below).
    b. Innocent endangered (prohibited).
    c. Warning shots (prohibited).
    d. Summon assistance (with exceptions as listed below).
    e. Moving vehicle (with exceptions as listed below).
    f. Animals (with exceptions as listed below).
2. Reasonable means, minimum force:
   Every reasonable means will be utilized when arresting, preventing, or terminating a felony or for the defense of oneself or another before a police officer uses his firearm. In all cases, only the minimum amount of force will be used which is consistent with the accomplishment of a mission.
3. Innocent endangered:
   A firearm shall not be discharged if the lives of innocent persons may be endangered.
4. Warning shots prohibited:
   The firing of warning shots is prohibited. A ricocheted bullet or poorly aimed shot may result in death or injury to innocent persons.
5. Summon assistance prohibited:
   Discharging a firearm to summon assistance is prohibited, except where the police officer's safety is endangered.
6. Moving vehicle prohibited:
   Discharging a firearm from or at a moving vehicle is pro-

hibited, unless the occupants of the other vehicle are using deadly physical force against the officer or another by means other than the vehicle.

7. Animals prohibited:
   The discharges of a firearm at dogs or other animals should be an action employed only when no other means to bring the animal under control exists.

8. Police officers on the street are often called upon to make:
   a. Split-second decisions
   b. Under tense conditions
   c. About the use of their guns

9. The police officer has to make decisions right on the spot. If it's a wrong one:
   a. He can be injured, or
   b. He can cause injury to innocent persons, or
   c. He can be subject to disciplinary action.

10. The police officer on the street must understand thoroughly the principles that guides the Justification for the Use of Physical Force in Making an Arrest or Preventing an Escape.
    Primary Thrust
    a. Protection of people in the community
    b. Justification for the use of physical force in making an arrest or preventing an escape. P.L. 35.30
    c. Conduct during response to emergency.[12]

In addition to honoring the restrictions on discharging weapons, members of SCRU maintain a low weapon visibility; that is, weapons are almost always holstered and kept out of sight. Moreover, after a suspect is confronted and apprehended, all weapons are immediately holstered. This procedure minimizes the accidental discharge of a weapon in the event that the prisoner resists or attempts to escape, and the police must use force in order to restrain him. It also helps in reducing public hostility towards the police in critical situations.

Search and Seizure

Members of the SCRU, because they usually make arrests when they have observed a crime, are particularly likely to be concerned with Fourth Amendment restrictions: "The right of people to be secure in their persons, houses, papers and effects against unreasonable searches and seizures shall not be violated, and no warrants shall issue, but upon probable cause, supported by oath or affirmation, and particularly describing the place to be searched, the persons or things to be seized."

The right to be secure from unreasonable searches and seizures by the agents of the government is one of the most fundamental rights of a free people. The Fourth Amendment places this limitation upon the activities of the sovereign. For many years after its ratification, the amendment was considered to be a limitation only upon the activities of the national government. In due course, however, the Supreme Court selectively incorporated its provisions into the due process clause of the Fourteenth Amendment, thereby placing its limitations upon the activities of the state governments as well.

The amendment does not, of course, prohibit all searches and seizures. It only prohibits those that are unreasonable. Most unreasonable or uncontrolled actions are those in which the police officer, not having sufficient information to justify the search, exceeds the limits placed upon his authority by the amendment.

In most cases, the courts require that, whenever practicable, the police must obtain advance judicial approval of searches and seizures. In other words, the police must be able to convince a magistrate, through information contained in a sworn statement (usually an affidavit), that there is probable cause to justify the search. A properly executed warrant is the usual judicial instrument required to conduct a legal search.

The police are generally reluctant to seek a warrant, however, because of the stringent evidentiary standards courts require for obtaining the warrant and the availability of search and seizure alternatives. It follows that there are some exceptions to the search warrant requirement of the Fourth Amendment. Significant exceptions include (1) warrantless searches incident to a lawful arrest, (2) field interrogation, (3) consent searches, and (4) automobile searches.[13] Senior citizens robbery unit searches are usually justified as warrantless searches incident to a lawful arrest. The nature of SCRU decoy team activities does not permit the court to issue search warrants prior to searches and seizures. Hence, members of the backup team must either arrest the suspect prior to the search, obtain a search warrant, or obtain the suspect's consent for the search. In the absence of any of these conditions a search is not permitted.

In order to assist street anti-crime personnel in complying with Fourth Amendment requirements, the New York State Legislature enacted Section 140.50 of the Criminal Procedure Law. Section 140.50 provides in part, that: "A police officer may stop any person in a public place, located within the officer's geographic area of employment, whom he reasonably suspects is committing, has committed, or is about to commit a felony or misdemeanor listed in the penal law."[14]

Traditionally a search without a search warrant is allowable if it is made incident to a lawful arrest.[15] For example, if shortly after the decoy is robbed, members of the backup team arrest the suspect on the street, and, as a result of the subsequent search of the suspect's person, his "victim's" wallet is recovered, this action would be considered a proper search incident to a lawful arrest and, consequently, a search not requiring a warrant. Thus, in making searches incidental to arrests, the initial arrest must be able to stand without the search, but the search cannot stand without the arrest.

The Arrest

To the policeman, the arrest procedure is not a routine matter. Through training and experience he has been made aware that there is always an element of danger present in an arrest. Sometimes the danger may come from the prisoner himself; at other times it may come from a hostile crowd. In all arrests, therefore the policeman is obliged to follow certain basic procedures to minimize any dangers to himself, his prisoner, or to innocent bystanders.

In the first instance, when making an arrest process, the officer must assume and maintain control of the situation. Here, the manner in which he speaks to the subject is of paramount importance. He must speak to the prisoner in a clear, controlled, and commanding voice. Abusive language, particularly language with racial overtones is to be avoided at all times. Second, extremes in behavior are to be avoided as they can excite a panic response from a youthful offender or from bystanders. Third, the prisoner must be thoroughly searched for weapons and escape devices. Too frequently an improper search or no search at all has resulted in the injury or death of an unsuspecting police officer.[16] Fourth, the prisoner must be hand-cuffed with his hands placed behind his back. This form of restraint will prevent the prisoner from reaching for a unsuspecting officer's weapon and affecting escape. A prisoner restrained in this manner will not be able to run very fast and maintain his balance. Finally, the prisoner is not permitted to talk to bystanders, as he may be con-tacting a friend or an accomplice. If he attempts to incite a crowd to interfere with the arrest he must be immediately removed from the crime scene. Further, if the arrest is effected in an area where people are hostile to the police, the arresting officer will effect the removal of the prisoner from the crime scene as promptly as possible.[17]

Initially, the prisoner is taken to the precinct that has jurisdiction of the area in which the crime was committed. As a matter of rou-tine, the prisoner is asked for his name, address, telephone number, age, and the names of his parents. No further questioning is per-mitted. After the arrest is recorded and the necessary paperwork is completed, the prisoner is then transported to the Central Booking Division, which is located in another area of the borough. It is at central booking that the prisoner is formally processed into the crim-inal justice system.

Minors (criminals under 16 years of age) are also transferred to the Central Booking Division. After the necessary reports are com-pleted and authorization for the prisoner's release comes down, the juvenile is remanded to the custody of the juvenile authorities. In all cases involving juvenile arrests, the police authorities immediately notify the juveniles' parents or guardians.

NOTES

1. Taped interview with Rosemary "Rip-off Rosie" Carbonaro, Brooklyn, New York, June 15, 1979.
2. Halper, Andrew and Ku, Richard, An Exemplary Project, New York Police Department — Street Crime Unit (New York: Abt Associates, Inc., 1975; Su-perintendant of Documents, U.S. Government Printing Office, Washington, D.C., S.N. 027-000-0038-9), p. 9.
3. Halper and Ku, pp. 33-34.
4. Halper and Ku, p. 34.
5. Carbonaro
6. Carbonaro
7. Carbonaro

8. Skolnick, Jerome, Justice Without Trial: Law Enforcement in Democratic Society (New York: Wiley, 1966), p. 42.

9. Daudistel, Howard, C., et al., Criminal Justice, Situations and Decisions (New York: Holt, Rinehart and Winston, 1979), pp. 87-88.

10. Lewis, Peter and Peoples, Kenneth, The Supreme Court and The Criminal Process — Cases and Comments (Philadelphia: W. B. Saunders Co., 1978), p. 484.

11. Kerper, Hazel, Introduction to the Criminal Justice System, as revised by Joseph H. Israel (St. Paul: West Publishing Co., 1979), p. 123.

12. New York City Police Department, Precinct Anti-Crime Tactical Training Manual (New York: Police Academy, 1976), pp. 15-17.

13. Senna, Joseph and Siegal, Larry, Introduction to Criminal Justice (St. Paul, 1978), pp. 199-200.

14. Precinct Anti-Crime Tactical Training Manual, p. 59.

15. Senna and Siegal, Introduction to Criminal Justice, p. 200.

16. Precinct Anti-Crime Tactical Training Manual, p. 84.

17. Interview with Sergeant Richard Fitzpatrick, June 6, 1979.

CHAPTER 4

THE DECOY TEAM IN ACTION

IN the preceding chapter we examined the com-
position of a decoy team, its mission, and the concept of how a team
operates in the field. This chapter will focus on the actual operations
of a SCRU decoy team. The chronology of events, from the stakeout
to the apprehension and arrest of the suspect, will be described
precisely as witnessed and recorded by the author. Two of the three
decoy operations that will be discussed here were successful, and it
should be noted that the reverse ratio is most often the case. As a
matter of record, a study of SCRU crime statistics has disclosed that
approximately 20 percent of decoy operations are successful.

A CHRONOLOGY OF DECOY TEAM OPERATIONS

The Identification, Contact, Apprehension,
and Arrest of Jacques LeDuc

The decoy team for this day's operation was composed of Officer
William (Billy) Lohse, team leader; Officer Eileen (code name,
"Easy Eileen") Thompson, decoy; and Officers Joseph Dailey and
Thomas Meehan, backup team.

Before the team proceeded to its target area, Sergeant Richard
Fitzpatrick assigned it to surveillance duty at a senior citizen's picnic
in Prospect Park in Brooklyn. On this day, SCRU was to receive a
commendation award in recognition of its service to the elderly. The
picnic and the award ceremony were arranged by the Flatbush
Inter-Agency for the Aged. After the award ceremony, the team proceeded to its assigned area.

Officer Thompson rode in the command car with Officer Lohse
and the author. She left the car at Flatbush Avenue and Regents
Place and walked one block north to the target area, which was
located at the intersection of Flatbush Avenue and Albemarle Road.

After she arrived in the target area, Officer Thompson located a
a suitable apartment building on Albemarle Road. The building was

located approximately forty yards from the intersection. Officer Lohse and Officer Thompson agreed that she would "work" the stores on Flatbush Avenue and proceed to the building after she made her play. Officer Lohse parked the command car on the right side of Flatbush Avenue, south of Albemarle Road, and approximately fifteen feet from the intersection. Officer Thompson was to work the left side of Flatbush Avenue, north of Albemarle Road. From the vantage point chosen, Officer Lohse had a clear view of both the north side of Flatbush Avenue, where the stores were located, and the west side of Albemarle Road where the apartment building was located. He was also in position to turn west on Albemarle Road. The backup team parked the observation van on the right side of Albemarle Road, approximately fifty feet west of the entrance to the apartment building. The operation began at 1:45 PM.

The Chronology of the Operation

1:50 PM OFFICER LOHSE: "Eileen, on your right. Blue shirt, tan pants, get ready. Come out (pause) No good, Eileen, go back."

OFFICER THOMPSON: "The decoy acknowledged Officer Lohse's instructions by depressing the button on her microphone twice.

In this instance, the subject observed the play, but he walked past the decoy.

1:58 PM OFFICER LOHSE: "All right, Eileen, on your right we're going to have two. One with a white shirt, black pants. The other one is wearing a black hat. They're coming fast. Start coming out now. They're in the middle of the sidewalk. (pause) The guy in the black took a good look at you. Start walking towards the corner. (pause) No good, Eileen, go back."

The subjects stopped at the corner and watched the decoy for several seconds. They looked around the area — probably for plainclothes police — then crossed Albemarle Road and continued south on Flatbush.

2:05 PM OFFICER LOHSE: "Eileen, on your right. White shirt, black pants, white sneakers. He is carrying a small bag. (pause) He got a good look, Eileen, he is slowing down."

(To the author: "I think we got a 'goer.' ")

At this point the subject stopped at the corner and then walked back toward the decoy. Officer Thompson walked into a storefront, counted some money, and put it in her wallet. She put the wallet in her shopping bag.

2:11 PM OFFICER LOHSE: "Come out, Eileen, he's waiting for you. Walk to the corner and head for the building. He's on you, Eileen, keep going."

The subject stopped at the corner and waited for the decoy. A radio patrol car stopped at the opposite side of the street as the decoy turned right on Albemarle Road. The decoy continued to walk toward the apartment building.

2:16 PM OFFICER THOMPSON: "Billy, I'm going in."

OFFICER LOHSE: "Okay, but slow down a little, there's a radio car on the corner."

As the radio patrol car left the scene, the subject continued his pursuit of the decoy.

OFFICER LOHSE (to the backup team): "Joe, do you have Eileen in sight?"

BACKUP TEAM: "Yeah."

OFFICER LOHSE: "Keep going, Eileen, he's closing in."

The decoy entered the building, and the subject followed her inside. After several seconds he emerged from the building, and the decoy signalled that the subject had the wallet.

2:18 PM OFFICER LOHSE: "Okay, he's got it. Let's go!"

Officer Lohse turned west on Albemarle Road and parked the command car approximately thirty feet from the entrance to the apartment building. By the time he arrived at the scene, the backup team had the subject in custody. Officer Lohse entered the building and spoke to the decoy. Upon determining that she was not hurt, he returned to the street.

In the meantime, a small crowd had gathered in the vicinity of the building. A police radio patrol car stopped, and the officers inquired if assistance was needed. Upon being informed that the situation was under control they left the scene. Officer Dailey escorted the prisoner to the observation van, and he was taken to the sixty-seventh precinct. As the crowd began to disperse, Officer Thompson left the building and walked west on Albemarle Road. Officer Lohse, in the command car, was waiting for her at the corner.

At the precinct, the decoy went to a dressing room and removed her disguise. At no time, except for the initial encounter during the robbery, is the prisoner allowed to come into contact with the decoy. This procedure is necesary to protect her identity.

The prisoner was taken to the detective squad room where Officer Dailey, the arresting officer, advised him of his rights. As is the practice in all SCRU arrests, his picture was taken for the unit's identification files. Officer Dailey asked the prisoner for his name, age, home address, telephone number, and for the names of his parents. No further questions were asked, and no other police officers were permitted to talk to the prisoner. Upon receiving the necessary information, Officer Dailey telephoned the prisoner's father — a podiatrist at a local hospital — and informed him of his son's arrest.

After the preliminary arrest procedures were completed, Officers Lohse and Thompson returned to SCRU headquarters. Officers Dailey and Meehan transported the prisoner to the Central Booking Division, which is located at the eighty-fourth precinct. The author received permission from Lieutenant Ray Coles, the task force commander, to accompany the arresting officers to central booking. Ordinarily, civilians, including attorneys, are not allowed in the processing area at central booking.

Formal processing of prisoners into the criminal justice system begins at central booking. In the case of Jacques LeDuc, the following procedures were effected:

First, the prisoner was booked, "mugged" (photographed), and assigned a New York state identification number — in this case, number 26500. Once a prisoner receives an identification number, it remains with him for the rest of his life.

Second, Officer Dailey took the prisoner into an enclosed room, where he was strip-searched. The strip-search procedure is as follows. The prisoner is made to undress completely. He is then ordered to stand in the far corner of the room, facing the wall. The officer will then proceed to search all of his garments for weapons or contraband. Finally, he is moved to the middle of the room and is told to spread his buttocks and squat down in a quick movement. This procedure will expell any contraband that he may have hidden in his body cavity.

Third, the prisoner was fingerprinted.

Fourth, Officer Daily took the prisoner to a detention room. He told him that he could make one phone call, and the prisoner called his parents.

The detention room is a square room with walls twenty-five feet long. Along each wall there is a long wooden bench. Behind the bench, at shoulder height, there is a long steel rod that runs the length of the wall. In front of the bench there are a number of small desks, perhaps six or seven for each bench. The prisoner is seated on the bench, one hand is handcuffed, and the other portion of the handcuff is secured to the rod in the wall. The desk is for the arresting officers use.

After the prisoner completed his call, Officer Dailey sat him at a bench, secured him to the rod, and sat at the desk to write the arrest report. Some of the information included in the report is as follows:

NAME OF ASSAILANT: Jacques LeDuc
TIME OF ARREST: 2:18 PM
PLACE: 2111 Albemarle Road, Brooklyn
AGE: 17
OCCUPATION: Schoolboy — Erasmus Hall Senior High School
PLACE OF BIRTH: Port Au Prince, Haiti
PROPERTY SEIZED: Small wallet, containing money

While Officer Dailey was completing his report, the prisoner's fingerprints were sent to the FAX (Facsimile) unit, and each print was assigned a FAX control number. All numbers were then coded and recorded. The print card was then sent by computer to the main FAX unit at Albany, New York. This procedure was completed in approximately five minutes. About an hour-and-a-half later, the FAX unit at central booking received a report of the prisoner's criminal history. A copy of the report was made available to Officer Dailey. The information contained in the report disclosed that Jacques LeDuc had a previous conviction for robbery.

Through the FAX report, the police are also told whether the prisoner is on parole or probation, or whether there is an outstanding warrant against him, or whether he uses an alias. In police terminology, a person who uses an alias is known as an AKA (also known as). If the prisoner does use one or more aliases, the AKAs are sent to the warrant investigating unit. Here, a check is made for warrants that may have been issued against the prisoner under one of his aliases. A copy of the FAX report is also forwarded to ROR (release on recognizance). At ROR a determination is made as to whether the prisoner is bailable.

Fifth, after all of the information on the prisoner was recorded on the report, Officer Dailey remanded the prisoner to the custody of the precinct officers. The prisoner was then lodged (locked-up). (*Note*: Prisoners are lodged in three separate cell areas. Females are lodged in one cell area, according to age group. Males over sixteen years of age are lodged in a second cell area. Male juveniles, homosexuals, and transvestites are lodged in a third cell area.)

Sixth, when the victim is an elderly citizen, the arresting officer will contact the Victim Services Agency (located at central booking). The arresting officer will inform agency personnel of the crime and of the name of the victim. Agency personnel will then render assistance to the victim. If she is at central booking, she will be taken home. She will be advised that her assailant is in jail, and that he will be of no danger to her. The agency will provide for medical and financial assistance from other help agencies, if required. This step is eliminated when the criminal's *victim* is a police decoy.

Seventh, Officer Dailey went to the Early Case Assessment Bureau (ECAB) for classification of the prisoner. At ECAB, he reviewed the case with an assistant district attorney. After discussing the case with Officer Dailey and examining the prisoner's criminal history, the ADA decided to classify Jacques LeDuc, C (up). The following list will identify the classifications — any one of which an assistant district attorney may assign to a prisoner.

A — The case goes directly to the grand jury. No plea will be accepted at this time.

B — The case may be taken to the grand jury or to a hearing.

C — (up) The case will go to the grand jury. No plea will be allowed at this time. The prisoner will be arraigned. At a future date, however, the prosecutor may allow a plea. If the prosecutor does not allow a plea, the defense may request a hearing in order to determine whether a plea may be allowed. If the pleas are denied, the case will go to the grand jury.

C — At a later date the assistant district attorney may reclassify the prisoner C (up) or C (down).

C — (down) The felony charge is dropped. The crime will be classified as a misdemeanor.

D — The case will be disposed of at the arraignment.

The police have no voice in determining classifications. The procedure is a power vested in the assistant district attorney. A classification is subject to revision or reversal only by the district attorney.

The following forms were completed by various law enforcement personnel as a result of this arrest:

1. Arrest report
2. Supplementary arraignment report
3. Pre-arraignment/arraignment report
4. Arrest/bench warrant (In the event that the prisoner is released and does not report to the court at the appointed date.)
5. Victim Services Agency report
6. Narcotics addiction report
7. Arraignment card
8. Property clerk's invoice (voucher)
9. Complaint report
10. Arresting officer's affidavit

On June 21, 1979, Jacques LeDuc was allowed to plead guilty to a Class A misdemeanor. He was fined fifty dollars and released.

The Decoy Operation of July 18, 1979

This operation was conducted during a lull in Operation Silk Stocking — the search for a particularly vicious killer. Silk Stocking commenced on June 15, 1979, as a result of a series of push-in robberies, at least three of which resulted in the death of the assailant's elderly victims. The operation, which will be discussed in detail in a subsequent chapter, continued almost without interruption for eight of the nine weeks during which the author conducted his study of SCRU.

The decoy team for this day's operation was composed of Officer

Abe Hurtado, team leader; Officer Carol (code name "Courageous Carol") Conry, decoy; Officers Thomas Meehan and Joseph Dailey, backup team. In addition, Officers Robert Gibbons and Ellen Alwill were assigned to conduct a continuing surveillance of the area in an unmarked observation van. They were to cruise the area in a continuing search for the Silk Stocking robber and to act as a second backup team in the event of a decoy's encountering a possible suspect.

The operation began at 11:05 AM. Because of a heavy rain, the decoy remained in the command car with Officer Hurtado and the author. As the rain continued unabated, Officer Hurtado decided to cruise the area until it subsided. Officers Dailey and Meehan were instructed to do the same and to maintain contact with the command car and the observation van.

All command cars are equipped with a division receiver-transmitter, which is kept in operation at all times. During the time Officer Hurtado was cruising in the crime area, division dispatchers continually informed all cruising units of crimes and accidents that had occurred or were occurring in the area. The following taken from the author's notes is a chronology of such occurrences:

The Chronology of the Events

11:10 AM Cardiac attack, white male — on the street. 1018 Bedford Avenue.

11:14 AM Child struck by car. 6270 Linden Blvd. Ambulance and police unit responding.

11:16 AM Female, black. Beaten by male, black. Going to Kings County Hospital. Police unit responding.

11:18 AM Hold-up alarm from 1002 Rutland Road — Supermarket. Radio car responding.

11:22 AM All units advised to be on look-out for a runaway child: female, Hispanic, fourteen years, five feet seven inches, brown blouse, blue denims, white sneakers, Flora Martinez.

11:26 AM Break-in, apartment at 2351 Caton Avenue, radio car responding.

11:31 AM Woman with a knife. Dispute with neighbor. 7201 Church Avenue. Police unit responding.

11:34 AM Prowler, top floor, Apartment 6-C, 5628 Empire Boulevard. Radio car responding.

11:37 AM Male, black, with a hatchet, on a bike. He is after a female postal worker. Foster and Bedford avenues. (pause) Street crime unit personnel called in and reported that they have had this male under observation. Request all units to stay away. They will handle this one.

11:40 AM Child fell from a sixth floor window. 2704 Kings Highway. Ambulance and radio car responding.

11:44 AM Black male, black hat, and black clothes; carrying a gun. 2305 Flatbush Avenue. Radio car responding.

It stopped raining at approximately 12:30 PM. Officer Hurtado discussed several possible target areas for the day's operation. It was decided that the team would work on Church Avenue, between Flatbush and Bedford avenues. This portion of Church Avenue was selected because it contained eight to ten stores from which the decoy could make her plays. Officer Hurtado contacted the backup teams and advised them of the location of the target area. Officers Gibbons and Alwill were to continue to cruise in the area.

At the target area, Officer Conry decided to work out of a carpet store on the right of side of Church Avenue. Officers Meehan and Dailey decided to leave the car and set up an observation post at the Manufacturer — Hanover Bank — to the left of the carpet store on the corner of Flatbush and Church avenues. The command car was positioned approximately 100 feet from the carpet store and thirty feet from the driveway of a funeral parlor. The operation began at 1:15 PM.

The Chronology of the Operation

1:20 PM OFFICER HURTADO: "Carol, there are two mutts walking towards from your left, but they were the ones who walked by you a few minutes ago, so I'm not going to play these guys, they're local."

1:30 PM OFFICER HURTADO: "Carol, on your left. He has a tank shirt with a number "12," rust-colored pants, white sneakers, and a blue rain hat. (The decoy acknowledged.) He's walking fairly close to the carpet store. You can start coming out."

The decoy made her play, but the subject, after taking a look at her, walked away.

1:32 PM OFFICER HURTADO: (to the backup team) "Heads up,

guys. The guy that Carol just played walked into the shoe store."

1:33 PM OFFICER HURTADO: "Disregard him, Carol. He's walking towards Flatbush. I've got a guy coming in a black raincoat, leather hat, dungarees, white socks, and black sneakers. He's hugging the wall. He's coming to you from your left. (pause) You got that guys? (The backup team acknowledged.) (pause) I'm sorry, Carol, he came up so fast that I couldn't give you the okay to come out."

The team leader explained to the author that there were too many people in the vicinity of the carpet store, and he momentarily lost sight of the subject. He said, "Sometimes we'll lose a few that way."

1:45 PM OFFICER HURTADO: "Tommy, I've got a hearse in the driveway. It's blocking my view of the carpet store. I won't play anything from my end. You guys take it. Let Carol know when to come out. Just give me a good description." (The backup team acknowledged.)

There was no activity for almost fifteen minutes. During this time, the hearse moved out. The team leader resumed command of the operation.

2:05 PM OFFICER HURTADO: "Carol, I've got two coming on your right. Blue T-shirt, brown pants, white tank top, dungarees; he is carrying an umbrella. They are in the middle of the sidewalk. (pause) Okay, start out. It looks like the guy in the blue shirt saw the play. He said something to the guy in the white tank top. Neither one of them has looked back yet. Just take a little stroll. Don't go too far. They are out of my view now. Tommy, let me know what they do."

OFFICER MEEHAN: "They just went into a discount store."

OFFICER HURTADO: "Did you notice if they looked back at Carol?"

OFFICER MEEHAN:"No."

OFFICER HURTADO: "Tommy, from what exit will you leave the bank if he goes towards Flatbush?"

OFFICER MEEHAN: "I'll be coming out of the Church

Avenue exit."

OFFICER HURTADO: "Will you be able to cover him from that corner if he breaks into a gallop?"

OFFICER MEEHAN: "Hopefully, yes. (pause) Abe, Carol, they're coming out. Get ready, Carol. (pause) Forget them. They just crossed the street and are heading towards Bedford."

2:25 PM OFFICER HURTADO: "Carol, we are going to make plays from both ends. If you get a play from Tommy's end remember what I told you yesterday at Fifty-first and Church. Angle out towards the guy. Angle out and meet him halfway. Don't meet him at the doorway." (The decoy acknowledged.)

2:27 PM OFFICER MEEHAN: "Carol, on your left. Brown hat, white shirt, dungarees, white sneakers. He's coming up fast — in the middle of the sidewalk. (pause) Move out Carol."

OFFICER HURTADO: "Too late, too late, too late. No good, Carol, he never broke stride. You came out too late.

2:31 PM OFFICER MEEHAN: "Abe, there's a guy in a red tank shirt, black cap. He is directly across the street from me. He is hanging out at 2211.

OFFICER HURTADO: "That's the senior citizen center. I can't see him because of the garbage that's on the sidewalk. Keep an eye on him, Tom, a lot of old people go into the place."

OFFICER CONRY: "I don't think that I should make a play on him. I would prefer to go into the lobby and look at the directory. He might pick me up while I'm inside. (pause) Tom, have you seen any old people coming in or out?"

OFFICER MEEHAN: "No, I haven't seen any."

OFFICER HURTADO: "All right, Carol, you can go do that. Don't spend more than thirty seconds looking at the directory. Leave the building and walk towards Flatbush. We'll break the operation off from there."

OFFICER MEEHAN: "Carol, how about if on the way out you just check your money for a second or so?"

OFFICER CONRY: "It doesn't make sense to be taking money out in that place."

OFFICER MEEHAN: "Okay, I believe you're right."

OFFICER CONRY: "What if I make a light play on him as I enter the building? That would be better than taking it out while I am in the lobby or after I leave."

OFFICER HURTADO: "That's good, Carol, make your play before you go into the building. Remember what I said to you. I want you in there no more than thirty seconds. If he doesn't pick up on you, I want you to walk out after you finish reading the directory."

The decoy acknowledged the team leader's instructions and proceeded towards the senior citizen center. As she passed the subject, she made her play and walked into the lobby; after reading the directory, she left the building.

2:37 PM OFFICER HURTADO: "Tom, did he get a look at her?"

OFFICER MEEHAN: "Yes, he gave her a good look, but there is no movement."

OFFICER HURTADO: "Where is Carol now?"

OFFICER MEEHAN: "She is nearing the corner of Flatbush. He is still watching her, but there is no movement."

OFFICER HURTADO: "Okay. Keep me informed of Carol's position, as I'm going to start rolling."

OFFICER MEEHAN: "She is on the other side of Flatbush. He is still watching her, but there is no movement."

At this point, Officer John Lohse who was in the area working on the Silk Stocking case contacted the team leader and advised him that he had the decoy in sight.

OFFICER HURTADO: "Okay, Tom, John has her in sight."

OFFICER CONRY: "Abe, where do you want me to go from here?"

OFFICER HURTADO: "Cross over to Twenty-first Street and walk towards the cemetery. If he doesn't make a move by that time, we'll pick you up. (pause) Keep going that way, Carol. I can see him in the doorway. I don't think we're going to get any movement from this guy."

OFFICER MEEHAN: "He's still looking her way, Abe, but he hasn't moved. (pause) There's a guy walking east on Church. (pause) Ha! Ha! He is completely naked."

A few minutes later, division radio reported the incident. A radio car was dispatched to intercept the man.

The subject remained at the senior citizen center, and the operation was called off at 2:50 PM. It was resumed at a different location at 3:10 PM. After several unsuccessful plays at the new location, the day's activities were terminated at 4:30 PM.

At SCRU headquarters the team held a rap session, and the events of the day were discussed in detail. Much of the discussion centered on the necessity of improving the timing techniques.

The Identification, Contact, Apprehension and Arrest of Lemuel Willard

Although the stakeout phase of Silk Stocking was terminated on July 6, 1979, the investigative phase continued without interruption. Concurrent with the investigative activities, SCRU supervisors assigned some decoy team members to surveillance duty in the suspect's target areas. All SCRU members were supplied with a composite drawing of the suspect that was developed from information obtained from his victims.

The plan of operations as developed by SCRU supervisors was as follows:

(a) The decoy team was to conduct its normal activities in the assigned crime area. The team leader was, to the greatest extent possible, however, to select those subjects who fit the general description of the Silk Stocking Robber;

(b) The surveillance team was to cruise throughout the crime area and to maintain contact with the decoy team;

(c) If the activities of the investigative team extended into the crime area, it was to advise both the decoy team and the surveillance team of its presence; and

(d) The surveillance team would act as a floating support unit for either the decoy team or the investigative team.

Hence, although the three teams were operating as independent units within the crime area, the main purpose was to make contact with and apprehend the Silk Stocking suspect.

The decoy team for this day's operation was composed of Officer William Lohse (team leader), Officer Eileen Thompson (decoy), and Officers Abe Hurtado and Thomas Meehan (backup team). Officers John Lohse, Robert Gibbons, and Carol Conry were assigned to surveillance duty. The author was assigned to work with Officer Lohse.

On this day, Officer Thompson elected to work out of the European American Bank, located on the east corner of Nostrand and Newkirk avenues. Earlier she had selected two buildings into which she could enter after she made her play. Both buildings were located on Newkirk Avenue: one at 3013 and the other at 3019. The command car was parked on the west side of Newkirk Avenue, north of Nostrand, and approximately sixty feet diagonally away from the bank. The backup team was south on Newkirk Avenue near the intersection of East Thirty-first Street and approximately 200 feet from the building at 3019. It was agreed that the decoy would make her play from the bank and proceed south on Newkirk Avenue to one of the buildings. The operation began at 11:25 AM.

The Operation

11:25 AM OFFICER LOHSE: "Abe, can you give me a reading?"

OFFICER HURTADO: "I read you five by five, Billy. I moved to the west side of Newkirk. I have a better view of the apartment buildings and the bank."

OFFICER LOHSE: "I was going to suggest that, because if I have to move out this truck is blocking my lane, and if there are any cars at the red light, I'll have to go out on foot."

OFFICER HURTADO: "Okay, I'm on the same side of the street you are — I'm facing New York Avenue. I have the entrance to the buildings and to the (housing) project secured."

11:31 AM OFFICER LOHSE: "Eileen, from your right. Red shirt, blue pants, white sneakers. He's moving across Nostrand. Start moving out. (pause) He got a look, but he kept on going. Go back."

11:35 AM OFFICER LOHSE: "Alright, Eileen, we've got a kid com-

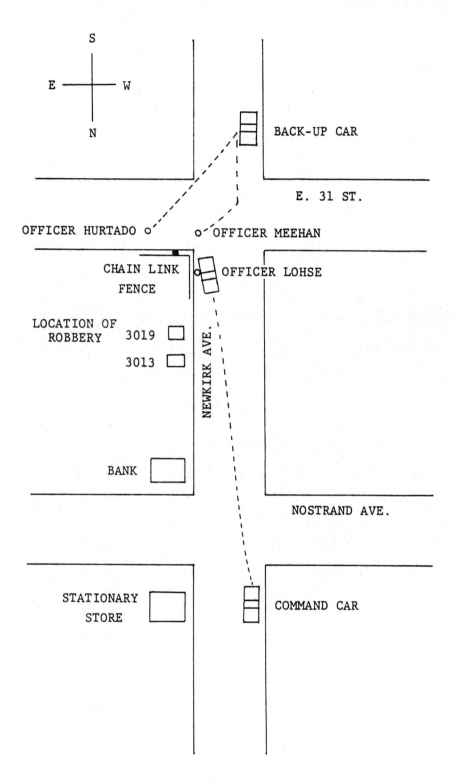

Figure 4-1. THE DECOY OPERATION OF JULY 24, 1979

ing down Newkirk, he is on your left, same side as the
bank. He has a brown jogging suit. Okay, Eileen, you
can start coming out now. He saw it. He got a good
look at it, Eileen. He looked just once. Keep calm, let's
see his reactions. (pause) We've got a "goer" here. He
crossed the street and is standing by the candy store.
He is giving you a good look."

11:37 AM OFFICER LOHSE: "Okay, Eileen, he went into the candy store. He might be looking at you through the window. Keep walking towards the building. (pause) He
just walked out. He took a look at you and walked
back inside. Keep going."

At this point, the decoy entered the building. The team leader
advised her that the subject was still in the candy store. After a few
minutes, the team leader told the decoy to leave the building and to
proceed to the bank.

11:41 AM OFFICER LOHSE: "He's out. Abe, can you see him? I
have this oil truck blocking my view."
OFFICER HURTADO: "Yes. He's looking at Eileen. He's
crossing the street and is walking in her direction."
OFFICER LOHSE: "Let me know what's going on, Abe."
OFFICER HURTADO: "Eileen is returning to the building. He's picking up his pace. I think there is someone
in the hallway. She is not going in. She went in.
(pause) Somebody chased her out of the hallway. The
kid is following right behind her."
OFFICER LOHSE: "Damn it, the same thing happened
yesterday."

The decoy moved towards the second building. The subject walked up to her and he spoke to her briefly and then walked to a
building some thirty feet away and sat on an iron railing.

11:46 AM OFFICER LOHSE: "Eileen, did he say anything to you?"
OFFICER THOMPSON: "He asked me if I was lost."
OFFICER LOHSE: "Okay. Go to the building and start
reading the names on the mailboxes. Eileen, he's starting to walk towards you. Be sharp on this, Abe; I've
got this freaking truck in my way. We've got a goer
here. He wants that money."

OFFICER HURTADO: "He broke it off. He just went back to the place (iron railing) he was before, Bill. I think he is looking around for a backup."

OFFICER LOHSE: "Yeah, he is still looking at her. He's coming again, Eileen. Keep moving. Son of a bitch. He walked away."

OFFICER HURTADO: "He is on the corner. He is looking toward East Thirty-first Street.

OFFICER LOHSE: "She got chased out the hall again; ain't that a bitch!"

11:50 AM OFFICER HURTADO: "He's coming back. He stopped at 3013 and is looking up at the windows. He moved back to the railing. (pause) He's coming back."

OFFICER LOHSE: "I have a good view now. He's taking off his jacket, Abe. This guy is going to be a runner on us, so be ready."

OFFICER LOHSE: "Okay, Eileen, don't come out, he's starting to walk up real slow. He has his jacket off. What he'll probably do is take it (the wallet) and stick it under the jacket."

At that moment a woman walked out of 3013, and the suspect walked away. He returned to the iron railing and then walked to the corner of East Thirty-first Street.

11:54 AM OFFICER LOHSE: "Eileen, that woman fouled it up. You will have to move out. Is that building near where he was sitting any good? (The decoy acknowledged in the affirmative.) Okay, then work that one. He's waiting for you near the corner. He is looking your way. He wants the bread."

OFFICER LOHSE: "Abe, this traffic has me blocked — I can't move. What's going on?"

OFFICER HURTADO: "That woman is still there, but he is still on Eileen."

OFFICER LOHSE: "Okay, I'm clear now. He's still there. He wants that money. (The decoy is now in 3019.) (pause) Okay, Eileen, Abe, he's coming down now — get ready. He's going in. (After several seconds, the decoy signalled the team leader.) Okay, he's got it! Let's go!"

The subject emerged from the building and strode quickly towards East Thirty-first Street. Officer Lohse moved the command car to the corner of East Thirty-first Street and Newkirk Avenue. As the command car moved into position, Officers Hurtado and Meehan, moving on foot, apprehended the suspect on the East Thirty-first Street side of the corner. As soon as the officers holstered their weapons, the suspect began to resist the arrest. He quickly moved to a chain link fence, placed his upper torso over the railing, and held on to the fence from the inside and began yelling for help. It was difficult for the arresting officers to break his grip from the fence. Lohse went to their assistance (*see* Fig. 4).

12:06 PM SUBJECT: "I just crossed the street from East Thirty-first Street. Get off me. What the fuck are you doing to me? Eddie! Eddie! Help! Eddie! Eddie! Oh shit! Let me go! Eddie! Eddie! Help! Come and help me!"

OFFICER MEEHAN: "Let go of the fence, kid. We don't want to hurt you."

SUBJECT: "Get off of me, man! Eddie! Eddie! Help me!"

OFFICER LOHSE (displaying his shield to a gathering crowd): "Police, stand back!"

SUBJECT: "Get off! Get off! Eddie! Eddie! They're killing me! Help!

As the struggle continued, the crowd grew larger. Lohse returned to the command car and attempted to summon assistance. He could not contact headquarters or any of the support units because of the tall buildings in the area and because of the limited range of the transmitter.

In the meantime, two of the subject's older brothers and his mother responded to his calls for help. One of his brother's had a golf club.

OFFICER HURTADO (displaying his shield to the subject's family): "Police, move back!" (They obeyed his command.)

Officer Lohse returned to assist his fellow officers. By this time the crowd was growing larger and somewhat hostile. The suspect's mother asked, "Why are they arresting him?" The author told her that her son had just robbed an old lady. One of his brother's re-

sponded, "That can't be. He just left the house a few minutes ago."
The author walked away and joined Lohse, who was trying to contact headquarters from the backup vehicle. This effort also failed.

> 12:12 PM OFFICER LOHSE (to the team): "I can't get anybody on
> the radio. We've got to get this kid out of here before
> all hell breaks loose!"
>
> THE SUBJECT: "Get off me! Get off me! Eddie, help
> me! I don't want to go back to jail! Help me, Eddie! I
> don't want to get locked up again!"
>
> THE AUTHOR (to a woman looking out of an apartment window): "Dial 911, lady, okay? (The woman
> did not respond.) (pause) Lady, dial 911 — get the
> police! (She moved away from the window and did not
> return.)

The arresting officers were finally able to break the suspect's grip
on the fence, though the suspect continued to struggle with his captors. They forcibly moved him to a parked automobile where they
placed his upper torso on the hood and proceeded to handcuff him.

> 12:20 PM HEADQUARTERS RADIO: "We have a 10-13 (police
> officer in need of assistance). We have a 10-13 at East
> Thirty-first Street and Newkirk. (pause) Available unit
> responding."

Within ninety seconds, two radio patrol cars and the SCRU support team responded to the call, and a second SCRU unit arrived
shortly thereafter. The team later learned that the woman at the
window did not call the police. The emergency call was placed by a
local trucker who had recognized one of the team members.

> 12:24 PM HEADQUARTERS RADIO: "No further on that 10-13, repeat, no further on that 10-13." (No further assistance
> required. The officers at the scene are in control of the
> situation.)

The subject was finally subdued. He was searched, and the
decoy's wallet was recovered. He was then escorted to the backup
vehicle and transported to the sixty-seventh police precinct. The
SCRU support team left the area and contacted the decoy. After the
robbery, Officer Thompson left the building and went to Nostrand
Avenue where she was met by the support team. She was unaware of

the events that occurred at East Thirty-first Street and Newkirk. The uniformed police remained in the area until the crowd dispersed.

12:35 PM THE AUTHOR: "Come on, Billy, let's get out of here. (in the command car): He sure was a tough bastard."
OFFICER LOHSE: "Damned right he was. He knew we had him. He didn't want to get arrested again."

During the drive to the sixty-seventh precinct, Officer Lohse explained the gravity of the situation. He said, "This is a particularly bad area. In the past two weeks there have been six separate shootings here. Most of the shootings were done by the Rastafarians (Rasty's). They are a vicious cult group from the island of Jamaica. The use of marijuana is part of their cult ritual. Most of them carry .9-mm pistols — this is a particularly lethal weapon . . . just one hit is enough to kill a guy or cripple him for life. They are very hostile to the police. . . .

We were very lucky on that corner. And that is because the kid wasn't a Rasty. If he were, we would have had a shoot-out. . . . Another thing that helped us was the fact that we used minimum force — something else helped — we didn't use our weapons. The kid knew what he was doing. He wanted us to beat him up. If we 'drew blood' we might not be here talking about it." He then added: "We have to be very careful how we treat these kids when we arrest them. Since you've been with us, you've seen the attitude of these people toward us. Most of these kids are about fifteen or sixteen years old and they're black. We're white. Mobs don't know what the kid has done and some don't even care. All they see is a black kid being arrested and beaten up by white cops. That's all they need to start a riot. That's the situation we were in today."

At the sixty-seventh precinct the prisoner was taken to the detective squad room on the second floor, where he was photographed. He was led to a small anteroom for questioning.

OFFICER MEEHAN: "What is your name, and where do you live?"
THE PRISONER: "You guys trapped me. You set me up."
OFFICER MEEHAN: "What is your name, and where do you live?"
THE PRISONER: "Officer, you didn't arrest me legally.

When you arrested me you didn't say, 'We're police officers.' You just jumped me."

OFFICER MEEHAN: "We showed you our police shields, and we said, 'Police, don't move.' What is your name, and where do you live?"

THE PRISONER: "I don't have to tell you a damned thing."

At that point, Officer Robert Gibbons, one of the support team members, approached the prisoner. He stared at the prisoner for a few seconds and in a calm but firm voice asked, "Want any help?" The prisoner looked up at Officer Gibbons and recited his name, address, phone number, and his mother's name. He was then permitted to call his mother.

THE PRISONER: "I didn't do anything, Ma, they're lying. (pause) You know that I wouldn't lie to you, Ma; they're lying. (pause) I don't want to go back to jail. (pause) Okay, but hurry up. They're going to take me away from here."

A preliminary investigation disclosed that Lemuel Willard was scheduled for a court appearance on July 25, 1979, to answer an earlier charge of robbery. The prisoner was subsequently transferred to the Central Booking Division for processing into the criminal justice system.

Willard was convicted upon a plea of guilty to the charge of robbery in the second degree. He was sentenced to serve a six-month term at the Brooklyn Correctional Institution.

The chronology of events as reported in the preceding cases is typical of the procedures and innovative techniques utilized by SCRU in its efforts to protect the elderly and to reduce the crime rate in the inner city. The events are also accurate indicators of the problems and dangers that often confront plainclothes policemen in the performance of their duties in a hostile environment.

Most policemen, and policewomen, of course, with whom the author came into contact during the summer of 1979 accept the dangers inherent in their duties as part of the job. They are aware that the public is, for the most part, insensitive to these dangers and often openly hostile to them. Some are bitter and make no attempt to disguise their resentment of the community and of the criminal justice system. The greater majority, however, are aware that the ally of the policeman is an enlightened and cooperative public. Hence, they are continually working to improve relations between the police and members of the community. During a discussion on the subject of community relations, Lieutenant Ray Coles, said, "The improvement of relations between the public and the police is a major concern to me and to police administrators. We must help people when they are in trouble. We must let them know that we need them and that they can depend on us. Our relationship should be one of mutual understanding and respect."

The single factor that frustrates the police and the one that most are unwilling to accept is the concept of diversion. As a police officer said to the author: "This guy beat the hell out of an eighty-three-year-old woman. He is fifteen years old. It just kills me to think that he'll be out on the streets in a few months. You know what he will be doing when he gets out? He'll go looking for another old lady!"

During a discussion on the subjects of entrapment and of diversion, an official of the New York City Supreme Court told the author, "Entrapment is not the problem. The defense has accused the police of entrapment on many occasions; particularly in the cases of decoy arrests. The charges have never held up in court. The problem is diversion. The courts cannot continue to let these kids out on the streets and expect the police to maintain order." When asked if he had a solution to the problem, he said: "Build more jails!"

Perhaps the court official's statement may be considered to be a crass and insensitive oversimplification of a serious and complex social and legal problem to those who believe in the concepts of diversion or restitution or rehabilitation. But to the policeman who must deal with the recidivist on a daily basis and to the court official who has no influence over the decisions of the judge, the problem is developing into a crisis of major proportion that will result in a breakdown of law and order. Hence, they see no alternative to incarceration.

CHAPTER 5

UNIT INVESTIGATIVE TEAMS

Functions

CHAPTERS Five and Six contain a detailed analysis of the investigative component of SCRU. The investigative teams play a significant role in crime control by virtue of their information gathering, crime analysis, and law enforcement functions. Unlike the decoy teams, unit investigators do not effect disguises or utilize special deployment tactics, and, therefore, they are more visible to the members of the community,

The teams, consisting of two or three members, are primarily responsible for responding to and investigating complaints from elderly citizens. During the investigation of a complaint or a crime, a team may coordinate its activities with one or more of the following departmental groups: (a) street crime personnel, (b) uniformed precinct personnel, (c) division detective squads (for example, homicide or narcotics of burglary squad), (d) latent fingerprint section, (e) department artist, and (f) CATCH system personnel.

In addition to their investigative functions, the teams are responsible for the continuing surveillance of high-crime areas under SCRU jurisdiction, assisting decoy teams or other street crime units when the need arises,.and rendering assistance to elderly crime victims. This latter function may include transporting the victim home or to the hospital, securing the victim's apartment (having the locks changed), or providing for medical or financial assistance.

In instances when a victim has been assaulted in her apartment as a result of a push-in robbery (the victim is seized by the assailant at the entrance to her apartment and is pushed inside), the investigator will arrange to have the victim stay with a relative or with a friend for a few days. If this is not possible, an elderly citizen help agency will be called and advised of the victim's situation. Agency personnel will visit the victim regularly until she has recovered from her experience.

The interest by SCRU personnel in the welfare and safety of the elderly is one of genuine concern. It is not uncommon for an investigator to visit a victim at the hospital or at home to inquire about her general health or her needs. Most investigators will return to the victim's apartment, clean it up, and then arrange for transportation home after she is released.

Senior citizen robbery unit investigators also perform an important educational function. As liaison between the police and the community they are in daily contact with the various public and private agencies that have been established to assist elderly citizens. Team members are regularly assigned to speak at picnics, rallies, and other functions for elderly citizens. In addition, investigators conduct regularly scheduled seminars and workshops for the elderly, where they outline the various measures that the elderly must take to ensure maximum personal safety. Among other precautionary measures are (1) never resist an assailant. Resistance almost always leads to violence by the criminal, which could result in serious injury or death; (2) do not travel alone, particularly at night; (3) arrange to have social security benefit checks or pension checks sent directly to the bank; (4) never display money in public places; (5) avoid wearing jewelry, particularly watches, bracelets, earrings, and neck chains; (6) do not carry large sums of money; (7) when on the street, keep alert at all times; (8) do not enter a building if there are unfamiliar people loitering near the entrance or in the immediate vicinity; and (9) never enter an elevator with a stranger.

After the investigator has finished his remarks he opens a question session. Most of the questions are directed to the problems of building security, the need for increased uniformed police patrols, transportation, and financial assistance. At the close of the session, the elderly are provided with a number of instructional pamphlets. The pamphlets contain additional reminders on security and safety and a listing of the addresses, telephone numbers, emergency call numbers, and the location of the area agencies that will assist victims and of the local police precinct.

Crime analysis is an essential police function that enables departmental planners to coordinate activities among the various commands and to develop crime control strategies in high-crime areas.

The senior citizen robbery unit does not have its own crime analysis section, therefore, it receives crime statistics data on a daily, weekly, and monthly basis from such sources as precinct crime analysis sections, the citywide crime analysis section, and PBBS crime data section. The data are combined with the daily crime reports submitted by the unit's field teams. As a minimum, the data will include (a) name, address, age, and sex of the victim, (b) time and place of the crime, (c) type of crime, (d) injury to the victim, (e) property loss, and, if possible, (f) identification of the offender.

An analysis of the accumulated data will allow SCRU supervisors to identify high-crime areas, watch for the development of crime patterns, and plan for team assignments.

After the data have been compiled and analyzed, SCRU supervisors then plot the information on the respective area zonal maps on a precinct-by-precinct basis. As discussed earlier, SCRU activities encompass the entire area under PBBS control. The area has been subdivided into four operational zones for ease of crime area identification and SCRU team assignment and deployment. The zones and precincts are then ranked according to the level of crimes committed against the elderly. These rankings are then submitted to the task force commander for approval.

In addition to the zone maps (spot maps), a crime information folder for each zone is provided for the use of SCRU personnel. Among other data, the folder will contain information on the place and the time of the crime, age and sex of the victim, a description of the offender (including a composite drawing), a description of whatever property was stolen, and the type of crime committed. The various crimes that come under the categories of robbery or personal grand larceny are (1) vestibule, (2) lobby, (3) stairway, (4) elevator, (5) hallway, (6) push-in/follow-in, and (7) miscellaneous, which includes street robberies. To these categories are added the separate crimes of assault and battery, manslaughter, and homicide.

Completing the data contained in the crime information folder is a comprehensive study of crime patterns that may be developing in one or more of the four zones of Patrol Borough Brooklyn South. To discover crime patterns, SCRU supervisors compare crimes committed in one precinct with similar crimes reported from the other precincts of the same zone. They then compare the results of their study with similar crimes committed in the precincts of the remaining three zones. In this manner, SCRU supervisors are able to determine whether the developing crime pattern is limited to one or more precincts in a single zone, spreading to one or more precincts in two or more zones, or area wide. Team assignments or deployments, therefore, may be determined by the level of criminal activity in a given area, by existing or developing crime patterns, or by both.

Unit supervisors normally assign cases to investigative teams based on their areas of operation. For example, if a crime occurs in zone one, the team assigned to that zone will receive the case. It follows that a team operating in an assigned zone will respond to a citizen's complaint and will assume responsibility for the conduct of the investigation. Sometimes a team is passed over by SCRU supervisors if it has a heavy case load or if it is on a special assignment.

For purposes of continuity in the investigation of a case and in order to eliminate dual responsibility, SCRU supervisors will assign a case to one member of a team. For example, if a case is assigned to the team of Officers DiCostanzo and Brown, Officer DiConstanzo may be designated as the prime investigator. In this instance, although Officer Brown will participate in every aspect of the case, he will assume a supportive role. When Officer Brown is designated as the prime investigator, the roles are reversed. The team member to whom the case is assigned will assume full responsibility for the conduct of the investigation. Some of the responsibilities of the investigator include (1) interviewing the victim, (2) determining the conditions under which the crime occurred, (3) gathering evidence, (4) listing property loss, (5) coordinating the team's activities with police support units and with civilian support agencies, (6) searching for the suspect, (7) evaluating evidence, and (8) conducting follow-up investigations.

Ordinarily, people making emergency calls to the police use widely publicized police-call channels. A complaint from an elderly citizen, therefore, may be received by a PBBS headquarters dispatcher, a local precinct dispatcher, or a police administrative assistant at SCRU headquarters. In any event, whoever receives the complaint will report it to the responsible police field units. Unless otherwise directed, only those units located in the immediate vicinity of the crime will acknowledge and respond to the call. In the event that an investigative team is not located in the immediate crime area, the SCRU supervisor on duty will dispatch an available team to the scene. Normally, unit decoy teams on assignment, even though they may be located in the immediate vicinity of the crime, will not respond to the complaint. In an emergency situation, however, the unit supervisor may call off a decoy operation and order the team to proceed to the crime scene. Upon the arrival of an investigative team, the decoy team will resume its previous activities.

Sometimes a uniformed police patrol or a street anti-crime unit will arrive at the crime scene before the SCRU investigative team. Whichever unit arrives first will remain at the scene until relieved by a SCRU investigative team, which will assume command of the investigation.

The first concern of the investigator is to assess the physical and mental condition of the elderly victim. If she is injured or is unable to respond, the investigator will arrange to have the victim transported to a hospital. The interview will be postponed to a later date. The investigator will locate a relative or a friend of the victim and will report on the crime and on the condition of the victim. He will also tell the relative or the friend where the victim is.

If the victim is able to respond to the investigator's questions, the interview begins almost at once. Years of experience in the art of interviewing has taught the police that most victims will offer more detailed and more accurate information about the crime and the offender if questioned as soon as possible after the crime was committed. If the interview is conducted at a later date, the victim may forget or be confused. The police have found, moreover, the more the victim thinks about the crime later on or about the possible reprisals, the less inclined she is to risk providing information to identify the offender.

The investigator, well aware of the victim's anxieties and fears, will begin the interview by asking her a few questions about her family or her health. When he is satisfied that she is in a relaxed frame of mind he will begin to question her about the crime. Investigators use a number of techniques or styles when conducting interviews. The use of a specific technique or style will depend upon the physical and mental condition of the victim at the time of the interview.

The following technique was used by detective Phil De Angelo when he interviewed Mrs. Gertrude Rapfogel a few hours after she was assaulted and robbed:

DETECTIVE DE ANGELO: "How are you feeling? Do you want

me to call for an ambulance or a doctor?"

MRS. RAPFOGEL: "No. I'm feeling better now, but I'm still a little nervous."

DETECTIVE DE ANGELO: "I understand. Try to relax. We won't stay very long. Do you have any children?"

MRS. RAPFOGEL: "I have a daughter who lives in Brooklyn Heights."

DETECTIVE DE ANGELO: "Can you give us her telephone number? We would like to call her."

Mrs. Rapfogel gave Detective De Angelo the telephone number. Officer Ellen Alwill went to Mrs. Rapfogel's neighbor's apartment and made a telephone call to her daughter. (Mrs. Rapfogel's telephone wires had been cut by the perpetrator.)

DETECTIVE DE ANGELO: "Are you taking any medication?"

MRS. RAPFOGEL: "I'm taking some pills for my heart."

DETECTIVE DE ANGELO: "How do you feel now? Do you want me to break off the interview? I can come back at another time."

MRS. RAPFOGEL: "I feel fine."

DETECTIVE DE ANGELO: "Who is that good-looking young man in that picture?"

MRS. RAPFOGEL: "That's my grandson. He's an officer in the Navy. He always writes to me. He's a darling boy. I'm very proud of him."

DETECTIVE DE ANGELO: "I can understand why. Gertrude, can you remember anything about the fellow who robbed you? Anything you tell us will remain strictly confidential."

MRS. RAPFOGEL: "Are you sure? I'm afraid that he might come back and hurt me again."

DETECTIVE DE ANGELO: "We want this guy off the streets. The more you can tell us about him, the easier it will be for us to catch him. When we do get him, we'll try to put him away for a long time. Try to relax now, and tell us all you can remember about him."

After some gentle questioning, Mrs. Rapfogel was able to recall some identifying characteristics of her assailant.[1]

As we discussed earlier, SCRU investigators often utilize several investigative techniques when they are conducting an interview. Some will open the interview by asking questions of a personal nature about the victim herself and will then proceed to the more formal questioning about the crime, concluding the interview with the more personal questions. Sometimes, an investigator will utilize a combination of the two techniques, interspersing personal questions with the formal questions. In almost all instances, the investigator will address the victim by her first name.

Although SCRU training manuals provide investigators with a number of techniques and sample questions that may be employed during an interview, unit supervisors are quick to emphasize that there is no single technique that can be considered as the model for the investigator. It is generally recognized, however, that the success of any interview will depend, primarily, upon the state of mind of the victim and upon the skill of the investigator.

It will suffice to say at this time that no question, no matter how innocuous it may appear, is unimportant. Each question serves the purpose of informing the investigator of the circumstances peculiar to the commission of the crime, of the identifying characteristics of the offender, and of the personal statistics of the victim. In addition, the results of the interview become part of the overall crime data that are evaluated by the department's analysts in the development of reports of crime statistics for high-crime areas.

The following interview was conducted by SCRU Investigator Robert Noblin on Monday, July 9, 1979.[2] The crime, a push-in robbery, was committed on Monday, June 4, 1979. The victim, Mrs. Julia Beckel, a seventy-eight-year-old widow, sustained head injuries that required sending her to the hospital. Detective Thomas Matioli had conducted the preliminary interview on the date of the crime. The case was reassigned to Officer Noblin as one of the "pattern" cases to be investigated in the unit's search for the Silk Stocking robber. The interview is typical of those conducted by SCRU investigators. The dialogue follows:

OFFICER NOBLIN: "Julia, I'm here to review your case with you. I know that you discussed it with Detective Matioli on the day of the robbery. But we are conducting a thorough investigation on this guy, and we need more information. The fellow who robbed you is still out there."

MRS. BECKEL: "Here? He's over here?"

OFFICER NOBLIN: "No. We don't think he is still in this particular area. But he has robbed and hurt some other women. The last robbery was Tuesday. We believe it is the same man, and we need more information on him. We don't have very much to go on."

MRS. BECKEL: "Do you think he'll come back?"

OFFICER NOBLIN: "No. Don't worry about him, Julia. There are detectives looking for him right now. Julia, what we want to do is to go over everything that you can remember. Maybe there are some details that were overlooked during the original investigation. So we'll go over everything again, if it is okay with you."

MRS. BECKEL: "It's okay. I hope they catch him."

OFFICER NOBLIN: "How old are you, Julia."

MRS. BECKEL: "I'm seventy-eight years old."

OFFICER NOBLIN: "Really? You don't look that old!"

MRS. BECKEL (laughing): "That's because I don't look my age. But believe me, I am that old. I feel it."

OFFICER NOBLIN: "Do you live with anyone, Julia?"

MRS. BECKEL: "All alone, my dear. All alone. I'm afraid to go out anymore. But I have to because I need to eat. And I got to buy my medicines."

OFFICER NOBLIN: "Try not to go out alone. Ask one of your neighbors to go with you. Here is my card. If you notice anything suspicious or if you need help, call me right away. I'll come right down. If I can't, someone else will."

MRS. BECKEL: "I have some other numbers also. I'll be careful."

OFFICER NOBLIN: "How do you feel, Julia? How is your health?"

MRS. BECKEL: "I feel better now. But I have a heart condition and some other things wrong with me. See all those pills? They're pills for everything I got wrong with me."

OFFICER NOBLIN: "Julia, after the robbery, did you have any money to get along?"

MRS. BECKEL: "I took home some money to eat, for the rent, for the gas and electric, for the telephone . . . he cleaned it out."

OFFICER NOBLIN: "By any chance, when he took your money, did you have anything to get by for the week? How are you making out now?"

MRS. BECKEL: "Now, I have my social security check. And then they gave me a hundred dollars."

OFFICER NOBLIN: "They did through SCAN?"

MRS. BECKEL: "The senior citizen's, ah. . . ."
OFFICER NOBLIN: "Anti-crime network?"
MRS. BECKEL: "Yes."
OFFICER NOBLIN: "Yes, okay. They gave you money to get by, then?"
MRS. BECKEL: "That's right."
OFFICER NOBLIN: "I'm glad there was somebody there to help you out a little bit."
MRS. BECKEL: "Yes, they helped me. It was very nice of them."
OFFICER NOBLIN: "Mrs. Ivy, from SCAN?"
MRS. BECKEL: "Yes, yes, she is very nice. Very sweet."
OFFICER NOBLIN: "Good. Julia, can we take a picture of you?"
MRS. BECKEL: "My picture? (laughing) Why not? Why don't you want to take my picture? Look how pretty I am!"

At this point in the interview, Officer Noblin directed his questions to the day of the robbery and to the circumstances under which it occurred.

OFFICER NOBLIN: "Basically, Julia what we want to do is to kind of go over the story on what happened. How about if we start from the beginning? Where were you coming from that day?"
MRS. BECKEL: "You see, I have a retarded son (42 years old), so Saturday I took out the social security money. I said, 'This is for the light, this is for the eat, this is for the rent, and this I had to pay for the mental hygiene.'

"I had to pay them thirty dollars because he was transferred to a group home on Decatur Street and Fulton. They (the Group Home authorities) wanted sixty dollars. I said, 'Look, I'll pay you the sixty dollars. I'll give you one check for thirty dollars, and you'll get another check from the mental hygiene for thirty dollars, and then I'll pay them.' But then I said, 'Why should I pay them the thirty dollars? I'll pay them fifteen dollars, so I'll have some money here in the home. I'll pay them the rest when I get my social security check.'

"I have a little box that I put the money in. So I said, 'Let me go buy some things. Maybe he won't be transferred so soon.' Because when he was transferred they (the group home authorities) wanted his social security check. I said, 'Look, you can have his check as long as I know that you're taking good care of him.' So, I bought him six pairs of underwear, tops and bottoms, six pairs of socks, four polo shirts, and a pair of pants.

"He (the suspect) took all of my money. You know, I don't take all my money home. Just what I need. I had seven dollars and fifty cents in my pocketbook, and he took that too. He left me with nothing.

"I get one hundred and eighty dollars of social security and ninety dollars and fifteen cents from the SSI (supplementary security income). Now, they raised the social security so they took off seventeen dollars, so I get only seventy dollars and twenty-five cents from the SSI, and with the social security it makes two hundred and seventy dollars and twenty-five cents. Am I right?"

OFFICER NOBLIN: "That's not much money to get by on for a month."

MRS. BECKEL: "So you see? I said, 'Look, this is for the telephone, this is for the electric, this is for the gas, and this is for the eat.' "

OFFICER NOBLIN: "And that doesn't leave you much!"

MRS. BECKEL: "How much does it leave me, my dear? How much I ask you? How much? And stamps, you know? They used to give me food stamps. I use to pay for them from the same money I used to save. I said, 'This is all right, I can eat.' So it cost me forty-four dollars a month, food stamps they used to send every two weeks. So twenty-two dollars for twenty-seven dollars worth of stamps. So they took that away, and now they give me ten dollars worth of stamps and I don't have to pay. Isn't that something? Now what could you buy for ten dollars? For a sick woman like me. When I need a diet. Who looks at a diet already? My sugar is up to 225."

OFFICER NOBLIN: "Oh, that's way over."

MRS. BECKEL: "Yes. It's way over. And everything. And my heart is no good. And he had to come and take away all my money."

OFFICER NOBLIN: "Okay, Julia. Now, can you tell me where you went that day?"

MRS. BECKEL: "I went to the bank and send away the fifteen dollars. And all of the money was here."

OFFICER NOBLIN: "This is the day of the robbery?"

MRS. BECKEL: "Yes, this was on June 4."

OFFICER NOBLIN: "What bank was it?"

MRS. BECKEL: "The Lincoln Bank. On Saturday I took out the money I needed. I said, 'Why should I go Monday? I have to dress myself. Maybe I won't be able to go Monday. Monday, I'll go pay this (group home bill).'

"So I ate my lunch, and I said, 'Let me go down to the bank and pay the fifteen dollars and be done with it.' Well, I went Monday, after lunch. It must have been after twelve. And I went to the bank. You know, I don't see so good."

OFFICER NOBLIN: "After you left the bank, did you go shopping?"

MRS. BECKEL: "I went to the bank, and the man wrote me out a money order. And he knows me. He's my boyfriend over there, and he said, 'Look, mama. You could put it (the money order) in the mailbox or you could drop it. I'll put it in the mailbox for you.' I said, 'All right.' And I went (pause). I needed milk, I needed orange juice, and I needed bread. I went to the Key. You know, the Key on Nostrand and Church?"

OFFICER NOBLIN: "The Key Food Store?"

MRS. BECKEL: "Yes. And I bought the milk, the juice and the bread. I was walking home, because, you know, I can't walk fast. And I don't know — I told the doctor. I can't breathe and I can't breathe, and I don't know, I get so weak that I have to go in someplace and have something. He said 'That's good, you do that.' So, there's a coffee shop, as you know, on Nostrand and Church."

OFFICER NOBLIN: "Right off the corner, next to the candy store?"

MRS. BECKEL: "Yes. I went in there. The girl knows me. And she said, 'All right.' They all know me. They all call me either grandma or mama. The girl said, ' I'll give you a dietetic cupcake and coffee.' I said, 'Okay, you give me the cupcake and coffee. I don't know, I feel so weak. My heart is something. I want to eat and then maybe I'll take a pill. I have some at home and one in my pocketbook.' I said, 'On the way back I'll put the pill in my mouth and then I'll be alright.' She said, 'Look, I hope you get home soon, and be well, and take care.' I said, 'Alright.' "

OFFICER NOBLIN: "And you walked straight down. . . .?"

MRS. BECKEL: "And I walked straight down to Nostrand Avenue. I had my key in my hand. I have only one lock — it's a police lock. And I turned around this way to open up the door (Mrs. Beckel looked over her shoulder), and he grabs me from the back, closes up my mouth and my eyes, and throws off my glasses. And he says, 'If you scream, I'll kill you!' And I says, 'What do you want from me? You want money?' I said, 'Here, I have money in my pocketbook.' He dragged me in the house. I have a chair, standing near the telephone. He opened up my drawer, took out my pajamas, tied up my face — my eyes, so I wouldn't see him, and he started choking me. If he would give me one more choke, I would be dead. But the good Lord said, "No, you have a sick boy, you can't be dead." And my heart was going like this (Mrs. Beckel pounded her hand rapidly on her chest), and I was thinking, 'Oh, the pill, the pill, the pill, the pill, I'm dying, the pill.' And the good Lord heard me and said, 'You'll be alright.'

"And he cleaned me out. He went to the closet, found the box, and he took every cent of it. But you know, I know that the landlord has to come. So I said, 'Why should I crawl in the closet to get the money? I'll have the money in an envelope, put it in the yellow bag, and put under that linen.' So I did that. That he didn't get."

Officer Noblin interrupted the interview at this point. He then directed his questions to the injuries sustained by Mrs. Beckel during the assault and to the actions of the suspect after he pushed her into the apartment. The purpose of the latter series of questions was to determine the *modus operandi* of the suspect. This information would be useful to department analysts in determining the existence of crime patterns in this area. Some of the questions were also related to the search for the "Silk-Stocking" robber.

MRS. BECKEL: "That's when he went away. I was bleeding from top to bottom."
OFFICER NOBLIN: "Now, why? Did he hit you on the head with something?"
MRS. BECKEL: "He must have. I was unconscious."
OFFICER NOBLIN: "Okay, let's kind of go back a little bit, Julia. After he tied you up, he put you on a chair in the bedroom.'
MRS. BECKEL: "Yes."
OFFICER NOBLIN: "And he tied you with pajamas?"
MRS. BECKEL: "Yes, with pajamas, and he found some, uh, you

see my feet swell up, so he found a pair of support hose. He must have had a knife, so he cut them, and he tied me up by the hands, the feet, and the eyes."

OFFICER NOBLIN: "Now, did he place any stocking or anything around your neck to choke you?"

MRS. BECKEL: "I don't (pause) he must have. Because I was all black and blue."

OFFICER NOBLIN: "Around the neck?"

MRS. BECKEL: "Around the neck, and from here to here. I was black and blue."

OFFICER NOBLIN: "You have no idea what he hit you on the head with?"

MRS. BECKEL: "I have no idea. I don't know. . . ."

OFFICER NOBLIN: "All right. You felt like you became unconscious?"

MRS. BECKEL: "I was unconscious. I was bleeding. And I have a neighbor upstairs. She has a cousin who lives next door. I heard her voice and tried to get my hand out and tried to take this off (the pajamas) and free my other hand and untie myself. And I went to the (pause) I don't know how I got to the door. I don't know! My heart was going, and I was looking for the pills, and I couldn't find them. I was like unconscious. And I said, 'Sadie!' And she said, 'Ohh, grandma! What's the matter! What's the matter!' I said, 'Nothing is the matter. Don't get scared. I'm all right, I'm all right."

"They called the police. They called the ambulance. She was with me. They took me to the emergency. And one of the doctors said, 'Lady you ought to thank God that you are alive. Look at your head! You have two holes in your head.' (to Officer Noblin) You want to see the holes he made me in the head?"

OFFICER NOBLIN: "That's okay, Julia. I've already checked with the doctors at the hospital about your condition. They told me that you will be okay."

The questioning now turned to the suspect. Officer Noblin asked Mrs. Beckel if she could recall anything about him.

OFFICER NOBLIN: "One or two more questions, Julia. Apparently you were unconscious. You have no idea of what he did in the apartment?"

MRS. BECKEL: "I have no idea."

OFFICER NOBLIN: "Do you remember at any time while you were conscious if he was wearing gloves?"

MRS. BECKEL: "I don't know. No, I don't think so. You see, I don't see so good, and he threw my glasses off!"

OFFICER NOBLIN: "Can you tell me what he looked like or what he wore?"

MRS. BECKEL: "I couldn't tell you what he looked like. I couldn't tell you what he had on."

OFFICER NOBLIN: "You have no idea what he looked like?"

MRS. BECKEL: "I couldn't see his face. He wouldn't let me! If my eyes were good, maybe. And then I was all mixed up. So how could I know what he looked like or what he was wearing?"

OFFICER NOBLIN: "Did he make any sort of statements that he was taking a plane and that he was leaving the country?"

MRS. BECKEL: "Not to me!"

OFFICER NOBLIN: "Did he mention anything about having a car parked outside?"

MRS. BECKEL: "Not to me!"

OFFICER NOBLIN: "Do you have a telephone here?"

MRS. BECKEL: "Yes."

OFFICER NOBLIN: "Did he cut the telephone wires?"

MRS. BECKEL: "No. But he took everything."

Officer Noblin then asked Mrs. Beckel to list and describe the property that she had lost.

OFFICER NOBLIN: "Julia, besides the money he stole, what else did he take?"

MRS. BECKEL: "He took my son's polo shirts, socks, and underwear. The tops only. New from the store. He didn't take the pants."

OFFICER NOBLIN: "Anything else, Julia?"

MRS. BECKEL: "He took presents that people gave me for my birthday or Christmas — things I couldn't afford to buy. All right, they weren't fourteen-karat gold, but he took that! You know, my brother, before he died, he was in the jewelry business, and he said, 'Look, here is a cameo for you. Never, never give it to anyone. That's for you as long as you live.' And that he didn't take. But what did he do? He took the chain off it. It was a fourteen-karat chain. He took it off and tore it to pieces. Later, when I felt a little better, I saw it tore up in pieces."

OFFICER NOBLIN: "Now the day you were shopping, were you wearing any sort of jewelry?"

MRS. BECKEL: "No. I never wear anything on my fingers."

OFFICER NOBLIN: "How tall are you, Julia?"

MRS. BECKEL (laughing): "I don't know how tall I am."

OFFICER NOBLIN: "Oh, you're a tiny girl. I would say about five feet. What do you weigh, Julia?"

MRS. BECKEL: "Oh, I must weigh about ninety or a little over. That's all."

OFFICER NOBLIN: "And you walk very slowly when you go out?"

MRS. BECKEL: "Yes, I can't walk fast."

OFFICER NOBLIN: "Now, here (apartment building) you came up the steps?"

MRS. BECKEL: "He came up on the steps in back of me and grabbed me in the back."

OFFICER NOBLIN: "When you first came into the building, did you notice any of your neighbors outside?"

MRS. BECKEL: "No one, but no one! Usually they are all standing by the door. But, no one was there! Otherwise they see me carrying something and they'll take it from me and say, 'Grandma, you ain't going to carry it. I'll carry it for you.' The whole house calls me grandma."

OFFICER NOBLIN: "So there was nobody outside and nobody inside?"

MRS. BECKEL: "There wasn't a soul inside; there wasn't a soul outside."

OFFICER NOBLIN: "Okay."

MRS. BECKEL: "And, you know, this door downstairs is always open. And, you know, I smell such a funny smoke. You know, I don't know what it is."

OFFICER NOBLIN: "It's marijuana."

MRS. BECKEL: "Yes, and they don't even live here. They sit on that big window (in the lobby of the building) over there. (pause) Maybe it was one of them. I don't know!"

OFFICER NOBLIN: "Did he have an accent, by any chance?"

MRS. BECKEL: "No, I don't think so."

OFFICER NOBLIN: "How was his voice? Was it soft? Was it rough?"

MRS. BECKEL: "He was, you know . . . like a murderer — I'll

kill you, he says!"

OFFICER NOBLIN: "Did he mention anything that he wanted your gold? Did he say where's your gold, or give me your gold?"

MRS. BECKEL: "No, no, no. But he did say to me, 'You just now cashed the check.' He must have been watching me from the bank. But I didn't cash no check!"

OFFICER NOBLIN: "But you were in the bank before you went shopping?"

MRS. BECKEL: "Yes. I was in the bank to send this (showing her a money order for the group home). I says, 'Here is seven dollars. You want the money, take it.' But he wouldn't take it. He took it after he took all the others from the box. After he took all the others from the box, took my poor son's clothes that I bought him, took everything from me, and that was the end!"

OFFICER NOBLIN: "Did any detectives come and dust for fingerprints?"

MRS. BECKEL: "Yes. They came on the day that I went to the hospital. Later a policeman, I think it was Detective Matioli, gave me my key. They put a new lock on the door for me while I was in the hospital."

OFFICER NOBLIN: "Was it the SCAN people? We put the locks on for nothing."

MRS. BECKEL: "I don't know. But I didn't pay for it."

OFFICER NOBLIN: "Sweetheart, did you incur any expenses at the hospital, or did medicaid or medicare take care of it for you?"

MRS. BECKEL: "No. But I still go to the hospital. I have something wrong with my skin. It gets red and it itches, so I go there for treatments."

OFFICER NOBLIN: "How did Detective Matioli treat you? Pretty good?"

MRS. BECKEL: "Yes. He was very nice."

OFFICER NOBLIN: "Okay, Julia, thank you very much. You have been a great help to us. We'll keep you informed on this guy. Take care of yourself, and call us if you need anything, okay?"

MRS. BECKEL: "Yes, okay. Are you going to come back?"

OFFICER NOBLIN: "We'll try to keep in touch with you, Julia. If we don't, the people from SCAN will. Thank you, Julia."

Although Mrs. Beckel had recovered from her physical injuries, it was apparent to the observers that this frail, seventy-eight-year-old widow had not yet recovered from the psychological impact of the assault. On several occasions during the interview Officer Noblin and the author observed that her moods would change from exuberance, to pensiveness, to expressions of anger, and then to fear. At one point in the interview Officer Noblin cautioned Mrs. Beckel about going shopping without a companion.

OFFICER NOBLIN: "What you have to try and do is to go with a neighbor or a friend. Go to the bank and return together."

MRS. BECKEL: "I hope that you get him. (pause) You know, I'm afraid to go to the bank. You know, the super (superintendent) (pause), I knew him when he was in the carriage. . . ."

OFFICER NOBLIN: "Oh, you must have been here a long time."

MRS. BECKEL: "Oh, I'm here thirty-nine years!"

OFFICER NOBLIN: "Thirty-nine years!"

MRS. BECKEL: "That's right. And my husband died here. My husband was forty-nine years a man (at this point, Mrs. Beckel began to cry). And he left me with a sick boy. That's why I'm sick from that. (pause) Well, anyway, this super I know when he was a baby, I says, 'Billy, will you come to the bank with me?' He says, 'Sure!' And he went to the bank with me. . . ."

OFFICER NOBLIN: "Good, good."

MRS. BECKEL: "So I gave him a couple of cents. He didn't want to take it. So I said, 'Look I don't want you to go for nothing. You have a lot of work in the house. Here's a couple of cents for you. I'll give them to you.' And he thanked me."

OFFICER NOBLIN: "Well, that's what you are going to have to do."

MRS. BECKEL: "I'll have to take somebody to go with me to the bank."

OFFICER NOBLIN: "Anybody. Just as long as you are with someone."

MRS. BECKEL: "Because I'm afraid to go near that bank."

OFFICER NOBLIN: "I don't blame you."

MRS. BECKEL: "You know, today I had to pay me electric bill. So, I went to the doctor. My doctor is on Ocean Avenue. I said, 'Why should I come here to the Lincoln Bank? I'll go to the bank which used to be the Fulton Bank.' I don't know what you call it now. So, I went in there and I got a money order and sent the electric bill. But I think somebody is there. Because, I didn't go in! I didn't go in. There was somebody there. And you know, I didn't have no lunch. I get very weak. So there is a little donut shop, further down. I went in there, and I got a piece of toast and a cup of coffee. I came back. I went back into the bank, and he was inside already. He wasn't outside. See?"

OFFICER NOBLIN: "This was awhile back?"

MRS. BECKEL: "This is today! But I didn't go in the bank."

OFFICER NOBLIN: "That's what you are going to have to do. You must remain alert."

MRS. BECKEL: "And he went away. And I met some woman that I know. Her niece has a retarded boy where my boy was. So I met her in the bank, and I sat and talked to her. And I didn't go out, but when I went out, I went to the Courtesy (pharmacy), got my medicine, took the bus, and went right home."

OFFICER NOBLIN: "Very good. Well, let us go now, Julia. Thank you very much for your time."

MRS. BECKEL: "Yes, so what's going to be with this, ah, this. . . ."

OFFICER NOBLIN: "By any chance if we catch him, we'll give you a call. Then we would want your cooperation, and maybe you'll come down to court. And if you do that, we will take you down and we will be with you."

MRS. BECKEL: "I would be afraid."

OFFICER NOBLIN: "No, don't be afraid."

MRS. BECKEL: "He'll send somebody to kill me!"

OFFICER NOBLIN: "No, listen, we'll be with you. He won't know anything about you. We keep everything confidential. He won't see you. He won't know anything about you. And we'll be with you at all times. There won't be any problems."

MRS. BECKEL: "But, I don't know what he looks like."

OFFICER NOBLIN: "Hopefully, when we do catch him, if, say, for instance, he makes some sort of an admission that he did rob you, or he was here in this building, then we would need you to go to court and just tell the judge what happened."

MRS. BECKEL: "I don't have to identify him! Well, I hope you find him. I hope you catch him."

OFFICER NOBLIN: "Well, we'll keep in touch. We'll let you know."

MRS. BECKEL: "He shouldn't use one cent, that, that he took from a poor think like me (Mrs. Beckel began to cry). That I didn't have what to eat until they (SCAN) gave me money."

OFFICER NOBLIN: "He should walk across the street and get hit by a bus."

MRS. BECKEL: "He should! He should! The good Lord should punish him! He should be punished good! From a poor thing like me. If they wouldn't give me money, I wouldn't have anything. I'd starve! A sick woman, with all this here. I've got to have that!

"You want to see a picture of my son? They gave him a birthday party. (pause) See, that's him by the candles. They made him a birthday cake."

OFFICER NOBLIN: "He's a handsome fellow. (pause) Okay, Julia, don't worry. We'll keep in touch with you."

At SCRU headquarters Officer Noblin discussed the case with his supervisors. After studying the circumstances under which the crime was committed and the *modus operandi* of the suspect, the case was added to the growing number of Silk Stocking crime pattern cases. The key factors leading to this decision were: (1) the crime was a push-in robbery; (2) the victim was taken to a bedroom and bound to a chair; and (3) the suspect used panty hose and pajamas to bind and choke his victim. This combination of characteristics was peculiar to the *modus operandi* of the Silk Stocking robber.

As the preceding report of the Beckel case indicates, when an elderly citizen is robbed or assaulted, the offender is seldom arrested at the scene of the crime. In such instances, the police are informed that a woman has been robbed or assaulted and that her assailant has escaped. The investigative team has the responsibility of gathering the information and evidence that will lead to the identification, apprehension, and eventual conviction of the perpetrator. The investigators will interview the victim, canvass the area for possible witnesses, examine the crime scene for physical evidence, and search the area for clues as to the identification of the offender. Because an investigator usually develops his own methods and techniques, the degree to which a crime is investigated often depends on the skill and resourcefulness of the investigator.

In order to determine the conditions under which the crime occurred, the investigator must assemble, in proper sequence, all of the information supplied by the victim or by a witness of the crime.

There are a number of factors that are to be determined by the investigator during the interview, and when they are ascertained, they will form the basis of his search for the perpetrator. The investigator must determine the time of the robbery (day and hour). This information is important not only to the investigation of the case, but also in discovering the existence of a crime pattern in a given area. A study of crime reports has disclosed that most robberies and assaults of elderly citizens have occurred during the hours of 11:00 AM to 4:00 PM on Mondays, Tuesdays, or Fridays.

The investigator will need to know the time she left her apartment and returned and also the routes she used to and from her destination. He will also need to know if she regularly uses the same routes. The time and route factors are important in establishing the *modus operandi* of the criminal. He may spot her on one day, study her habits for a few days, and then rob her.

The investigator will ask the victim to give him a sequential account of her activities after she left her apartment. Did she go to the bank? Did she go shopping? Did she stop and talk to anyone? Did she have lunch? Was she alone?

He will also need to know all the physical disabilities of the victim. Does she have impaired sight or hearing? Does she have a heart condition? Does she have difficulty in walking? Does she use a cane or a walker? In addition, was she encumbered by a shopping bag or a shopping cart?

The place of the assault is important. Did it occur on the street? Did it occur in the vestibule, the lobby, or the elevator of the apartment building where she lives? Was it a push-in robbery? Did she use the elevator or the stairs to reach the floor to her apartment? How many locks did she have to unlock?

Provided with this type of information, the investigator and SCRU supervisors may reasonably conclude whether the robbery was planned or unplanned. They may also discover a developing crime pattern. In the Beckel case, it was determined that the offender spotted Mrs. Beckel in the bank and then followed her home. The obvious clue in this robbery was the offender's saying to the victim, "You just now cashed a check."[3] Although the information indicated that the criminal could have planned the robbery, the police did not consider it as a conclusion of fact.

In almost all instances when a complainant reports the commission of a crime, a uniformed patrol officer is the first to respond to the call for assistance. If the crime is reported during its commission, the police may be able to apprehend the perpetrator at or near the scene of the crime. Because most criminal actions are reported after they have been committed, it is extremely rare for the criminal to be caught at or near the scene of the crime.

At the scene of the crime, the uniformed patrol officer will take information for a preliminary crime report. Most reports of this type contain little or no information that will lead to the identity of the criminal. It follows that the police must rely on a thorough investigation if they are to identify, locate, and eventually arrest the criminal. It is these reports, lacking in significant investigative leads, that challenge the skill and resourcefulness of the police investigator. In discussing the search for the criminal, Professor Alan Kalmanoff said: "The task of identifying, locating, and arresting a suspect — and perhaps successfully introducing the accused into the criminal justice system — is fascinating to most investigators."[4]

On the other hand, because SCRU has primary responsibility for all crimes committed against the elderly (with the exception of murder), its investigators are not hampered by inadequate preliminary crime reports. In most instances, the investigative team that is assigned to the case is at the scene of the crime right after the crime is reported. Once SCRU jurisdiction over the case is established, the team will begin to search for evidence. It is not possible to determine whether or not SCRU investigators have an advantage over other police investigators who normally rely on preliminary crime reports because no studies have been conducted in this area.

The push-in robbery offers the SCRU investigator the best opportunity for discovering and evaluating evidence. In most crimes of this type, the victim is tied either to a chair or to a bedpost while the criminal proceeds to ransack the apartment in search of money, furs, or jewelry. It is during this stage of the robbery that the criminal is likely to leave a fingerprint or some other evidence that may link him to the crime.

Evidence used in this context needs some definition. Hazel Kerper has defined it as follows:

> Evidence is every species of proof legally presented in a court of law through the medium of witnesses, records, documents, objects, etc., for the purpose of inducing belief in the minds of the court or jury on the issues in the case. Evidence can be classified as real evidence, testimony, direct evidence, circumstantial evidence, and in other ways. *Real evidence* includes objects of any kind (guns, maps, fingerprints, etc.) placed before the court or jury; *testimony* is the statements of competent witnesses. *Direct*

evidence is eyewitness evidence; *circumstantial evidence* is evidence of circumstances which tend to prove the truth or falsity of a fact in issue. . . .[5]

Because of the conditions and circumstances under which push-
in robberies and assaults against the elderly are committed, SCRU
investigators rely, primarily, on real evidence in their search for the
criminal. Direct evidence and testimony are considered less reliable
for several reasons. In the first instance, push-in robberies are
always initiated at the victim's apartment door, in dimly lighted
hallways, and in the absence of witnesses. Second, persons who may
have observed the suspect enter the building or the elevator with the
victim, or who may have noticed him in the area during the time of
the crime are, most often, reluctant to cooperate with the police
because they do not want to get "involved." For example, some people consider it a bother to testify in court, particularly when it may
mean a loss of a day's wages. Others will not cooperate because they
fear retaliation from the criminal or from his friends. In some instances, witnesses will not come forward with any information because they "identify" with the criminal. This attitude is not uncommon in many low-income ethnic neighborhoods, where the protection of one's "own kind" is the unwritten rule. Finally, the police have
long recognized the general unreliability of eyewitness testimony.
Many studies have shown that people are often unable to recall, with
reasonable accuracy, the events that took place during the commission of a crime. This is particularly true with the passage of time or
when the action took place so quickly that the sequence of events remains a blur of confusion in the mind of the observer. Real evidence, therefore, is often the only source of evidence available to the
investigating officers.

In most push-in robberies, SCRU personnel will conduct an independent search for evidence. Specialized police crime units will be
called to the crime scene, however, in the event that the loss of property is extensive (valuable jewelry, furs, silverware, etc.) or if the
victim is murdered. In all murder cases, the homicide detective
squad will, normally, assume overall control of the investigation. All
investigative activities will then be combined into a single effort until
the case is solved or is terminated for lack of evidence and/or progress. Depending upon the importance of a case, as determined by
the SCRU commanding officer, SCRU investigative personnel may
be assigned to work directly with the homicide detective squad for

the duration of the case.

To the student of criminal justice there are few problems that match the perplexities and frustrations of attempting to find the answers to the causes of crime. What are the biological, sociological or psychological factors that impel people to commit crimes? Why is it that some people will commit only one serious crime during a lifetime, while others, in approximately the same situation, will become habitual offenders? Although scholars agree that the answers to these questions are not easily found, criminologists continue to offer explanations and theories as the causes of crime.

The theories of the causes range from Cesare Lombroso's "natural biological factors" or Sigmund Freud's concept of "natural drive" to the "crime-specific" theories of Marshall Clinard and Richard Quinney.[6] Of course, there is some value and truth in each theory, as each attempts to explain crime from a biological, sociological, or psychological basis. Most are deficient, however, and cannot be considered satisfactory explanations of criminal behavior because they are limited in scope. Biological theories have very little empirical support. Psychological theories do not take into account social aspects of criminal behavior. Social-psychological theories rely to heavily on rational motives. Sociological theories do not adequately explain white-collar crime. And crime-specific theories are not well enough developed to enable investigators to predict the various types of crimes and the conditions that will produce them.[7].

In the area under investigation, a study conducted by department criminologists into the causes of crimes against the elderly has produced some evidence that at least one reason for crime in this area is economical. The consensus among SCRU personnel is that crime is a way of life for many juveniles of the inner city. Most are of school age or are unemployed and have little or no income. The streetwise juvenile is almost always on the alert for a possible source of income. The elderly female has been selected as the most likely victim for a robbery because she usually carries some money on her person and is the least likely to offer any resistance.

A robbery that occurred during the summer of 1978 may serve as an example. During a surveillance operation in the Flatbush section of Brooklyn, Officers McCafferty and Carbonaro arrested a thirteen-year-old youth on a charge of robbery. During the questioning of the youth at the police precinct, Officer Carbonaro, noting that the youth was fairly well dressed and that he had twenty-five dollars on his person, asked him why he robbed the elderly woman. The youth replied that he went to a sports store to buy a pair of Adidas® basketball shoes. The Adidas cost thirty dollars and he needed an additional five dollars. The elderly woman just happened to be a convenient supply source.

The Development of Crime Patterns

Most SCRU investigators consider motive discovery to be the task of the department's socio-psychological analysts rather than a matter of concern for field personnel. Hence, the discovery of the motive factor is given a low priority, if it is given any priority at all, during the course of an investigation. The highest priority is, of necessity, placed upon the discovery of real evidence: the type of evidence that will assist in the identification and, perhaps, the eventual arrest of the offender.

Daily crime reports by SCRU, SCU, uniformed patrols, and other field units are compiled by the crime analysis section on a weekly and monthly basis. A study of the resulting crime statistics from the accumulated data will, at times, disclose a developing or an existing crime pattern in one or more precincts within a zone, or in one or more zones within a patrol borough.

Although SCRU supervisors will make extensive use of reports released by the crime analysis section, they will conduct concurrent independent studies of crime committed against the elderly when they discover the existence of crime patterns.

The existence of crime patterns is determined by a detailed study of individual cases for some recurring evidence that would lead investigators to conclude that a series of crimes have been committed by the same person or persons. Some characteristics of the offender may identify him as a member of an ethnic group. For example, distinctive speech and voice patterns can sometimes identify the criminal as an Hispanic, an American black, or a West Indian black.

In other crimes, the *modus operandi* of the perpetrator may give the police evidence of a crime pattern. For example, the offender says the same statement to his victims ("I have to catch a plane"), or he may cut the telephone wires during the robberies.

As a result of such studies, SCRU supervisors can plot for each precinct and zone activities that indicate the existence of a crime pattern. In addition to the zone maps, a pattern case chart is established. The chart will contain the name and address of the victim; date, day, and time of the assault; precinct and zone; and identification of the assailant, if possible. Other common factors are included such as the route the victim took to her apartment building, the store or stores where she shopped, the amount of money she carried, and the persons she encountered when entering her apartment building.

The data developed from the various studies are transposed to precinct and area zone maps on a weekly basis. Crimes reported by unit decoy and investigative teams, however, are added to the zone maps as the information is received. Each type of crime (street robbery, off-street robbery, or push-in robbery) is identified by different-colored map pins and plotted on a street-by-street and house-by-house basis within each precinct. Using such zone maps, SCRU supervisors can identify high-crime areas, changes or shifts in criminal activities, as well as existing or developing crime patterns within each precinct or zone. Hence, SCRU field personnel are provided with current and highly accurate information on the total range of criminal activities that have taken place (and which may, predictably, continue to take place) within each precinct or zone.

Senior citizen robbery unit supervisors will assign a decoy team only to areas where the crime rate is high. Depending upon the intensity of the criminal activity, they may also assign an investigative team to surveillance duty in the same area. An investigative team in a high-crime area serves three important functions: First, by adding to the area's manpower, it will increase police opportunities for apprehending criminals; second, the team will be in a position to make an immediate response to a victim's complaint; and third, the team will be in position to function as a support unit for decoy operations in the event of an emergency situation.

If supervisors discover a crime pattern in one or more precincts or zones, a single investigative team is normally assigned prime responsibility for the conduct of the investigation. If, however, the crime pattern is one of major proportions or is nearing an out-of-control situation, the task force commander will assume overall direction of the investigation, and SCRU supervisors will be responsible for the day-to-day conduct of the investigation. In such situations, all available personnel will be utilized in a major effort to apprehend the criminal.

One of the most difficult aspects of the police investigative process is the physical identification of the suspect. It is a common misconception of most laymen that once the police have discovered a suspect's fingerprints, his apprehension, arrest, and eventual conviction will follow. This is more a matter of fiction than of fact. Fingerprints are useful only if the suspect has an arrest record, which puts his fingerprints on file. Although all servicemen, federal employees, most state employees, and employees of major corporations are fingerprinted for identification and security purposes, the files on these people are not readily available to local police authorities.

In addition, partial prints (e.g. fingertip prints, palmprints, or a partial print of a finger) are normally considered as of no value by police investigators, because, when suspects are arrested and fingerprinted, palmprints and fingertip prints are not taken and, therefore, are not on file. This does not mean, however, that police latent fingerprint experts cannot work with such prints. In some instances, when only fingertip prints or palmprints have been discovered by investigators, latent print experts have been able to match the discovered partial prints with fingertip prints and palmprints taken from arrested suspects.

The problem of identifying the suspect from the description provided to the investigator by the victim is about as difficult as trying to locate an offender without a police record through the use of discovered fingerprints. This is particularly true when a single assault has taken place or when there is no discernible crime pattern. As discussed earlier, the victim's information is not always reliable. Much of its reliability depends on how soon after the assault the interview took place and on the victim's state of mind. The victim's description is usually the only description of the offender available to the police, and it may provide some clue to a positive identification.

Sometimes the existence of a crime pattern may work to ease the task of the investigator. In crime pattern cases the investigator can compare the descriptions of a suspect provided by more than one victim. The various descriptions will be submitted to a police artist, who will then select characteristics mentioned by several victims and develop a composite drawing of the suspect. The composite drawing will be distributed to all police precincts throughout PBBS, as well as to the SCRU investigating team.

In discussing the victim's description of her assailant, a police artist said: "Her description of the suspect is not what the suspect actually looks like. It is a description of what she thinks he looks like, and I could be drawing a sketch of a person entirely different than the one you are looking for."

Because of the limited nature of the SCRU mission — to protect the elderly citizen from the crimes of robbery and assault — unit personnel operate under strict departmental guidelines in the conduct of their activities. It follows that unit investigative personnel, under normal operating guidelines, do not become involved in the typical search-and-seizure/stop-and-frisk situation. Hence, Fourth Amendment prohibitions pose few, if any, problems for the unit.

Typically, SCRU investigators begin their activities after the crime had been committed — that is, in response to a senior citizen's complaint. Usually the criminal has long departed from the immediate area by the time the investigators arrive at the crime scene. During the course of an investigation, however, an investigator will canvass the victim's neighbors in a search for information or witnesses. But he will not enter any apartment without a warrant or without the permission of the occupant. On occasions when strangers are encountered in a building where a crime was committed, the subject will be questioned in accordance with the guidelines provided in Section 140.50 of the Criminal Procedure Law (CPL).

During those times when investigators are assigned to surveillance duty in a high-crime area or when on routine surveillance duty, they are careful to operate within the confines of section 140.50 of the CPL. A suspicious subject may be placed under observation and followed for a period of time, but he may not be harassed or stopped. The subject will be confronted, however, if he actually commits a crime.

The *reasonableness* requirement of the Fourth Amendment is normally satisfied through the application of Section 140.50, CPL. Although a stop, question, and search is in fact a "detention and search," the Miranda warnings do not apply in most stop-and-frisk cases. While courts have not clearly defined the stop-and-frisk technique as "custodial interrogation," the officer always gives the Miranda warnings in the following cases:

A. When he/she has ground for, or plans to, arrest the suspect, regardless of the results of the search.

B. When it has been necessary to detain a suspect forcibly for the purpose of question or search.

C. When he/she questions a suspect at gunpoint.[8]*

The Miranda rules apply only to "custodial interrogation." Custodial interrogation may be defined as *that situation when a person has been arrested and is about to be questioned.*

The legal requirements for a valid juvenile arrest are the same as those for an adult.[9] In addition, the child's parent or guardian is immediately notified that he has been taken into custody. Also, if the arresting officer determines that it is necessary to question the child, the juvenile is taken to a specific room in the precinct station house that has been designated for this purpose by the appellate division of the first and second departments. The child is not questioned relative to a crime, however, unless both he and his parent or guardian voluntarily, knowingly, and intelligently waive his Miranda rights.[10]

NOTES

1. From tapes and notes of the author, 6-14-79.
2. From tapes and notes of the author, 7-9-79.
3. Supra.
4. Kalmanoff, Alan, Criminal Justice, Enforcement and Administration (Boston: Little, Brown and Co., 1976), p. 79.
5. Kerper, Hazel, Introduction to the Criminal Justice System, 2nd Ed., as revised by Herold H. Israel (St. Paul: West Publishing Co., 1979), p. 318.
6. Levine, James, Musheno, Michael, and Palumbo, Dennis, Criminal Justice, A Public Policy Approach (New York: Harcourt-Brace-Jovanovich, Inc., 1980), p. 73.
7. *Ibid* at 78.
8. New York City Police Department, Precinct Anti-Crime Tactical Training Manual (New York: Police Academy, 1976), p. 63.
9. In re Gault, 378 U.S. 1 (1967).
10. Halper, Andrew and Ku, Richard, An Exemplary Project — New York City Police Department — Street Crime Unit (New York: Abt Associates Inc., 1975; Superintendant of Documents, U.S. Government Printing Office, Washington, D.C., S.N. 027-000-00338-9), p. 69.

---

*From the Precinct Anti-Crime Tactical Training Manual, 1976. Reprinted by permission of the New York City Police Academy.

CHAPTER 6

INVESTIGATIVE TEAMS IN ACTION

ALL investigative teams are assigned a specific case load. Ordinarily, the case load varies from three to four active cases and four to six inactive but nonterminated cases.

Sometimes the SCRU supervisor will terminate an unsolved case. If the case is reopened at a later date it is usually reassigned to the original investigative team. It is not unusual when conditions may warrant it or when it becomes part of a crime pattern for a supervisor to reopen a case that may have been closed out several months earlier.

As a rule, investigative teams are not assigned to surveillance duties. When the situation may warrant it, however, investigative teams will assist decoy teams in high-crime areas, or they may be assigned to assist special teams in the search for a criminal. Although unmarked squad cars are used to maintain a low profile, team members wear regular street clothes.

The senior citizen robbery unit has achieved a high rate of convictions in proportion to the arrests its members have made, but the violence against the elderly continues. It can be said that, for a number of reasons, the criminal has the advantage in this insidious game where the criminals hunt the victim and the police hunt the criminal. First and foremost is a lack of police manpower. At present strength, the police simply cannot cope with the rising crime rate in the inner city. Second, the guilty plea returns the recidivist criminal to the streets too soon. Third, the police particularly in the inner city, operate in a hostile environment. Hence, without cooperation from the public, the criminal is in control of the situation. And fourth, many policemen feel that the restrictions of the Fourth Amendment, particularly its prohibition of warrantless search and seizure, limits the effectiveness of the police.

The following incident, which occurred on June 7, 1979, may serve as an example of the restrictions placed upon the police by the exclusionary rule. On that day, the author accompanied the investigative team of Officers Larry Salzano and Joe Rainone on a surveillance tour of the East New York section of Brooklyn, a high-crime area.

After three hours of surveillance in the business district, Officer Salzano, the team leader, decided to move the operation to the apartment house complexes in the area. As the team approached the new location Officer Rainone asked Salzano to stop near a park bench where six youths were drinking. Rainone said, "I know all of these guys. I put four of them away (in jail). I see something that I want to check out."

As he approached the youths they all greeted him. Some started to joke with him, and one youth offered him a paper cup that contained some wine. Rainone spoke with the youths for approximately fifteen minutes. During the conversation, he appeared to concentrate on a tall youth standing to his right. Before Rainone departed, the youths allowed the author to snap a picture.

When he returned to the squad car, Salzano asked, "What was that all about, Joe?" Rainone said, "I spotted gold medallions on four of them. It's two-thirty in the afternoon; these guys aren't working. Where in the hell do they get the money to buy gold medallions, and wine? The big guy, Tony, had a large one on him, and I was trying to get close enough to him so that I could read the inscription on it. He got wise to me, and he threw a towel over his head. I couldn't read the damned thing."

Salzano turned to the author and said, "We run into this sort of thing every day. We know that they're either mugging some old lady or breaking into an apartment. But we can't do anything to them. We have to have probable cause. And, besides, without a complainant or a witness we would never get a conviction." Rainone said, "It just bothers the hell out of me to know that sooner or later they're going to hit another old lady."

The use of informers is extremely useful in police work, but SCRU does not make extensive use of such sources. This is not meant to imply that the unit does not have contacts who can provide valuable information to the police when it is needed. It is merely that for SCRU the role of the informer in the investigative process is minimal. For example, the majority of crimes that are committed against the elderly are committed by youths whose average age is seventeen to eighteen years. Most are crimes of chance and involve the taking of money. Decoy operation investigations responding to victim complaints are best suited to the situation.

It should be observed, however, that informers are utilized when jewelry, furs, or other items such as silverware and television sets are stolen or when crime pattern cases develop. In such instances the informer can provide a valuable service to the police.

How an investigator responds to a complaint from a victim depends upon his personal experience, his expertness, and his motivation. The following cases have been selected because of the varied nature of the crimes committed against the elderly, because of their psychological and sociological impact, and because they demonstrate the different techniques used by SCRU investigators.

The Identification, Apprehension, and Arrest of James Vincenzo Carley

On the morning of June 5, 1979, Officer Vance Herlihy briefed the author on a case that he and his partner, Officer Rosemary Carbonaro, were currently investigating. The background of the case is as follows:

A group of youths ranging in age from five to thirteen years had been harassing, attacking, and robbing elderly citizens in the Coney Island section of Brooklyn for two months. The area included single-resident homes, apartment house complexes, restaurants, business establishments, an amusement area, a mile of beaches, and an accompanying boardwalk.

The gang would snatch purses, pull chains from the necks of elderly women, and harass the elderly into giving them money. One tactic employed by the gang was the use of a five-year-old boy as a pickpocket. The gang would begin its operation by harassing an elderly man or woman. While the victim's attention was distracted the dip (pickpocket) would pick the keys from the pocket of the man or from the woman's purse or shopping bag. The gang would then demand money to ransom the keys. After the keys were returned to the victim, the youths would leave the area. Sometimes, the gang leader or some other member of the gang would notice that the victim had more money on his person. The gang would then follow the victim to his apartment building and proceed to rob him in the vestibule or lobby. The second robbery was usually preceded by a physical assault of the victim.

In the present case a gang of youths, using the tactics just described, attacked and robbed Mrs. Selma Hirshfeld, a seventy-six-year-old widow in the lobby of her apartment building. As a result of being pushed and slapped, Mrs. Hirshfeld fell down a flight of stairs and sustained facial injuries and a broken hip. After she was able to crawl to her apartment (where she remained for a day), she was then taken to the hospital where she is now recovering from her injuries.

Earlier, Officer Herlihy had apprehended Arlen Johnson, age thirteen. Johnson, apparently the ringleader, is now in police custody awaiting a hearing on this matter.

On June 5, 1979, the author accompanied Officers Herlihy, Carbonaro, and Rainone to the Coney Island area. Working on information received from the victim and from Arlen Johnson, the team lead by Herlihy began a search for another suspect, James Vincenzo Carley, eleven years old.

Vincenzo, as he is known to the police and his friends, lives at 1421 W. Thirty-third Street. Upon arriving at the building, which is a low-income public housing project, the team passed through a courtyard where several men and women were sitting on benches and stoops. As the team approached the entrance to 1421, all conversation ceased, and the people just stared at them. It was an uncomfortable moment, and Rainone advised the team to be on the alert for possible trouble.

The team entered the building and took an elevator to the eleventh floor, where they proceeded to apartment 11E. Vincenzo's brother came to the door and was quickly joined by his mother. Officer Herlihy asked where Vincenzo was. Mrs. Carley became hostile and wanted to know why the police wanted her son. During the discussion an unidentified male joined the mother and brother. Herlihy informed Mrs. Carley that her son was wanted on a felony charge and again asked her about his whereabouts. Mrs. Carley said that he was in school and would return at 2:30 PM. She denied any knowledge of her son's participation in the attack on Mrs. Hirshfeld and said, rather angrily, that she did not believe that he was a participant.

Herlihy told Mrs. Carley that her son would be picked up as soon as he was located. With that the team left the building and proceeded to the neighborhood school. At the school, Herlihy discussed the case with Mr. Lowenberg, the assistant principal. Herlihy asked for a copy of Vincenzo's record and discovered that the boy had been either late or absent from class on the day that Mrs. Hirshfeld was robbed. Furthermore, Vincenzo was late or absent on the days that other similar crimes were committed. Herlihy asked the boy's teacher, Mr. Glickman, how late Vincenzo had been on the days he was recorded as late. Mr. Glickman replied, "We don't keep such records. We just record that the student was late. A student could be late anywhere from ten minutes to four hours." Asked if students were required to explain their latenesses or if parents were notified, Mr. Glickman said, "We usually take the student's word for it. We don't usually advise the parents."

Mr. Lowenberg and Mr. Glickman became concerned. Mr. Lowenberg then asked what the police intended. They did not want Vincenzo removed from class. Normally, the police do not remove juveniles from class unless they are released by responsible school authorities. Herlihy made it clear that Vincenzo was wanted for a felony — in this case the beating and robbery of a seventy-six-year-old woman. He also pointed out that the beating resulted in the hospitalization of the woman because of a broken hip from being pushed down a flight of stairs. The school officials reiterated their concern about the removal of the student from class. Whereupon Herlihy advised them that, although he had the power to remove the boy on the spot, he would not arrest him until after he left school later in the day.

Mr. Glickman then informed the team that he was aware of the fact that Vincenzo had been "a participant in some crimes." He said that he came by this information during rap sessions that he and the school's guidance counselor had conducted with Vincenzo and some other students. Mr. Glickman said, "During the rap sessions he (Vincenzo) was not specific about the crimes he committed or those in which he participated. But he did admit that he was involved."

Mr. Glickman then asked Herlihy and Carbonaro if there was something that could be done for Vincenzo. He said, "Something should be done for him. Although his grades are still very low, he is improving." Carbonaro informed Mr. Glickman that her previous experiences with Vincenzo disclosed that he is a particularly vicious boy who apparently enjoys beating and robbing elderly people. Mr.

Glickman did not reply.

During this time, a secretary put in a call to a Mr. Bickel, a member of the board of education. Mr. Bickel called the principal's office and asked, "What is going on out there?" Herlihy took the telephone and told him the purpose of the team's visit. Mr. Bickel told Herlihy that he was concerned about the removal of the student from the school's premises. He said, "It cannot be done without a warrant for his arrest and without a release from the school authorities. To do so in any other manner would be a violation of the student's civil rights." Herlihy told Mr. Bickel that Vincenzo was wanted for the commission of a felony, and that he could indeed remove the boy from school. He would not, however, arrest him until the student left school. Mr. Bickel was satisfied with Herlihy's explanation, and the team departed.

Vincenzo was arrested by Herlihy and Carbonaro at his home later that afternoon. He was taken, accompanied by his mother, to the sixty-first precinct for custodial interrogation. Herlihy, in the presence of Mrs. Carley, read Vincenzo his Miranda rights. He then explained the Miranda rights to Mrs. Carley in order that she could fully understand the consequences of a waiver. Mrs. Carley said that she understood and voluntarily waived the rights. The following dialogue has been excerpt from the questioning by Herlihy and Carbonaro, in the presence of Mrs. Carley:[1]

HERLIHY: "She fell down, and Arlen was sitting on her then?"
VINCENZO: "Yes."
HERLIHY: "What were you doing?"
VINCENZO: "What? I was near the stairs."
HERLIHY: "Didn't you help?"
VINCENZO: "What? All I did was stand near the staircase and hold his books."
HERLIHY: "What made everybody run?"
VINCENZO: "Somebody came out."
HERLIHY: "Somebody came out of an apartment?"
VINCENZO: "Yes."
HERLIHY: "Who was kicking the lady?"
VINCENZO: "What? I remember one guy. I think it was Arlen."
HERLIHY: "This lady is still in the hospital. She has a broken hip."
VINCENZO: "Oh, in that one?"
HERLIHY: "Yes."

VINCENZO: "Uh, I, I. . . ."

HERLIHY: "Now don't go changing it. You describe the whole thing. One guy was holding her over the pillar, one guy was beating her, one guy was holding the staircase pillar, and a man came out of his apartment. We're talking about the same incident. She didn't go to the hospital right then and there because she crawled into her apartment, and she lay there for a full day because she didn't know it (that her hip was broken), and the next day they took her to the hospital. You guys were just having fun, right? They were just kicks."

VINCENZO: "I was just. . . ."

HERLIHY: "You had mentioned earlier, that Michael, no . . . What is the name of the five-year-old?"

VINCENZO: "Mark."

HERLIHY: "Mark, he took the woman's keys out of her pocketbook and tried to sell the keys back to the woman. And she went into the house. Who ran into the apartment and snatched the pocketbook?"

VINCENZO: "Judson Davids. I ran downstairs with the keys."

HERLIHY: "As I said, I arrested you for the robbery in which the lady got hurt. The other ones I am asking you about, you were present in them. But I'm not arresting you for those, understand? I have my own reasons not to arrest you. But I can arrest you if I wanted to. I could have you going to court from now until you become sixteen, but we are not doing that."

"The lady started to go into an elevator. Somebody chased her out of the lobby and she started to run to a maintenance door on Thirty-third Street. Somebody hit her alongside of the head with a rock. Who was it?"

VINCENZO: "It was Judson Davids. He punched her on the head."

HERLIHY: "Oh, he punched her — he didn't hit her with a rock? And that was Judson Davids? Was Arlen Johnson there?"

VINCENZO: "What? Yes."

HERLIHY: "There was you, Judson, and Arlen. Now that makes four of you. Now, the old lady who was robbed twice, you know the one who talks funny. Uh, one time someone took her television. She opened the door, they asked for a glass of water, and they went in and took her television. A couple of days later they came back and took money from her. You know which one I'm talking about? Were you there both times?"

VINCENZO: "No."

HERLIHY: "Which time were you there?"

VINCENZO: "The time they took the television."

HERLIHY: "We would like to get the television back for the lady. Do you think we could get it back? I'm sure that if we can, the judge will be very lenient on you. Who has the television now?"

VINCENZO: "I, uh, we sold it to somebody on the avenue."

HERLIHY: "Who sold it?"

VINCENZO: "What? I think it was Arlen."

HERLIHY: "Arlen sold it? How much did he get for it?"

VINCENZO: "What? Thirty-five dollars."

HERLIHY: "The woman paid one-hundred-and-fifty dollars for it just a week before that, and you got thirty-five dollars for it? How much did he give you?"

VINCENZO: "Seventeen-fifty."

HERLIHY: "Seventeen-fifty a piece? So there were only two of you who went after the television? Only you and Arlen? The other guys who went up with you didn't get anything?"

VINCENZO: "They were there. But they weren't with us when we sold it. Arlen owed me some money."

HERLIHY: "So there was only two of you when you stole the television?"

VINCENZO: "What? Arlen asked for a glass of water, and I went in with him."

HERLIHY: "Who slapped the lady? After you asked for a drink of water and she let you into the apartment. Who went over to the dresser drawer?"

VINCENZO: "Arlen."

HERLIHY: "And when the woman went over and said get away from the dresser, who slapped her?"

VINCENZO: "Arlen."

HERLIHY: "Did you see him slap her?"

VINCENZO: "Yes. He hit her when she was by the dresser. Then he pulled the plug out and grabbed the television and ran out the door."

HERLIHY: "And what did you do during this time?"

VINCENZO: "What? I pulled the plug out."

HERLIHY: "I thought you said Arlen pulled the plug out. Could it be that you took the television and you slapped the lady?"

VINCENZO: "Uh, no."

HERLIHY: "No? O.K. I am not going to pursue this anymore. As I told you, I'm asking you questions about cases that I have arrested Arlen on. And, as I told you, I made you a promise: Any information you give me on those cases I will not arrest you for. I already spoke to the corporation counsel that will defend for you. Unless I am ordered to arrest you for the other cases. But that is very unlikely."

The only one I am arresting you for is the one where the lady broke her hip. That is the only one that I am interested in at this moment. I just want you to go over it step by step on that particular case. You know which one I am talking about? The one that they tried to get the pocketbook, the lady resisted and she fell down. What made you pick that woman out?"

VINCENZO: "What?"

HERLIHY: "What made you pick that woman out from anybody else?"

VINCENZO: "What? We just started to talk about it."

HERLIHY: "You just started talking about it? I mean did you plan it ahead of time? Like, let's go get this lady?"

VINCENZO: "What? Arlen wanted a gold chain. And he said, "Like if we see a lady coming down the block we'll go to her." So when the lady came he followed her to the building. I had to open the door for her, and he went for her when I let the door go. She didn't have a chain so he tried to get her pocketbook."

HERLIHY: "Oh, so that's how you do it. That is, you just see something. In other words, the woman that you picked out didn't have a chain, then Arlen was tugging at the pocketbook. Is it that you just saw her on the street or did you see her in the apartment? How did you get up to the tenth floor?"

VINCENZO: "We seen her coming off the bus, and we followed her."

HERLIHY: "How did you know what floor to go to?"

VINCENZO: "What? We looked around until she opened up her mailbox."

HERLIHY: "Oh, I see, okay. She opened up the mailbox and you saw what apartment she lived in, and you went upstairs ahead of her and waited for her upstairs. Did you know the lady was hurt when you left?"

VINCENZO: "What? No."

HERLIHY: "Did you think that Arlen knew she was hurt?"

VINCENZO: "I think so."

HERLIHY: "What makes you think that Arlen knew and you didn't? Did he say anything to you that. . . ."

VINCENZO: "He just said . . . he was the one that was beating her, and he said when we went away that she wasn't moving."

HERLIHY: "Okay. Now let's see, there was you. What was Mitchell doing?"

VINCENZO: "What? He, he was helping Arlen out."

HERLIHY: "When you say helping Arlen out, was Mitchell hitting the lady, too?"

VINCENZO: "What? I don't think so."

HERLIHY: "The lady said two people were hitting her — either Arlen and Mitchell or Arlen and you."

VINCENZO: "Arlen and Mitchell."

HERLIHY: "Are you sure now?"

VINCENZO: "Ah! Ah! I'm sure, all I did was holding the door."

HERLIHY: "The stairway door or the elevator door?"

VINCENZO: "The el . . . the stairway door."

HERLIHY: "When Arlen and Mitchell ran, did they go down the stairs or did they go in the elevator?"

VINCENZO: "They went down the stairs."

HERLIHY: "Did they run all the way down the stairs, or did they get off at another floor?"

VINCENZO: "All the way down the stairs."

HERLIHY: "After you left there, did you go do anything else?"

VINCENZO: "After we left there Arlen went home to change his clothes, because he said he and Mitchell might go do another thing. So me and Mitchell went home and changed our clothes."

HERLIHY: "Did you change your clothes so the cops couldn't find you?"

VINCENZO: "We changed them to warm up because it was getting cold."

HERLIHY: "Hmm. Okay. Just one more question. Hiram McCone, has he ever done anything with you guys?"

VINCENZO: "What? Uh! He done things with Arlen."

HERLIHY: "This Hiram, is he mean? Is he meaner than Arlen?"

VINCENZO: "He could beat Arlen."

HERLIHY: "But I'm talking about when they're stealing people's chains and pocketbooks. Does he like to hurt the people?"

VINCENZO: "Hiram says not to hit the old people, but Arlen does."

HERLIHY: "So Hiram says not to whip the old people but Arlen likes to hit the old people. Is there any reason why Arlen likes to hit the old people?"

VINCENZO: "I don't know. I talked to Arlen's mother, and she said that he hit a lady on the head with a rock. She was an older woman. I don't know why he hit her."

HERLIHY: "How many times have you been arrested?"

VINCENZO: "Me? Six times."

MRS. CARLEY: "He was arrested last March. There was some kind of a necklace off this lady. They had him like, like Arlen do the thing. Vincenzo was like a lookout."

HERLIHY: "Yes, well, that's still involvement. He's just as guilty."

MRS. CARLEY: "Yes, I know."

HERLIHY: "In this particular case we have a group of youths. As you can see, I'm not making up a story because he just sat here — and this is only half of the cases he has been involved in, and there is no sense in me going into the rest of them at this time because I wouldn't be able to prosecute him for other reasons. But this particular case that he was arrested for I am going to go ahead and prosecute. Right now the only question is whether I should release him to you tonight or to send him to Spoffard (a juvenile detention home in the borough of the Bronx). He will remain there until the judge says he can come home. Right now I'm inclined to release him to you only because I feel that Arlen is the vicious one and the one who caused all this. But if I do release him to you and he gets involved again in another robbery of another person, then I'm going to take it personal, you understand? I will then feel that it will be my fault because I'm putting him back on the street. What is your feeling?"

MRS. CARLEY: "I already told him that if he ever do anything else I'm going to have him put away in a home. That's what I told him. If he don't stop hanging around with Arlen. He is a bad boy because I've seen things that Arlen do."

HERLIHY: "If he is released in your custody this evening will you sign for him?"

MRS. CARLEY: "I'll sign for him."

HERLIHY: "I don't want you to beat him when he gets home."

MRS. CARLEY: "I ain't going to beat him."

HERLIHY: "Because I already told him that he just needs a little more guidance to stay away from people like Arlen. Unfortunately this is not a minor charge. The woman has suffered a broken hip."

MRS. CARLEY: "I know."

HERLIHY: "The only thing that is convincing me is that Vincenzo has not been involved in any trouble since we took Arlen off the streets."

MRS. CARLEY: "That's what I'm telling you. He only go do these things when he be hanging around with Arlen, because Arlen be telling him he going to beat him bloody if he don't do it. So Vincenzo is scared so he is going to do it."

HERLIHY: "What Vincenzo told me today about Arlen I would like him to tell that to his probation officer and to his legal aid attorney. Naturally you will be guided on what to say to the legal aid attorney. What I would like to see is that Arlen gets some kind of psychiatric help. He needs it badly. How about Mitchell? He has been involved in everything you and Arlen have been involved in. Where does he live?"

VINCENZO: "He lives in the same buiding, apartment 14F."

MRS. CARLEY: "Detectives came to our house looking for guns. They said that somebody told them that Vincenzo had a shotgun. They had a warrant and they searched everyplace. They didn't find anything but some bullets. They told me to keep him out of trouble."

HERLIHY: "I know — I heard about it. When I came to your house this morning you were pretty hostile. You said we were accusing your son of something he didn't do. We don't work that way. We're ninety-nine and nine-tenths sure that we have the right person before we accuse anybody."

Officer Herlihy left the interrogation room to discuss Vincenzo's release with his supervisors. Officer Carbonaro remained in the room. Herlihy returned after thirty minutes and told Mrs. Carley that her son would be released to her custody just as soon as the necessary papers were prepared.

Of the five youths involved in this case only Arlen Johnson and James Vincenzo Carley were tried for the criminal action. Arlen Johnson was sent to the Spoffard detention home before his appearance in family court. He was sent to the juvenile home because his social worker and probation officer convinced the court that his mother was emotionally incompetent to care for him. Arlen Johnson was later released to the custody of his grandmother.

James Vincenzo Carley was released to the custody of his mother.

Some Observations

One sensitive problem facing the police in their attempt to cope with juvenile crime and violence is the liberal attitude that continues to prevail among some public school authorities and teachers; in spite of the widespread knowledge that juvenile crime and violence continue to rise in this city of more than 9 million people and only 23,000 police.

Although the mood of the teachers present during the inquiry by Officer Herlihy at Public School 752 appeared to be somewhat resentful, the most disturbing factor was the attitude of Mr. Glickman, Vincenzo's teacher. He was aware for at least two months that the boy was involved in criminal activities, yet he never considered telling the police what he knew. Mr. Glickman, not trained in police matters, decided instead to handle this and other problems in his own way. Perhaps if he had contacted the police in this matter some of the elderly citizens who were assaulted by this gang might have been spared their ordeals.

As for Mrs. Carley, it is apparent from the recorded testimony that she exercised little or no supervision over her son's activities. Once the boy left the apartment in the morning, she assumed that he went to school. The school authorities never told her that he was habitually late for class (sometimes up to four hours), and for this she cannot be faulted. She was aware of Vincenzo's previous encounters with the police, however, and of his association with Arlen Johnson. Yet, she never questioned her son about how he was able to obtain money without a job.

Both Vincenzo, now thirteen years old, and Arlen, now nearing his sixteenth year, are back on the street. Their previous deviant behavior, poor scholastic achievement, and lack of parental supervision may make one wonder about the eventual fate of these typical products of the inner city.

The Identification, Apprehension and Arrest of Walter Simpson, Alias Walter Curtis

On the afternoon of June 6, unit investigators Dennis Fitzgerald and Robert Noblin went to a boarding house located at 98 E. Eighteenth Street in response to an elderly citizen call for police assistance. The investigators spoke to five elderly persons, all of whom complained that they were continually being harassed, robbed, and beaten by young men who had free access to the building.

The building at 98 E. Eighteenth Street is the type of apartment complex in which single apartment units have been divided into four or five separate living quarters. Each tenant has his/her own room while sharing common kitchen, bath, and toilet facilities. There are about four apartment units that have been divided in this manner on each floor of this ten-story building.

After speaking to some of the elderly residents, Officers Fitzgerald and Noblin located the building superintendent and his wife. They asked about the presence of muggers or drifters in the building or its immediate vincinty. As they were discussing security conditions with the superintendent, Officer Noblin observed the subject, Walter Simpson, in an obviously disheveled condition, leaving an apartment unit. Noblin called to Simpson, and when he ran Noblin pursued and caught him.

In the meantime, Fitzgerald checked the rooms in the apartment unit. In one of the single occupancy rooms he found an eighty-three-year-old widow, May Fuller, lying on the bed. May Fuller had just been raped and was bleeding profusely. Fitzgerald put in a call for an ambulance and then went into the hallway where Noblin was questioning Simpson. It was at this time that the officers read the suspect his rights. The officers learned from other tenants that Simpson had beaten, robbed, and raped other elderly women in the building.

The ambulance arrived for Mrs. Fuller, and Officer Fitzgerald accompanied her to the hospital. Officer Noblin took the suspect to the seventieth police precinct where he was placed in a detention cell. The author accompanied Sergeant Richard Fitzpatrick, unit supervisor, to the seventieth precinct and was present during the interrogation of the suspect.[2]

A subsequent investigation of Simpson's activities disclosed the following:

1. He had robbed and raped three other elderly women in the building besides May Fuller. All were in their eighties.

2. The tenants and victims live in fear of the suspect, Simpson, a twenty-one-year-old drifter, and others of his type. Most are so fearful of their assailants that they do not report the incidents to the police. When they do report an attack, they often refuse to prosecute.

3. The suspect, Simpson, would gain entry to the Fuller room, rape her, and then force her to sign a bank withdrawal slip. He would then go to the bank and withdraw the money — perhaps five or ten dollars at a time. (He was never questioned by anyone at the bank.) Sometimes he would accompany the victim to the bank and have her withdraw the money. It was also learned (from May Fuller) that Simpson had raped her on an average of seven times a week for the past six to seven weeks.

4. In a separate crime at the same boarding house on June 2, 1979, Simpson robbed Mr. and Mrs. Edwin Helpern of approximately $125. Mr. Helpern is seventy-four, his wife is sixty-seven. Simpson pushed his way into their small apartment while they were home. He took their money and nonchalantly ransacked the apartment in a search for more money or any possessions that he could sell.

   The couple were left without money or food for the weekend and had little to eat during that time. Some other tenants gave them food. The Helpern's did not call the police because they feared Simpson. Anna Helpern identified him when Officer Noblin had him in custody after the Fuller attack.

At 7:45 PM, Detective De Angelo and Officer Noblin again read the suspect his Miranda rights. Simpson said he understood. A subsequent examination disclosed that the suspect was not wearing underwear, and that there were traces of blood and semen on the inside, left pocket of his trousers. The police made no mention of this finding.

Detective De Angelo continued to question the suspect who had given them several names besides Simpson and Curtis. He had also given different birth dates. De Angelo told the suspect, "I know you are lying. You are only delaying the inevitable. Why don't you just tell us who you are? We are going to find out sooner or later, so why don't you make it easier for both of us?" Simpson remained silent and expressionless.

In the meantime Officer Fitzgerald called Sergeant Fitzpatrick from the hospital and reported that the doctors were able to stop the bleeding. Although May Fuller had submitted to treatment, she had refused to be examined. She was to be released in an hour. Fitzgerald also reported that Mrs. Fuller did not want to press charges against Simpson. Fitzgerald said that he would try to convince her to appear at the seventieth precinct so that she could identify him.

At 8:05 PM, Sergeant Fitzpatrick and Officer Noblin removed Simpson from the holding cage and took him into a rear room for questioning. Fitzpatrick asked Simpson about the Helpern robbery. The suspect denied it. Noblin reminded that he had been identified by Mrs. Helpern. Simpson then told Fitzpatrick that he drank with the Helperns on occasion. On that day, June 2, 1979, Anna Helpern gave him twenty dollars and asked to buy a bottle of blackberry wine: He said, "I bought the wine and kept the change (about $16). I went back there, but I didn't rob any money or steal food stamps."

After disposing the Helpern matter, Fitzpatrick turned to the Fuller rape charge. Noblin reminded him that he had been advised of his Miranda rights and was free to exercise them. Simpson agreed and said he understood.

Fitzpatrick asked Simpson if he had raped May Fuller. Simpson said, "No!" Noblin asked him if he had ever has sex with the woman. Simpson said, "No. I don't even know the woman." Fitzpatrick then advised Simpson that evidence in police possession was very much against him. Fitzpatrick said, "Officer Noblin and the super saw you coming out of the apartment. May Fuller is coming to the seventieth precinct to identify you, and you have bloodstains on your pants."

Simpson again denied that he knew the Fuller woman or that he was in her room earlier in the day. He said, "I was drinking with a friend in an apartment upstairs." Then looking down at his pants he asked. "What blood? Where do you see any blood?"

Fitzpatrick told Simpson that it would be to his benefit to tell the truth. He said, "If you cooperate we will tell the district attorney that you were cooperative. If you don't work with us now and they get to you, then we can't help you." Simpson said, "You gotta be kidding. I didn't do what you are accusing me of. You want me to confess to something I didn't do. How could I do that?" At this point, Fitzpatrick and Noblin agreed to show Simpson the blood spots. Noblin ordered him to stand up and to drop his trousers. The blood spots were located and pointed out to the suspect who continued to deny the charge.

Noblin stepped out of the room. He was trying to locate an extra pair of trousers for Simpson. The police wanted to remove Simpson's trousers for testing. Fitzpatrick calmly continued to work on the suspect. He told him that the district attorney was on his way to take over the interrogation and that he could expect no help once the DA arrived. Then he said, "You know, Walter, we even found semen on the inside of your trousers. If I didn't want to help you, I wouldn't be telling you these things." Simpson was silent for awhile then he said, "I understand and appreciate that you're trying to help me, so I'll tell you everything." He admitted that he had had sex with May Fuller but denied that he raped her. He told Fitzpatrick that they were friends and she asked him to go to bed with her and he agreed. In Simpson's words, "We had a couple of drinks. She got undressed and so did I. Then I hugged her, and we had sex" (*see* Fig. 6-1).

The only time that he came close to admitting to rape was during Fitzpatrick's continued probing into the conditions that led directly to the last assault on May Fuller. To this probing Simpson replied, "I wanted to get her drunk first and then have sex with her." He justified his act by asking, "How would you like for somebody always walking in front of you in the nude?" He claimed that May Fuller did this on more than one occasion. When Fitzpatrick asked if she went to bed willingly, Simpson replied, "Maybe she didn't want to have sex then, but I didn't force her."

Noblin returned to the interrogation room, and Fitzpatrick told him that Simpson wanted to make a statement. He was advised of his Miranda rights for the third time. Noblin told him, "I want to make sure that you understand what it means to talk to us about May Fuller." Simpson said that he understood and then reiterated his previous statements. He again denied that he raped the woman. He claimed that the act was completely voluntary, and that he had

Figure 6-1. This picture of May Fuller was taken a few days after she was raped.

committed the sex act with May Fuller only one time.

After his admission, Fitzpatrick wanted the suspect's trousers for laboratory tests. An extra set of pants could not be located, therefore it was decided that the incriminating pocket would be cut out. Noblin walked up to Simpson and said, "I want you to listen to me carefully. I am going to ask you to drop your pants so that we could cut the pocket out. When you do, keep your hands on the outside. If you move them to the inside and try to disturb the blood or the semen, I'll break your face. Understand?" Noblin made the statement in a low but firm voice. Simpson replied, "I hear you." The pocket was removed and sent to the laboratory for testing.

The assistant district attorney and an aide arrived at 8:55 PM. These men took over the questioning of the suspect. At this point the author and Noblin were told by Sergeant Fitzpatrick that Officer Fitzgerald just brought May Fuller in, and we left the room. May Fuller was sitting on a chair in a second-floor interrogation room. She appeared to be angry with Fitzgerald. He wanted to keep her in the precinct until Sergeant Fitzpatrick could arrange for a lineup. He needed five men to appear in the lineup with Simpson. May

Fuller would have none of it. She told Fitzgerald, "I told you everything that you asked me. I gave you all the help you wanted. Now I want to go home."

Sergeant Fitzpatrick was told that the special assistant district attorney for sex crimes was on her way to the precinct to talk to May Fuller. The lineup procedure could not be conducted without the special assistant district attorney. By this time, 9:25 PM, May Fuller was very angry and would not cooperate with anyone. When Fitzpatrick asked her to talk about the rape, she screamed, "That's disgusting — I won't talk about it. It's over — he's in jail — that's disgusting." Then she wondered about what her friends would think of her. She complained, "They probably think that I'm out getting drunk."

At that moment the special assistant DA arrived to question the Fuller woman. The assistant special DA, a woman in her late twenties, arrived to question May Fuller. She sat down and began to ask questions. The victim, very upset, said, "I want to go home. This is all so disgusting — I am tired. I don't want to get anyone in trouble." She turned to Fitzgerald and said, "You told me that you would take me home in ten minutes. It's been a hell of a long ten minutes." In response to another question by the special assistant DA, Fuller said, "It's all over my head. I will not discuss this anymore. It is disgusting."

The seventieth precinct officers were able by this time to locate five men who agreed to appear in the lineup. They were to be paid five dollars each for their appearance.

Fitzgerald and Noblin were convinced that the Fuller woman would not identify Simpson. They discussed the matter with the special assistant DA and were able to convince her to charge Simpson on the basis of available evidence and without the lineup identification. Upon calling her office for approval of this procedure she was told that the lineup had to be held. She explained to the police: "Without a positive identification by the victim, we cannot prosecute him on the rape charge. We will have to proceed with other charges."

Noblin took May Fuller to another part of the room and attempted to persuade her to identify Simpson. She became upset and said, "I've been through all that. I am not going to do it. I am sick of it. I want that guy (pointing to Fitzgerald) to take me home." At that moment Sergeant Fitzpatrick came into the room and announced that the lineup procedure had been completed, and that the subject was ready for identification. Fitzgerald took May Fuller aside and spoke to her. She reluctantly accompanied him to the lineup observation room. She was assured by Fitzgerald that she could see the men but they could not see her. At the observation window she took a quick look, turned away, and said, "I don't know any of those people. I don't recognize anybody." There was nothing to do but to take her home.

The special assistant DA and Sergeant Fitzpatrick agreed that a few days rest and assurances from the police that Simpson would not harm her again would have a calming effect on May Fuller and that she might agree to identify him. In the meantime Fitzgerald took May Fuller home. Upon his return he produced her panties. He was somehow able to cajole her into surrendering the undergarment to him, and it was sent to the police laboratory for blood and semen tests.

After the assistant district attorney completed his interrogation of Simpson, he was remanded to police custody. Noblin then transported the prisoner to central booking for processing into the system. During the trip to central booking, Simpson — apparently confident that May Fuller would not identify him — admitted to Noblin that he had had sex with May Fuller some thirty to forty times. Although he continued to deny the rape charge, he bragged that he could have had sex from May Fuller whenever he wanted it.

A week later the special assistant DA visited the victim. May discussed some aspects of the case with her. She repeated the rape and robbery charges but refused to identify Simpson.

Meanwhile, Fitzgerald, concerned about her mental and physical well-being was trying to make arrangements through some city help agencies for psychiatric assistance. He also wanted her to be moved into a nursing home where she would have the necessary physical care. As he explained to the author: "The woman is sick. She has a brother in New Jersey, but he is too old to help her, and nobody else seems to give a damn. I just don't want to leave her in the flophouse. She needs supervision."

Walter Simpson was identified by Anna Helpern. As a result he was indicated on the following charges:

two counts of robbery — second degree

two counts of burglary — third degree
one count assault — second degree
one count assault — third degree
one count grand larceny — third degree

He was allowed to plead guilty to assault and robbery — second degree. He received a sentence of one year at Elmira State Prison, and he is now back on the street.

May Fuller died of natural causes in late-Septemper 1979.

It was the opinion of some members of SCRU that Simpson should have been indicted on the rape charge. They were convinced that the results of the blood and semen tests on his pant pocket and on Fuller's undergarment would have been sufficient grounds for conviction. They also pointed out some contradictions in his voluntary confession that implied that May Fuller was forced into the sex act.

As far as the police were concerned, the important thing was to get Simpson off the street for as long a period as possible. They felt that the district attorney should employ every legal means at his disposal to accomplish this end.

The district attorney, on the other hand, viewed the case from a different perspective. He was of the opinion that a positive identification of the suspect by the victim was necessary for an indictment. The rape charge had to be proved in court and that would require the presence of May Fuller at the trial. Taking into consideration the victim's refusal to identify the suspect, the district attorney reasoned that an indictment on the rape charge was useless. He had no choice but to indict Simpson on charges of assault, robbery, and larceny.

The Assault of Molly Ratner[3]

On June 11, 1979, the author was assigned to the unit investigative team of Detective Philip De Angelo and Officer Abe Hurtado. At approximately 5:12 PM, Sergeant Richard Fitzpatrick, SCRU supervisor, received a citizen's complaint. He ordered the team to proceed to 539 Ocean Avenue, Apartment 5B, and assume control over the case.

Upon entering the building the team was stopped by plainclothes members of the street crime unit who asked for identification. Detective De Angelo identified himself, and the team was escorted to the

victim's apartment where we were admitted by street crime unit
Officer Stan Long. Officer Long had responded to the complainant's
call and reported to Detective De Angelo that the apartment was occupied by Mrs. Molly Ratner, an eighty-six-year-old widow. She
was pushed into her apartment by an unknown black male when she
opened the door to enter. Her assailant took her into a bedroom, tied
her to a chair, gagged her, and proceeded to ransack the apartment.
After the briefing, Officer Long left the apartment, and the SCRU
team assumed responsibility.

De Angelo escorted Mrs. Ratner into the kitchen and began his
questioning. He asked her if she could remember just when the assault occurred and whether her assailant had taken her to any other
room besides the bedroom. She said that she could not remember
everything but that she would try to help him.

DETECTIVE DE ANGELO: "Why don't you tell me in your own
words exactly what happened?"

MRS. RATNER: "I went to the senior citizen's group on Bedford
Avenue near Clarkson. From there I went into the Waldaum's
Food Market, and I bought some items. And then I came home."

DE ANGELO: "How did you walk? Did you walk up Bedford
Avenue? Up Ocean Avenue?"

MRS. RATNER: "I walked on Clarkson, crossed Flatbush and then
walked down Woodridge to Ocean, then turned left and walked
to my building."

DE ANGELO: "What happened when you came to the building?"

MRS. RATNER: "When I came to the building I always look to the
left, to the right. There was absolutely nobody on the street; so I
took out my key and came inside. I went to the elevator. There
was absolutely nobody there."

DE ANGELO: "Then what happened?"

MRS. RATNER: "I got to my floor, and as I was opening my door
he came from behind me. He closed my mouth (the assailant put
his hand over Mrs. Ratner's mouth) so I couldn't scream. He
pushed me in and closed the door after me. I don't know where he
came from."

De Angelo asked her to tell him what happened after they entered
the apartment. She told the detective that her assailant took her into
the bedroom, sat her on a chair, and tied her to it with some scarves
that he found in a dresser drawer.

DE ANGELO: "Did he say anything to you?"

MRS. RATNER: "He wants money."

DE ANGELO: "What did he say to you?"

MRS. RATNER: "I can't tell you the exact words."

DE ANGELO: "Just take your time."

MRS. RATNER: "It was quite a shock. You can understand that."

DE ANGELO: "What can you remember? What was the most he said? In other words did he repeat things?"

MRS. RATNER: "He wants money. I took out my wallet and showed it to him. I said, 'See, I don't have any money. I just came back from shopping, and I don't have too much money in the house.' I told him that I was robbed a month ago, and all my costume jewelry was stolen."

DE ANGELO: "Did he say anything to you? What did he do?"

MRS. RATNER: "He wanted money. I showed a little box where I had a few dollars and a lot of quarters. He took them all."

DE ANGELO: "Then what did he do?"

MRS. RATNER: "Then he tied me up."

DE ANGELO: "Oh! He first asked you for money. You gave him the box with the bills and the coins and then he tied you up?"

MRS. RATNER: "Yes."

DE ANGELO: "Okay, Molly. Now take your time and try to remember what he said or did."

MRS. RATNER: "He tied my legs, arms, and waist. And then he started choking me."

DE ANGELO: "Did he say anything while he was choking you?"

MRS. RATNER: "Money, where's your money? That's all he wanted to know. I said 'Look, I don't have money. My daughter gives me every few days what I need.' But he kept asking me, 'Where is the money?' He started taking everything apart looking for the money."

DE ANGELO: "Did he at anytime try to gag you?"

MRS. RATNER: "Yes, he put it in my mouth."

DE ANGELO: "When did he do this?"

MRS. RATNER: "He used one of the scarves."

DE ANGELO: "Then what did he do?"

MRS. RATNER: "He went looking for money."

DE ANGELO: "Did he leave you in the bedroom and search the rest of the house?"

MRS. RATNER: "Yes, he went into the living room."

DE ANGELO: "Can you tell me about how long he was there?"

MRS. RATNER: "It must have been here almost two hours."

DE ANGELO: "When he left did he say anything to you?"

MRS. RATNER: "He told me that he was going to go in and make a long distance call. He had a car outside, and he was going to go to the airport, and he was leaving town. That's what he said."

DE ANGELO: "Then he left."

MRS. RATNER: "I thought I heard him leave, but I didn't dare try to get out because the bedroom door was closed. Then I tried to loosen some of the scarves, but when I walked into my neighbors I still has some scarves on my legs."

DE ANGELO: "Did you try to call for help?"

MRS. RATNER: "I got to the telephone, but he had cut the wires."

DE ANGELO: "Then you went to your neighbor?"

MRS. RATNER: "Yes. My neighbors untied me and called the police."

DE ANGELO: "Try and give me a description of this fellow as best as you can. Tell me anything that stands out in your mind."

MRS. RATNER: "I didn't see him too much because he was usually in back of me. But I imagine he was about five foot nine."

DE ANGELO: "Can you tell me anything else? How did he look? Was he fat?"

MRS. RATNER: "He was black. He had short hair. He was slim. And that's all I can remember."

DE ANGELO: "Can you tell me anything about his clothes? What was he wearing?"

MRS. RATNER: "I don't know. I couldn't see too well because he was never much in front if me. He was always in the back. He was smart enough for that."

DE ANGELO: "Now, let me ask you something else. He grabbed you with his hands, right? Did he have a ring or a watch?"

MRS. RATNER: "I don't know. The first thing he did was to take off my marriage band."

DE ANGELO: "Is there anything he did that stands out in your mind? Did you get a look at his shoes?"

MRS. RATNER: "I couldn't see too well. The first thing he did was to take my glasses off and throw them on the bed. He tied my eyes, he tied my mouth."

DE ANGELO: "Do you think you can identify him?"

MRS. RATNER: "I couldn't swear to it. Maybe I could. I don't know."

DE ANGELO: "What I am going to have to do is take you downtown to look at some photos. I don't want to disturb you too much today because you have had a bad experience."

MRS. RATNER: "And how!"

DE ANGELO: "Molly, I want you to go to the hospital. Your throat is bruised, and you have been bleeding."

MRS. RATNER: "I don't think I should go. My throat feels bad because he choked me. It's also irritated."

DE ANGELO: "Molly, if you don't want to go I want you to promise me that you will go to your own doctor tommorow."

MRS. RATNER: "Okay, I'll go, but he didn't hurt me too bad. He didn't break anything."

Earlier De Angelo asked Officer Hurtado to call the crime scene poeple — the forensic unit. He wanted them to dust for fingerprints. Normally, SCRU does its own work. In this instance the apartment is old and the texture of the paint (wrinkles, cracks, etc.) is such that if fingerprints were discovered it would take an expert in this science to lift them properly.

When Hurtado returned he advised De Angelo that he was going to canvass Mrs. Ratner's neighbors to get information on the suspect. He also told De Angelo that he had called Mrs. Ratner's daughter, and that she was on her way to the apartment. De Angelo resumed questioning Mrs. Ratner.

DE ANGELO: "Do you think anyone followed you on your home?"

MRS. RATNER: "I don't think so."

DE ANGELO: "It is very possible that he was in the building before you arrived."

MRS. RATNER: "He probably was, but I didn't see him. If he was, I don't know where he came from."

DE ANGELO: "We sent for the fingerprint experts, so please don't touch anything. You said that he put his hand on your mouth and later choked you. Does that mean that he didn't have gloves on?"

MRS. RATNER: "Yes. He didn't have gloves. I didn't see his hands much, but I know he didn't have gloves."

DE ANGELO: "Did he hit you with anything?"

MRS. RATNER: "No. He had a knife with a long blade. He put it on my dresser, and he said that he would stab me if I yelled."
DE ANGELO: "That means that he took the gag out of your mouth."
MRS. RATNER: "Yes."
DE ANGELO: "You said that you saw him put the knife on the dresser. Did you see which hand he used?"
MRS. RATNER: "No. He had his back to me."

De Angelo learned that the suspect had Mrs. Ratner in custody for two hours. He also learned that the suspect, at some time during his search for money, used a pair of gloves that he found in the apartment. The call for the crime scene people was put in anyway on the chance that the suspect might have left prints before he found the gloves.

With the questioning over, Mrs. Ratner was moved to the living room. She asked Officer Ellen Alwill, a unit decoy who had arrived earlier, if she could go to the bathroom. Alwill told her it was okay but to try not to touch too many things, as the forensic unit wanted to dust for prints. While she was in the bathroom Mrs. Ratner became hysterical. Alwill went to her assistance. This was the first time that she had seen her face since the attack. She cried and said, "I didn't know I had all that blood on my lips. I tried to wash some of it off with toilet paper. What is my daughter going to say? I didn't want to be a burden on them!"

About an hour later, Mrs. Ratner's daughter and her husband arrived. They expressed much concern over the elderly woman's well-being. De Angelo suggested that she should not stay in the apartment overnight. Her son-in-law said, "You can come home with us tonight." Her daughter said, "Of course!" Then, as an afterthought, she mused, "We'll see, we'll see." A few minutes later she told the SCRU team, "You don't know what a sweet, beautiful, and considerate woman my mother is. She has been a wonderful mother to me — so good." Turning to her husband she said, "We'll put her in a nursing home!"

Molly Ratner objected to the idea of being placed in a nursing home and announced that she was going to stay in the apartment. Detective De Angelo and Officer Alwill suggested that if she did remain in the apartment someone should stay with her. It was finally decided that Molly would spend a few days with her daughter. The decision as to whether she would enter a nursing home would be made at a later date.

Comments

Prior to the investigation of the Ratner case, SCRU supervisors were concerned about a developing crime pattern in at least one or perhaps two of its high-crime zones. Beginning in January, 1979, task force and department analysts observed that in certain push-in robberies the assailant or assailants used the same *modus opernadi*. For example, the victims were all elderly women, most had just returned from shopping, and all had been tied to chairs with silk scarves or pantyhose. The Ratner case was one of the crime pattern cases that later resulted in the establishment of a major operation by police administrators in an effort to put this series of attacks against the elderly to an end.

Molly Ratner refused to enter a nursing home. She returned to her apartment on June 14, 1979. The area social welfare agency and some private senior citizen assistance groups were advised of her return. Using field workers, these groups maintain regular contacts with the elderly and provide a number of services. Some are unique and one will be the subject of the next chapter.

NOTES

1. Taken from notes of the author and from Official Report of Investigator Vance Herlihy.
2. Taken from the notes of the author and from Official Report of Investigators Fitzgerald and Noblin.
3. Taken from the notes of the author and from Official Report of Detective Philip De Angelo.

CHAPTER 7

THE SENIOR CITIZEN
ANTI-CRIME NETWORK

DURING the early 1970s officials of the New York City Department for the Aging became increasingly concerned about the rising number of crimes being committed against the elderly. As a result of this concern they established a citywide program that was designed to protect, educate, and assist elderly citizens. This chapter deals with the work and goals of the Department for the Aging (DFTA) and the Senior Citizen Anti-Crime Network (SCAN).

In order to ascertain the scope of the crime problem, DFTA officials established SCAN projects in a number of selected high-crime areas. We shall give special consideration to the project located in the Flatbush area of Brooklyn because it is located in Patrol Borough Brooklyn South, which the author studied, and the area has experienced the highest crime rate against the elderly in the city.

The New York City Department for the Aging is the city's official advocate and planner for the needs of New York's older citizens. Through its own resources and through the receipt of two grants to establish special programs, the department has undertaken a citywide effort to mobilize the criminal justice and social service systems in a comprehensive attack on the problem of crimes against the elderly.

In 1976, as the problem of crimes against the elderly intensified, the DFTA developed a continuing relationship with the police administrators that resulted in the joint efforts described below:

1. The establishment of specialized senior citizen anti-crime network units, with increased police personnel, in every borough in the city.
2. Police department data on selected crimes against the elderly were made available to the research division of the DFTA for analysis.

3. A senior citizen escort program to which volunteers are to be recruited predominantly from high schools was established. The students who are selected from a list of applicants will be trained by local police community affairs officers and assigned to escort older persons to and from stores, banks, and senior centers in their neighborhoods.

4. The establishment of older citizens committees in local precincts to review the operations of the senior citizen escort programs and other specialized police programs. Older residents are to have formal input into the policies and procedures of their local precinct.

5. In each police precinct, one senior citizen center or some other social agency will serve as a crime victim referral center to which police officers will refer elderly victims of crime for assistance in overcoming the impacts of victimization.

6. Under the aegis of the police department, a citywide senior citizen committee, on which the Department for the Aging's director of field operations serves, meets regularly with the police commissioner and his top command staff to review the operations of each of the above programs and to develop additional innovative strategies.

After two years of operation, it can be said that the establishment of senior citizen anti-crime units has been highly successful. The lines of communication among senior citizen's action committees, the Department for the Aging's director of field operations, and the police commissioner have been successful. This open line of communication between these groups has helped to improve relations between the police department and the community. The escort service was not in operation in the Brooklyn South area during the time of this study — June through August 1979.

In March 1976, The Department for the Aging, in association with the New York City Foundation for Senior Citizens, received a grant of $129,000 from the Mayor's Criminal Justice Coordinating Council for the Establishment of a Crime Prevention Program for the Elderly. As a result, the DFTA established the senior citizens crime prevention program.

Program administrator's established three projects to meet the immediate needs of the elderly: victim assistance, training, and public information.

Two victim assistance centers were established. One was located in Precincts 44, 46, and 48 in the West Bronx. The other was located in Precincts 20 and 24 on the west side of Manhattan. The centers provided assistance and counselling to crime victims as well as advice on crime prevention to all elderly citizens. In addition, project personnel coordinated their activities with the police and community organizations in developing crime prevention programs in the affected precincts.

The police held training sessions in crime prevention and safety techniques regularly. Project personnel developed a number of training materials designed to meet a varied range of needs. They recruited paraprofessional crime victim aides to assist project personnel in implementing the program. The recruits were trained in interviewing and servicing techniques. The centers also provided training sessions for the elderly on a citywide basis.

Finally, program administrators have provided speakers to senior citizen centers and community organizations in all areas of the city. On several occasions, project personnel have appeared before state and local legislators and provided them with information on the issue of crimes against the elderly. The testimony and data presented at these hearings have resulted in the enactment of several laws designed to assist the elderly.[1]

Within a year these programs, established by DFTA in selected target areas, were incorporated into a new citywide federally funded program.

In March 1977, the Department for the Aging, in association with the New York City Foundation for Senior Citizens, received a grant of $250,000 from the Administration of Aging, a division of the United States Department of Health, Education, and Welfare. In New York City, a parallel grant was awarded to the Community Development Agency by the Community Services Administration.

The Community Development Agency established the senior citizen crime assistance and prevention program (SCCAPP). The DFTA established the senior citizen anti-crime network (SCAN).

The SCAN program is one of the seven anti-crime programs for the elderly that were funded in 1977 in five U.S. cities and in the District of Columbia by a consortium of federal agencies: The Department of Housing and Urban Development (HUD); The Law Enforcement Assistance Administration (LEAA) of the Department of Justice; the Community Services Administration (CSA); and the Administration of Aging (AOA). The latter two are divisions of the Department of Health, Education, and Welfare (HEW).

The programs operate in Washington, D.C., New Orleans, Chicago, Milwaukee, Los Angeles, and New York City. Collectively, the seven programs are referred to as the National Elderly Victimization Prevention Assistance Program.

The seven programs are evaluated on a yearly basis by the National Council of Senior Citizen's Legal Research and Services for the Elderly and by the University of Cincinnati's behavioral sciences laboratory.

Essentially, SCAN is a demonstration program designed to demonstrate new ways to deter crime against the elderly. Its full-time staff is a project director, a training specialist, two community organizers, a victim service coordinator, a research assistant, and a secretary. Its part-time staff includes a typist and twelve community aides recruited from the target areas of the earlier programs.

The central office of SCAN is located in the borough of Manhattan. It also has field offices located in the boroughs of the Bronx, Brooklyn, and Queens.[2] It is administered jointly by the New York City Department for the Aging and the New York City Foundation for Senior Citizens, Inc.

The administrators of DFTA established four district but complimentary operations designed to attain its primary goal of protecting the elderly from the criminal element. These are (1) public information, (2) victim assistance, (3) neighborhood organizing, and (4) court monitoring.

From previous experience DFTA administrators were aware that without the cooperation of a concerned and informed public its program would have little chance of success. High on the list of its priorities, therefore, was the development of a well-coordinated information exchange network to make the public aware of the plight of the elderly citizen.

As part of its public education program SCAN began publishing bulletins and newsletters covering a wide range of activities. Individual community groups are kept informed on the number of crimes committed against the elderly and of SCAN's efforts to cope with the problem. It suggests a number of precautions that citizens can take to prevent such crimes and lists agencies that will give assistance. In particular, SCAN urges cooperation with the police and other support agencies.

In its efforts to inform and assist local groups, SCAN has established an ongoing evaluation program of innovative and successful anti-crime activities on a citywide basis. It will assist other local groups in developing similar activities in their areas for training personnel and supplying information on the availability of resources necessary to maintain the programs.

The SCAN program has focused particular attention on the operations of the criminal justice system (police, prosecutors, courts, and probation and parole) and the social services system (health, mental health, housing, and financial services) as they affect the elderly victims of crime. Its evaluations, with appropriate recommendations, are forwarded to the DFTA and to the affected departments for action consistent with its recommendations.[3]

In its first year of operation, SCAN was directed by DFTA to establish a pilot project in the borough of the Bronx whereby elderly crime victims would be able to obtain financial restitution from the New York State Crime Victims Compensation Board. To assist the elderly through the city bureaucratic structure the DFTA hired community aides and trained them as advocates for the victims. The prime functions of the aides were to accompany the victims to the various social service agencies and to act as their representative.[4] The project proved successful and was later incorporated into a larger program on a citywide basis.

The major mechanism developed to assist the elderly is the crime victims referral network, which was established in 1977 by the Field Operations Division of the Department for the Aging and by the police department. The network is composed of seventy-three social service agencies (one for each precinct in the city) to which victims sixty years old or over can be referred for special services assistance. Among the services provided by the network are assistance as temporary subsistence allowances, psychological or psychiatric care, hospital and medical expenses, and transportation service. The DFTA selected the agencies operating in the network and trained all the personnel of participating agencies in providing aid for the victim.[5]

The SCAN victim service coordinator helped to organize the agency network. He is responsible for coordinating the activities of the various service agencies in the citywide operations of the network.

Shortly after the establishment of the SCAN, the DFTA directed its supervisors to mobilize the resources of two target neighborhoods in a comprehensive grass-roots strategy to reduce the incidence of the crimes against the elderly and to alleviate the climate of fear in each neighborhood. One of the target areas is in the Flatbush section of Brooklyn; the other is in the Astoria section of Queens.[6]

At the time of the pilot project, the Flatbush section had the highest rate of crime in the city against the elderly. It still ranks at or near the top in this category of crimes. The Astoria section was more stable than Flatbush, but is was experiencing a rising crime rate against the elderly.

The project staff organized a neighborhood task force on crimes against the elderly in each area. The task force was composed of representatives of local citizen organizations including churches, synagogues, tenants' organizations, schools, businesses, and the local police precinct.

Each task force developed a range of strategies and crime deterrence techniques designed to meet the specific needs of its neighborhood. Each task force made use of the following techniques:

1. The task force developed or strengthened tenant lobby patrols in buildings housing large numbers of elderly people and developed citizen's street patrols.
2. Members of the task force planned to make door-to-door surveys of isolated elderly residents, who were to get Freon horns from the SCAN. The horns were intended to deter criminals and to alert tenants to an elderly person's need of assistance.
3. The SCAN, with the assistance of the Community Service Society of Greater New York, operates an emergency financial aid project. The project provides immediate and direct financial assistance to elderly victims of crime.
4. As an after-the-fact crime prevention measure the SCAN established a policy of installing new door locks for elderly victims in the pilot area.
5. The SCAN arranged for telephone services for homebound, isolated elderly persons, which provided regular scheduled telephone contacts with responsible adults in the community

who check on all aspects of the recipient's welfare. The service was intended to provide a measure of emotional assurance to the victim.

6. Operation Identification (Operation I.D.) is basically a police department program. Under this program residents — particularly the elderly — are urged to engrave a number — preferably one's social security number — on all valuable possessions such as television sets, stereos, typewriters, radios, watches, silverware (if possible), and so on. Police have theorized that valuables identified in this manner will be difficult to pawn or fence and can be readily identified when recovered. As an additional deterrent, stickers showing that valuables on the premises have been identified were to be attached to house or apartment doors and to store windows.

7. In the police security survey the police visited the homes and apartments of elderly persons and conducted a security check of the premises. Security devices were installed on windows. Suitable locks for doors were provided free of charge where needed. In one case, an eighty-five-year-old man living in the Coney Island section of Brooklyn South was using a wire coat hanger to secure his door. He had been robbed by neighborhood youths on an average of two or three times a month. As Investigator Rosemary Carbonaro said, "Whenever the 'Skells' needed money they would 'hit' the old man."

8. For civilian auto patrols carefully screened civilians were recruited. The civilians were to use their own automobiles and were to be reimbursed for mileage. The SCAN was to provide mobile citizen band radio units to each participant.

9. Block watchers was an innovative police department program involving the mass enrollment of residents of the neighborhood, particularly the elderly, to serve as watchers. Under this program civilians were trained to observe and report all crimes or suspicious activities to the police. The police assigned a special call number for this activity, and each block watcher was assigned a secret code number for individual identification.[7]

Officials of SCAN are firmly committed to the proposition that the elderly are in a unique position to make a valuable contribution to the neighborhood crime deterrence program. According to these officials, "They have the time and the ability to play a key role in defending themselves, their peers, and their neighbors of all ages. For their own good, and for the good of their communities, we believe the elderly must shed the image of helpless victims and don the new role of capable crime deterrers.[8]

Most of the services provided to the elderly by the SCAN and police department programs during the pilot project have been continued on a citywide basis since it was terminated. Others, such as the civilian patrols and the door-to-door surveys have evidently been discontinued. This assumption is based on observations made by the author in the Brooklyn South area during the summer of 1979. At this time, there was no visible evidence that either the civilian patrols or the door-to-door survey teams were operating.

Finally, SCAN supervisors established a senior citizen court-monitoring program. Under the program a corps of elderly citizens, trained in courtroom procedures by SCAN specialists, attends all trials involving crimes against senior citizens.

In addition to learning courtroom procedures, the volunteers also receive extensive instruction on the operation of the criminal justice system of the city. The volunteers, or court monitors, do not receive a salary, but they are reimbursed for transportation and related expenses.[9] The court-monitoring program serves a number of purposes. First, the presence of monitors, some of whom are former victims, in the courtroom puts the judge on notice that he is under scrutiny, and his decisions will be protested vigorously by SCAN and other community organizations if the monitors report that justice was not being served. Second, elderly citizens who would normally have little else to do but stay at home or sit on a park bench are given the opportunity to participate actively in the campaign to eliminate crimes against their peers. Third, the continuous monitoring of court proceedings (it is hoped by the SCAN) will eventually improve the quality of justice. Finally, the court monitoring program provides the SCAN with a citywide reporting system, which it could not possibly afford under its limited budget if it had to employ full-time paralegal personnel.

The programs that have been established by the SCAN, in coordination with police department activities, have provided much needed assistance to the elderly residents of the city. Because of the success of its initial efforts the SCAN has been continued in existence by the DFTA.

The SCAN-Flatbush target area is one of the several sections of Brooklyn in which SCAN tried out its various methods.

The material in this profile is taken from a SCAN report on the Flatbush section of Brooklyn South. According to its authors, "The profile consists of both hard and impressionistic data. Hard data sources include the 1970 United States census, 1975 population estimates from the New York City Department of Planning, and statistics on crimes against the elderly since 1975 from the New York City Police Department. Impressionistic data include the perceptions, attitudes, and opinions about the target area by representatives of community groups, residents of the area, and the SCAN staff."[10]

The target area, which is part of the Flatbush section of Brooklyn South, is bounded by Parkside Avenue on the north, Beverly Road on the south, Nostrand Avenue on the east, and Coney Island Avenue on the west. It is composed of several diverse sections. Flatbush Avenue is the geographic center of the area and is its major commercial street. Church Avenue is the second major commercial thoroughfare in the area. Most of the business establishments on Flatbush Avenue are small stores of the "Mom and Pop" type, which offer a variety of foods and merchandise.

The area consists of a number of small commercial establishments, one-family homes, and apartment building complexes. For purposes of this profile the area has been subdivided into five minisections in order to highlight its racial mix and its commercial and residential diversity.

Section one is within the area bounded by Parkside Avenue to Caton Avenue and from Coney Island Avenue to Flatbush Avenue. This is known as the "parade grounds" area because of the recreational facilities located on its periphery. It consists of a number of four-story, walk-up apartment buildings. The residents here are predominantly low-income blacks.

Section two is the area that is across Flatbush Avenue from Parkside Avenue to Linden Boulevard and to Nostrand Avenue. This section is markedly different from the first one in that it contains a number of private brownstone homes, some small apartment buildings, a number of small business establishments, and a number of large apartment house complexes. Living here are a mixture of elderly whites — mostly Jewish, West Indians, and American Blacks.

Most of the West Indian and American Blacks are young.

Section three is actually two avenues that cut across the entire target area. These avenues, Church and Ocean, have distinctly different characteristics from those of the surround area. Church Avenue is composed almost entirely of small business establishments. Ocean Avenue is the most highly populated section in the area. Both sides of the avenue are lined with large and medium apartment house complexes. The population here is fairly evenly distributed between elderly whites and black families with school-age children.

Section four is within the area bounded by Caton Avenue to Beverly Road and from Coney Island Avenue to Flatbush Avenue. This area contains both private homes and apartment buildings. The Prospect Park South section is located in this area. It contains some of the most elegant homes in the borough of Brooklyn. The residents of the private homes are predominantly white. The residents of the remaining section are a mixture of whites, blacks, and some Hispanics.

Finally, the remaining section of the target area is bounded by Church Avenue to Beverly Road and by Flatbush Avenue to Nostrand Avenue. This section is composed of a mixture of commercial establishments and apartment house complexes. In the 1970 census this section had the largest proportion of minority group residents in the area. It still contains a large young minority population.

The target area consists of all or parts of census tracts 506, 508, 510, 512, 522, 524, 794, 796, 820, 822, and 824. These tracts are listed in the 1970 United States Census.

The area contains 24,069 housing units, 1,641 of which are private homes. Over two thirds of these units were built before 1939. The percentage of private homes varies in each census tract. This is indicative of the wide diversity of type and the density of housing, which often requires different anti-crime strategies within the same area. For example, census tracts that contain a large number of private homes may require crime prevention efforts that utilize street-oriented strategies, such as civilian patrols. On the other hand, areas containing large apartment-house complexes may require tenant patrols in the lobby or in other places in the building.

The percentage of private homes in each census tract is as

follows: 506 (7.9%), 508 (1.5%), 510 (2.3%), 512 (1.2%), 522 (60.6%), 524 (34.5%), 794 (19.6%), 796 (5.1%), 820 (3.2%), 824 (18.5%).

Of significance to this study in terms of crimes against the elderly are the major shifts in the ethnic composition of the area that took place during the 1960s and 1970s. The importance of these shifts are that as minority groups moved into the area there was a corresponding increase in crime.

Table 7-I gives the total of persons sixty years and older at 22.3 percent and the total non-white population at 2.8 percent. The profile data establishes the former at 18.7 percent and the latter at 14.4 percent. If the 1970 data is accepted as correct, then the initial phase of racial transition in the area did not begin until 1973 or 1974. On the other hand, if the data presented by the authors is accepted as correct — as indeed it appears to be — then it is reasonable to assume that racial transition began in 1968.

Hence, any study of the effects of racial transition on crimes against the elderly must start with the 1960s and not with the 1970s as the 1970 data suggest.

TABLE 7-I

DEMOGRAPHY OF SCAN-FLATBUSH TARGET AREA (1970 U.S. CENSUS)

Tract	Population	Percent 60 years or older	Percent White	Percent Non-White
506	5,000	20.0	98.6	2.8
508	10,650	17.8	99.1	0.9
510	6,700	26.9	98.8	1.2
512	5,700	17.9	99.5	0.5
522	1,100	20.5	98.5	1.5
524	2,040	21.6	93.3	0.7
794	1,824	15.3	59.1	40.9
796	8,400	21.1	96.1	3.9
820	4,050	19.8	98.9	1.1
822	6,900	21.0	98.6	1.4
824	4,339	16.1	98.2	1.8
Total	56,703	22.3 (12,680)	97.2 (55,101)	2.8 (1,602)

Table 7-II indicates a wide variation in mean income, from a high of $20,000 (Tract 522) to a low of $7,277 (Tract 794). There is also a wide variation in the percentage of residents living below the federal poverty level — from a high of 16.8 percent (Tract 794) to a low of 6.0 percent (Tract 522). In only one tract, 794, is there a sizable percentage of the population receiving public assistance.

TABLE 7-II

ECONOMICS OF SCAN FLATBUSH TARGET AREA (1970 U.S. CENSUS)

Tract	Mean Income	Percent Below Poverty Level	Percent Receiving Social Security or Public Assistance
506	$ 9,446	15.8	40.0
508	8,799	11.0	35.0
510	9,413	10.4	28.0
512	11.201	8.7	33.3
522	20,054	6.0	18.3
524	14,869	6.9	28.0
794	7,227	16.8	33.3*
796	8,641	10.0	33.3
820	9,262	9.7	33.3
822	8,462	10.2	33.3
824	10,468	11.2	27.0

*(10.7% Public Assistance).

The authors of the profile, citing data received from the staff of the Flatbush Development Corporation, consider the poverty portion of the 1970 data inaccurate and perhaps misleading. According to their information, the percentage of those living below the poverty level during the early 1970s was much higher than indicated in the census report.[13]

The 1980 United States Census offers a striking contrast from the results of the 1970 census. A comparison of the total population figures in Tables 7-II and 7-III indicates a complete reversal of the ethnic composition in the target area.

Although the precise time of the initial migration has not been fixed, it appears that the period from 1968 through 1970 witnessed the largest movement of people into the area in more than a decade. Prior to this time, the largest migration occurred during the late 1940s.

In an analysis of the population shift during the year 1960 through 1970, the authors of the profile reported: "The overall analysis population of the Borough of Brooklyn declined by 1 percent, while the borough's older population — sixty-five years or over — increased 12 percent. Within the target area, the percentage of elderly residents increased from 13.4 percent of the population in 1960 to 18.7 percent — an increase of 39.6 percent. The percentage of blacks and Hispanics (during the same period) increased from 2.5 percent to 14.4 percent."[11]

It follows, according to the authors, that at the time of the 1970 Unites State Census, the migration of minorities had significantly increased, and the area was in the initial phase of racial transition.[12] A study of the 1970 data for the area does not reflect their assumptions. The disparities between the data presented by the authors, as developed by the Department of City Planning and the 1970 U.S. Census report can be seen in Table 7-I, which illustrates the ethnic composition of the area.

Table 7-III indicates an increase in the population of the area from 56,703 (1970 U.S. Census) to 62,422 — a gain of 5,719. Significantly, there was a marked decrease in the white population in every tract except tracts 522 and 524. The black population registered the highest gain in all tracts.

In the 1980 data the non-white population has been subdivided and identified by ethnic group. This separate identification represents an accurate percentage of each non-white group in this racially transitional area.

American blacks and West Indian blacks were grouped together. The authors feel that these two groups should be counted separately because of their cultural and economic differences and because of their different effects on people in the community.[15]

In discussing the growth of the West Indian black population in the target area, city planning and department personnel told this author that they will have some meaningful statistics available in the spring of 1982. They did emphasize, however, that the West Indians are increasing in number and will soon be the dominant group in some tracts.[16]

TABLE 7-III

DEMOGRAPHY OF SCAN-FLATBUSH TARGET AREA (1980 U.S. CENSUS)[14]

Tract	Population	Percent White	Percent Black	Percent Asian	Percent Hispanic	Total Percent Non-White
506	5,308	19.21	44.57	8.68	27.54	80.79
508	12,508	8.09	62.75	13.23	15.93	91.91
510	8,278	7.11	68.80	3.21	20.88	92.89
512	5,679	15.49	59.90	5.84	18.68	84.51
522	1,028	72.10	15.75	3.40	8.75	27.90
524	2,012	63.69	18.43	8.94	9.24	36.61
794	1,351	4.53	85.19	0.88	9.40	95.47
796	9,314	2.92	82.02	1.67	13.39	97.04
820	5,099	1.40	85.84	2.90	9.86	98.60
822	7,429	8.59	85.74	0.71	4.96	91.41
824	4,416	3.80	86.02	0.88	9.30	96.20
Total	62,422	18.78	63.19	4.58	13.44	81.20

The growth of the West Indian population (also known as Rastafarians) could mean a higher and more violent crime rate in the area. As we said earlier, they have a religion that is drug related, and they are prone to violence.

In 1975, the police department began maintaining records of robberies and other crimes committed against persons sixty years old and over. From these records police administrators selected five categories of crimes that were committed most frequently. Statistics were then developed for the following crimes: (1) pocketbook — force or threat of force used; (2) purse snatchings — no force or threat; (3) open area robberies — street muggings; (4) robberies in residential premises — stairways, basements, halls, lobbies, and other public areas inside buildings; and (5) dwelling robberies — inside a person's living quarters.

The statistics revealed that Brooklyn South, the area under SCAN jurisdiction, ranked first in the city in crimes committed against the elderly in three of the five selected categories: open area robberies, robberies in residential premises, and push-in robberies. In the following year, 1976, Brooklyn South ranked first in every crime category except purse snatchings.[17]

From 1975 to 1976 there was a marked increase in robberies in residential premises and push-in robberies, and there was a decrease in the other three categories.

The statistics from these three target precincts for the years 1975 and 1976 indicate increases in four categories of crime: open area robberies (39.0%), purse snatching (26.8%), robberies in residential premises (33.0%), and push-in robberies (57.4%). There was a 5.4 percent decrease in pocketbook robberies. An analysis of the combined records of the target precincts for the years 1975-1976 disclosed at 27.7 percent increase in the total number of crimes committed in the five selected categories of crimes.

A comparison study of the five selected categories of crimes committed during two separate periods — March 1976 and March 1977 — disclosed some interesting parallels. There was a 23.1 percent decrease in category crimes in Brooklyn South. In the target precincts the decrease in category crimes was 19.8 percent.

Further, there was a decrease in the total number of crimes committed against the elderly in the target precincts. The largest decrease was recorded in purse snatchings (55%). Pocketbook robberies decreased by 38 percent, and dwelling robberies decreased by 42 percent. Robberies on residential premises, however, increased by 70 percent. There was no change in open area crimes. The total number of crimes committed against the elderly was equal to 45.5 percent of the total crimes against the elderly in Brooklyn South.

In Brooklyn South, excluding the target precincts, robberies on residential premises increased by 31.1 percent. There was a decline in the other category crimes. The largest decrease was recorded in purse snatching robberies (48.5%). Open area robberies decreased by 16.3 percent. Pocketbook robberies decreased by 25.3 percent, and dwelling robberies decreased by 41.6 percent.[18]

The study disclosed that similar trends occurred in all of the selected crime categories in the target precincts and in other areas of Brooklyn South. This information led SCAN supervisors to conclude that the major thrust of anti-crime strategies should be directed toward an increased use of lobby and other "in-building" patrols.

Eventually the SCAN "in-building" anti-crime strategies were extended to all high-crime areas in the city.

Although the authors in general accept the police department statistics on crimes against the elderly, they have some reservations:

> Most significantly, they reflect only crimes reported to the police. Conversations with senior citizens and staff of senior citizen centers in the target area indicate that many crimes against the elderly are not reported. Another limitation of police statistics is that some reported crimes are not catalogued by the age of the victim, often through oversight by the recording officer. It can thus be safely assumed that some of the reported crimes in which the age of the victim is not recorded are against the elderly victims.[19]

According to the authors, therefore, the number of crimes against the elderly may be far greater than indicated by police data.

Perceptions by Neighborhood Residents and Workers

During the course of their daily activities the SCAN staff, besides their interviews with victims, routinely conducted interviews with elderly residents and with businessmen, social workers, and other people who live or work in the area. The names, ages, and occupations of the persons commenting on conditions in the area have been omitted from the profile. The time span of the interview period and most direct quotes were omitted also.

The following is a summary of the feelings and attitudes of the residents and workers of the area as reported by the SCAN staff.[20]

Most residents expressed feelings of fear and mistrust of young blacks. In some of the high-crime sections some residents said that the prospect of being robbed or beaten was no longer a remote possibility but a reality with which they must live constantly.

Others talked of the feeling isolation. They said that they were being forced to live in isolation from the rest of the community because of the ever-present danger on the street. Most of these people will not leave their apartments or homes during the evening, and, therefore, they seldom are able to socialize with friends or go to prayer service.

At the Jay Senior Citizen Center at 2059 Bedford Avenue, most of the elderly said that pocketbook snatching was an everyday occurrence. For the most part, the members of this community center were concerned about their personal safety. (As a point of interest, the Jay Senior Citizen Center closed its doors in August 1979, on the grounds that funds were lacking and that there were few regular visitors to the center.)

According to the SCAN report many residents of the area, young and old, felt hopeless. They have come to the realization that they no longer can expect to reverse the deterioration of their neighborhoods. In 1978, the director of a major social service agency in Flatbush said, "The community is lost. It can no longer be stabilized."[21]

Some interesting observations were made by a number of residents on the role of the landlords in connection with deteriorating neighborhoods and crimes against the elderly. Some residents think that the area is deteriorating because the landlords have willed it. They point to the fact that many elderly residents live in rent-controlled apartments. When the elderly leave, the landlords can rent the apartments at a higher rate. Some tenants charge that the landlords are deliberately harassing them in order to encourage them to move out. One renter claimed that some landlords are actually paying young men to harass elderly tenants. Others speak of more subtle forms of harassment such as agreeing to correct violations of the building code and then not making the changes. As a result, the elderly are forced to live in rat-infested apartments or in others where poor wiring, broken or faulty water pipes, falling plaster, and no heat are common.

According to the SCAN staff, there are groups that are organizing to reclaim their streets and neighborhoods. These groups are actively working to improve living conditions for all residents and to encourage cooperation among the various racial groups. It is, however, much too early to gauge the success of these efforts.

The SCAN staff is of the opinion that among the major factors responsible for some of the areas problems is racial tension between the elderly whites of the area and the young blacks, and between American blacks and West Indian blacks. These hatreds tend to spill over and reach all segments of the community, contributing to the increase in criminal acts against the elderly.

Another contributing factor, according to the SCAN staff, may be economic. Both the elderly whites or at least a majority of them and most black families live at or below poverty level. Some whites would like to leave the area but lack the finances to do so. Others are content to remain in the area where they have lived all of their lives. The young blacks are mostly unemployed and without ready spending money. This combination sets the stage for the victimization of the elderly. The elderly have some money, the young have none; therefore, the elderly become the source of supply for the young.

Finally, the departure of a number of persons from most of the larger and more effective community organizations may, according to the SCAN staff, be a contributing factor.

In the past, these organizations were able to help the elderly with their problems and to maintain good relations with the minority groups of the area. As racial transition entered its second phase and more minorities moved into the area, the incidence of crime also increased. Eventually, many of the active members of these established organizations moved. Without experienced and competent staff to carry out their functions, most organizations in the area became weak and ineffective.

The SCAN staff, in coordination with other city agencies, the police department, and the remaining community organizations is actively working to reverse the situation. As with the smaller neighborhood groups and organizations, it is too early to determine whether their efforts will succeed.

NOTES

1. The New York City Department for the Aging, Bulletin: Combatting Crimes Against the Elderly (New York, June 16, 1977), pp. 1-3.
2. Senior Citizen Anti-Crime Network, The New York City Department for the Aging — The New York City Foundation for Senior Citizens Inc., Background Paper (New York, 1977), pp. 1-2.
3. N.Y.C. Department for the Aging, Bulletin: Combatting Crimes Against the Elderly, p. 4.
4. *Ibid.*
5. Senior Citizen Anti-Crime Network, Background paper, p. 4.
6. N.Y.C. Department for the Aging, Bulletin: Combatting Crimes Against the Elderly, p. 4.
7. Senior Citizen Anti-Crime Network, Background paper, pp. 5-6.
8. *Ibid.*, p. 6.
9. *Ibid.*, p. 7.
10. Senior Citizen Anti-Crime Network, New York City Department for the Aging — The New York City Foundation for Senior Citizens Inc., "SCAN-Profile — Flatbush Section, Brooklyn South" (New York — 1978).
11. *Ibid.*, p. 12.
12. *Ibid.*, p. 4.
13. *Ibid.*, p. 6.
14. The data on the 1980 U.S. Census report was obtained by the author on April

14, 1981, from the city of New York, Department of City Planning, Population Division via telephone communication. In addition to the data, the author was informed as follows:

a. Information on age group of elderly whites was not available. This information will be available during the winter of 1981; and

b. Data in connection with statistics referred to in Table 7-II will be available in the spring of 1982.

15. SCAN Profile, p. 6.
16. Telephone Communication, City Planning Department, April 14, 1981.
17. SCAN Profile, p. 6.
18. *Ibid.*, p. 5.
19. *Ibid.*, p. 6.
20. *Ibid.*, p. 7.
21. *Ibid.*

CHAPTER 8

OPERATION SILK STOCKING —
THE HUNT FOR A KILLER

D URING the first quarter of 1979, SCRU investigators responded to a number of complaints from elderly victims in the seventy-first police precinct of Brooklyn South, which eventually led unit supervisors to establish Operation Silk Stocking. This chapter chronicles the events that produced a pattern of crimes and the efforts of the police department to bring an end to a series of particularly vicious attacks against the elderly.

The first of the assaults, which were to continue for more than eight months, occurred on the twenty-third of February 1979. Two more occurred during March, one on the second and the other on the ninth. A fourth attack occurred on the nineteenth of April 1979.

In a review of crime scene reports on these robberies, department analysts and SCRU investigators independently concluded that the *modus operandi* of the offender was almost identical in each case. Both groups found that all of the victims were elderly females who had returned to their apartments after a shopping trip or a visit to a bank, that all were push-in robberies, that the criminal made similar statements to each victim, and that he took similar actions and precautions during each robbery.

Senior citizen robbery unit administrators recognizing that a definite crime pattern was emerging took a series of steps designed to establish immediate and effective control in the newly established target area. First, a crime pattern case chart was set up in the operations room. The chart was to contain current information on the date, time, place, and other data pertinent to each case (*see* Fig. 8-1). Second, in conjunction with the chart, an area spot map was set up in order to identify the exact geographical location of the business establishments visited by the victim on the day of the robbery, the route she took on her way home, and the building in which the crime occurred. Third, a separate file folder was established for each pattern case. Fourth, a unit investigative team was assigned overall

CRIME PATTERN CASE CHART

DAY DATE TIME	PCT. LOB 61#	COMPLAINANT ADDRESS	COMING FROM
FRI 2-23 12:30	71-129 3273	ESTHER BAKER 85 CLARKSON AVE. 6G	FLATBUSH AVE.
FRI 2-23 15:00	71-150 3722	BETTY CANTOR 184 CLARKSON AVE. 5F	WALDBAUM'S
FRI 2-23 16:00	67-165 2159	SARAH LIEBERMAN 40 LINDEN BLVD. 4E	WALDBAUM'S
THURS 4-19 15:15	70-225 4059	IRIS BALIN 255 E. 18 ST. 5B	KEY FOOD
WED 4-23 16:50	71-250 7069	EVA DELANSE 5 LINCOLN RD. 3B	ASSOCIATED FOODS
FRI 5-4 12:00	71-257 7190	MYRA ROSEN 310 LENOX RD. 5A	FLATBUSH AVE.
TUES 5-8 12:30	71-264 7441	SELMA TUCKER 255 E. 19 ST. 4B	WALDBAUM'S
WED 5-9 12:15	71-266 7494	MARY BAILEY 191 LENOX RD. C3	SHOPPING ROGERS AVE.
FRI 5-18 13:30	71-281	ETTA WEINSTEIN 49 LINDEN BLVD. 2B	KEY FOOD
TUES 5-29 14:20	71-299	SADIE EPSTEIN 301 LINCOLN BLVD. 4E	ASSOC. FOODS
MON 6-4 11:30	71-304 9195	HILDA ROSSMAN 223 LENOX RD. 6B	WALDBAUM'S
MON 6-4 14:30	71-306 9203	V. RAPFOGEL 1310 NOSTRAND AVE. 5C	KEY FOOD
MON 6-11 15:30	71-320	M. RATHER 359 OCEAN AVE. 3A	WALDBAUM'S
FRI 6-15 13:20	71-332 8609	JULIA KASTNER 2106 ALBEMARLE RD. 4E	FLATBUSH AVE.
MON 6-25 16:00	67-348 6094	RUBY BLACKNER 28 LINDEN BLVD. 6B	KEY FOOD
MON 6-25 11:00	67-349 6100	IRENE BROMBERG 248 OCEAN AVE. 5C	STOP AND SAVE DISCOUNT & KEY FOOD
WED 6-27 16:40	71 10753	LILIAN HOLTZMAN 70 LENOX RD. 4D	FLATBUSH AVE.
TUES 7-3 12:00	67-357 11821	IRENE SELZMAN 182 LINDEN BLVD. 4F	BUS CHURCH AND NOSTRAND
WED 7-11 13:00	71-385 12603	MARY GROSS 215 LENOX RD. 10B	FLATBUSH AVE.
WED 7-11 14:00	71-386 12604	GERTRUDE KAPLAN 206 LENOX RD. 5C	FLATBUSH AVE.
WED 7-11 14:30	71-387 12605	STELLA SAPERSTEIN 206 LENOX RD. 5F	KAPLAN APARTMENT
TUES 7-24 16:30	71-405 13143	HARRIET LOESSER 252 STERLING ST.	ROGERS AVE.
WED 7-25 20:45	67-408 12503	IRENE SELZMAN 182 LINDEN BLVD 4F	APARTMENT
WED 8-1 13:20	71-417 12762	RUTH MARGOLIN 181 LENOX RD. C8	ROGERS AVE.
WED 8-1 13:00	71-419 12764	MARY BAILEY 191 LENOX RD. C3	FLATBUSH AVE.

COMMON FACTORS

8- COMPLAINANT PRESCRIPTIONS FILLED AT COURTESY DRUGS

4- COMPLAINANT'S HAVE ACCOUNTS AT METROPOLITAN SAVINGS.

2- WITHDREW MONEY ON DAY OF MUGGING- CATON AND FLATBUSH

CASE 165 SARAH LIEBERMAN RE: DD STATEMENT FOLLOW-UP #3 JAN. 10- MADE OUT CHECK TO CAMERA STORE

3- COMPLAINATS BELONG TO JAY SENIOR CENTER ACROSS FROM WALDBAUM'S

CASE #150 COMPLAINANT CASHED CHECK AT MANHATTAN-HANOVER CHURCH AVE.: SUSPECT SAID: "I SAW YOU IN BANK. GIVE ME YOUR MONEY OR I'LL KILL YOU."

SUSPECT MADE STATEMENTS TO AT LEAST 4 COMPLAINANTS ABOUT MAKING PHONE CALLS

STORES FREQUENTED BY COMPLAINANTS: HEALTHWISE DRUGS- CHURCH AVE.; GROCERY STORE- WASHINGTON AVE.; JEWELRY- CHURCH AVE.; FIESTA- CHURCH AVE.; BETTER PAID DRUGS- FLATBUSH AVE.

MALE- BLACK, 19-21, 5'9" TO 5'11", 145-155 LBS., DARK SKINNED, NEATLY DRESSED, SOFT SPOKEN.

Figure 8-1. OPERATION SILK STOCKING CRIME PATTERN CHART

responsibility for pattern cases. Finally, decoy team operations were increased in the target area.

As the number of crime pattern cases increased, the *modus operandi* of the criminal became clear to police administrators. From the victims' testimony and from their own investigative efforts, unit investigators learned that the criminal would repeat certain statements. He would say, "I have to catch a plane," or "I have my car double-parked downstairs," or "I'm in a hurry — I have to leave town." They also found that most crimes were committed between the hours of eleven o'clock in the morning and five o'clock in the afternoon, and that most of these crimes were committed on Mondays, Tuesdays, and Fridays.

From this data the police reasoned that the criminal was familiar with the habits of the elderly, and that he planned some of the robberies by observing the habits of his victims. The police were now reasonably certain that these crimes were being committed by one man.

In this action the investigators also learned that in all of the robberies the criminal took one or more of the following actions or precautions: (1) He waited until the victim opened the door before attacking her; (2) he seized the victim from behind. In this one action, the offender either put his arm around her neck or placed his hand over her mouth, knocked off her glasses and pushed her into the apartment — hence, the term, "push-in" robbery; (3) keeping behind the victim throughout the attack to avoid identification he pushed or dragged the victim into a bedroom; (4) he tied the victim to a chair or a bedpost with pantyhose, scarves, or strips of cloth torn from pajamas; (5) he choked the victim repeatedly — by means of a pantyhose or scarf tied into a slipknot — until she revealed where she hid her money and other valuables; (6) he wore gloves or searched the apartment for a pair to use; (7) he pulled out the telephone wires; (8) turned on the radio or the television set in order to block out the victim's screams; and (9) pulled the shades.

Despite the increased police decoy and surveillance activities in the target area, attacks upon the elderly continued into the summer.

As a result of the increasing data that made clear the emergence of a crime pattern, police administrators decided to put a new plan into operation. This plan, designed to apprehend the Silk Stocking Robber, was put into operation on Friday, June 15, 1979.

On the previous afternoon, Lieutenant Coles assembled eight

SCRU personnel (six males and two females) and advised them that they were to participate in Operation Silk Stocking, which was to begin the next day. The operation was to be conducted from 11:00 AM to 6:00 PM on Mondays, Tuesdays, and Fridays. It was to continue for a period of three weeks unless terminated earlier by the capture of the suspect.

On the morning of the fifteenth the officers assembled in the operations room where they were briefed on the details of the operation by Lieutenant Coles.

The operation was to be conducted in the seventy-first police precinct area — specifically in the vicinity of Bedford Avenue and Clarkson Avenue. In this area SCRU administrators established four bases for the conduct of operations. The first was located at the Jay Senior Citizen Center at 2059 Bedford Avenue. This base was designated as the control center for operations. The second was Waldbaum's Supermarket located at the corner of Bedford Avenue and Clarkson Avenue. The supermarket is located directly across the street from the Jay Center. The third was the stakeout apartment. This apartment, Number 2A, is located at 60 Clarkson Avenue approximately 150 feet from the corner of Waldbaum's. The fourth base was an observation post on the roof of a building at 2031 Bedford Avenue. This building, also known as Casey's house or Casey's roof, is located on the corner of Bedford and Clarkson avenues diagonally away from Waldbaum's. Because it offered the best view of the area under surveillance, the director of operations selected it as the center of operations and primary observation post instead of the Jay Center.

In addition to the four bases, a specially equipped observation van was to be parked on Clarkson Avenue on the east side of Bedford Avenue. The van, manned by two officers, was to be used as a secondary observation post and as a backup and pursuit vehicle.

The building on Clarkson Avenue was to be manned by four officers. Two officers were to occupy Apartment 2A. One officer, dressed as a telephone linesman, was to be stationed in the courtyard. The other, dressed as a janitor, was to be stationed on the third floor.

The decoys were told to operate from three locations — the Jay Center, the apartment, and Waldbaum's Supermarket.

When operating from the Jay Center, the decoy will walk to

Waldbaum's, make a purchase, and then proceed to Apartment 2A. When operating out of the apartment, she was to walk to Waldbaum's make a purchase, and then return to the apartment or cross the street to the Jay Center, after which she might return to the apartment.

The procedure was to be different when she operated out of Waldbaum's store. At Waldbaum's both decoys were to be stationed in the rear of the store. If a potential suspect is spotted, one of the decoys is to move into the public section of the store and purchase some groceries. After leaving the store she will proceed to the apartment. If she is being followed she will be alerted to this fact by the director, who will be stationed on Casey's roof. After she enters the building, the "telephone linesman" and the "janitor" are to move into position. In the meantime, the backup team in the van will proceed to the Clarkson Avenue building and will secure the front and rear entrances.

Hence, if the offender pushes the decoy into the apartment, he will be confronted by the two officers stationed there. If he eludes this officer, he will be met by the officer who has moved upstairs from the courtyard and into the hall. Eluding this officer, he will be met by the backup team, or if he tries to go to the roof, he will be confronted by the officer stationed at the floor landing.

Figure 8-2 illustrates the location of the four bases of operation, the layout of Apartment 2A, and the assignments for the first day's operation (decoys not included).

In the event that the decoy is not followed, she will return to the Waldbaum store and enter the premises through a rear entrance. The decoy will return the groceries for the purchase money. The second decoy will repeat the procedure when another possible offender appears.

On June 15, 1979 (the first day of Operation Silk Stocking) after the morning's briefing, the special teams departed for the target area. Sergeant Byrnes, director of operations, Officer Lohse, and the author proceeded to Casey's roof — the command post for the day's operation.

On the way to the command post the police dispatcher at base radio called in a 10-10. Responding units were advised that a man with a shotgun was reported to be on the roof of a building located at 284 East Thirty-fourth Street. Sergeant Byrnes ordered Officer

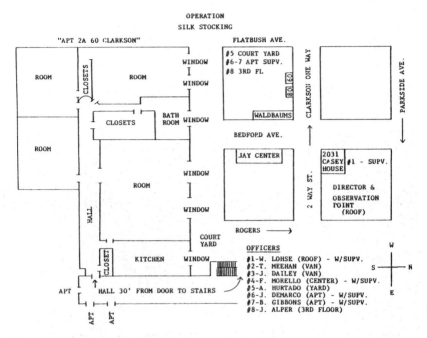

Figure 8-2. Shown here are the four bases of operation, the layout of the stakeout apartment, and personnel assignments.

DeCostanzo, driver of the command car, to proceed to the Thirty-fourth Street address.

Four other police units responded to this call — three uniformed police patrols and a SCRU plainclothes unit. Upon arriving at the scene, Sergeant Byrnes led the officers into the building. After a thorough search of the building and the area the police could not locate the man with a shotgun. Sergeant Byrnes ordered the SCRU out of the area. The uniformed police patrols remained on the scene.

On the trip to the command post Sergeant Byrnes surmised that the call could have been a ruse by local criminals. They know that all police units in the area will respond to such calls. In this manner, therefore, the criminals are able to identify the plainclothes police and the unmarked vehicles they use.

Before proceeding to Casey's roof Sergeant Byrnes went to the stakeout apartment at 60 Clarkson Avenue to discuss strategy with Sergeant Fitzpatrick and Officer De Marco. Fitzpatrick told him that De Marco was to be stationed in a bedroom approximately eight feet to the right of the entrance. He (Fitzpatrick) was to be in a bedroom directly opposite De Marco. If the suspect pushed the decoy into the apartment, De Marco was to make the first move for him. The suspect would be given the usual command, "Police, don't move!" At the moment of the command, the decoy would "go to the floor." Fitzpatrick said that he would act in a backup role because of the restricted area in which they were to be operating. After a brief discussion the three men agreed that De Marco would be the arresting officer if the suspect were to be captured.

At 1:15 PM Sergeant Byrnes gave the order for Operation Silk Stocking to begin. While the first decoy was getting ready to move out on the street the following incident occurred at the Waldbaum Supermarket. At 1:18 PM, some boys who were loitering near the entrance were told to leave by a uniformed security guard from the store. When the boys refused to leave, the guard slapped one of them on the mouth. Observing the altercation Sergeant Byrnes said, "If these kids run true to form they will be back with a gun. If not, they'll come back with more kids, and they'll beat the hell out of that guard."[1]

At 1:25 PM Officer Thompson left the apartment and walked to Waldbaum's. Before she entered the store she stopped at the corner and conversed with Officer Lohse who was at the command post on Casey's roof. Lohse told her to move into the store right away because a fifteen- or sixteen-year-old boy went in just before she got to the corner. After she entered the store, Thompson reported that she could not locate the young man.

As Lohse was talking to the decoy, Sergeant Byrnes spotted a young boy following an elderly woman on Clarkson Avenue. The boy followed her for several yards, crossed the street, stood watched her for thirty or forty seconds, and then followed her again. At that point Sergeant Byrnes suspended the SCRU operation. Officer Lohse instructed the decoy to move to the rear of the store and stall while the team picked up on this action.

The boy recrossed the street, walked past the woman, and waited for her at the entrance of an apartment building. He resumed following her as she passed him. As they turned the corner to Flatbush Avenue they were no longer in sight. Sergeant Byrnes ordered Officers Meehan and Gibbons, who were in the van, to keep them in sight. At 1:50 PM, Meehan reported that he had them in sight. At

1:55 PM, Gibbons reported that the boy was no longer following the woman, but that they would keep her under observation until she reached her home.

The van returned to its post at 2:08 PM, and the operation resumed shortly thereafter. Officer Thompson left Waldbaum's at 2:15 PM and returned to the apartment without incident (*see* Fig. 8-3).

Figure 8-3. Officer Thompson is on her way to the stakeout apartment.

From the time the operation was called off to the time it was resumed (a period of about twenty minutes), two incidents took place directly across the street from Casey's roof. In the first incident the owner of the Bedford Laundromat was taking numbers. The officers observed four people handing her money after she wrote "something" on a small pad. In the second incident, the owner of the shoe repair store next to the Laundromat was selling a controlled substance. Sergeant Byrnes reported these crimes to the police intelligence unit. At 2:25 PM Officer Alwill, the second decoy, left the apartment and proceeded to Waldbaum's. Officer Lohse told her that she was being followed by a young man from across the street. (*see* Fig. 8-4). He followed her until she entered the store. The officers regarded the young man with suspicion because he loitered

Figure 8-4. Sergeant Byrnes (left) and Officer Lohse (right) watch a suspect following Officer Thompson (decoy) at the command post on Casey's roof.

near the entrance waiting for her to emerge. Officer Lohse warned the decoy, but by the time she left the checkout counter the young man had decided to leave. Officer Alwill returned to the apartment without incident.

The decoys continued this procedure for the remainder of the afternoon, and the operation was called off at 5:30 PM.

On Monday, June 18, 1979, Sergeant Fitzpatrick was in charge. He was to work out of the apartment with Officer De Marco. Detective Frank Dattolico was to be stationed on the third-floor landing, and Officer Hurtado was to patrol the lobby of the building.

Officer Lohse directed operations from Casey's roof. Officers J. Dailey and T. Meehan were to operate from an unmarked squad car. The van was not available on this day.

Sergeant Fitzpatrick decided to have Officers Thompson and Conry — this day's decoys — operate from the Jay Center. They were instructed to leave the center, shop at Waldbaum's, and then proceed to the apartment. On the return trip they were to leave the apartment and proceed directly to the center. Fitzpatrick told the team members not to call for a decoy play unless they spotted a person who fit the description of the suspect. The team moved into position at 12:15 PM.

Conry decided to make the first run because she wanted to familiarize herself with the area. After her run, Officer Thompson followed the same procedure. Although there were a number of elderly women shopping that day, there were no incidents.

Thompson and Conry repeated the procedure until 3:25 PM. A heavy rain began to fall at that time, and when it failed to show any sign of abating, Sergeant Fitzpatrick called a halt to the day's activities.

During this morning's briefing, on Tuesday, June 19, 1979, Investigator Robert Noblin supplied team members with a picture of an offender named Gregorio Nelson. This criminal has a record of robbing and assaulting elderly women. He is a light-skinned black, eighteen years old, five feet ten inches tall, and he is well dressed and soft spoken.

Noblin also told team members that Gregorio Nelson is a particularly vicious person who was then out on the street. He lived at 598 Flatbush Avenue in the vicinity of the target area. Senior citizen robbery unit administrators considered him to be a prime suspect in this case. On this day the team was operating without the services of two members: Officer De Marco had been injured while on another assignment, and Officer Gibbons had been assigned temporarily to duty in another high-crime area of Brooklyn South.

Sergeant Byrnes was at the command post with Officer Lohse. Officers Meehan and Dailey were operating the observation van. The decoys were to work out of the Jay Center. Officers Hurtado and Alper were assigned to the apartment. The author had received permission from Sergeant Byrnes to observe from the apartment.

Because there were no backup officers in the building, Hurtado and Alper modified the strategy established by Sergeant Fitzpatrick. As before, Alper was to be stationed in the bedroom to the right of the entrance. When the decoy was enroute to the apartment, Hurtado would leave the apartment and go to the lobby. After the decoy was in the building and on her way to the apartment, Hurtado would take the stairway to the second floor. If the suspect entered the apartment, Hurtado would move to the door to support Alper, who would inform him if he should have the suspect under control.

If the suspect should break away from Alper, Hurtado would be in a position to prevent his escape. In the meantime Meehan and Dailey would have had time to enter the building to assist the apartment team.

The team moved into position at 12:05 PM. At 12:20 PM, Thompson left the Jay Center and walked to the corner of Bedford and Clarkson avenues. As she crossed Bedford Avenue, two young boys passed her. One of the boys stopped at the corner and watched her as she walked toward the apartment. After several seconds he turned away and joined his companion. Sergeant Byrnes told the decoy to return to the Jay Center.

At 1:02 PM, Conry left the Jay Center and walked toward the apartment. As she neared the building, Hurtado moved to the lobby. In the meantime Lohse reported that she was followed into the building by a man. Conry climbed the stairs to the second floor. The man walked past her and entered the elevator. Hurtado walked up the rear stairway and waited for the decoy. Within a few seconds she arrived at the second floor landing and proceeded to the apartment.

At 1:25 PM, Thompson left the Jay Center and walked to Waldbaum's. She purchased some groceries and walked toward the apartment. As she left the store, two youths spotted her and followed her as she walked on Clarkson Avenue. They stopped about twenty feet from the building and returned to Waldbaum's. The decoy entered the apartment without incident.

At 1:37 PM, Conry left the apartment. Alper followed her through the lobby. The decoy walked to Waldbaum's and purchased some groceries. As she left the store and turned on Clarkson Avenue, Lohse informed her that she was being followed by a youth wearing brown clothes. Hurtado returned to the lobby. Thompson maintained radio contact with the command post and with Conry. Alper took his position by the door to the bedroom. The decoy entered the building, but the youth did not follow her. Conry took the elevator to the second floor and returned to the apartment.

Thompson and Conry continued making trips to Waldbaum's and the Jay Center until Sergeant Byrnes called off the day's activities at 5:00 PM. When they arrived at the office, Lieutenant Coles told them that Operation Silk Stocking would not be resumed until Friday.

As the teams prepared to resume normal operations on the morning of Wednesday, June 20, 1979, some members of the Silk Stocking team discussed the tactics used during the past week. Officer Thompson said that the decoys should not make more than three runs in one day. She suggested, however, that they should stay on the street for a longer period of time.

As the discussion continued, Sergeant Byrnes joined the group. Lohse suggested that it was possible that the suspect might have been arrested and now be in jail. Officers Meehan and Dailey believe that he may be operating in another area of the city. Finally, Sergeant Byrnes asked them if they wanted to go back and try again. The consensus of the team was to go back.

It was evident to the author that most of the team members were frustrated. They were annoyed that the suspect had eluded them so far. More important, they were aware that he was a vicious and dangerous person. Hurtado summed up the team's feelings when he said, "We have to get that mean bastard off the street!"[2]

Later in the morning, the author discussed the suspect with Sergeant Byrnes. Byrnes said:

> We want this fellow badly because we feel that sooner or later he will murder one of his victims. It could be that he already has killed a couple of people. We are looking into that possibility.

This mutt does not initially hurt his victims. He pushes them into the apartment, ties them up, and then asks for money, gold, or jewelry. If he doesn't get the right answers, he chokes them with either a stocking or a scarf.

He has bloodied some of his victims, and we feel that the next time out we might be involved in a homicide.

The day's operation started at 12:32 PM. Sergeant Byrnes and Officer Lohse returned to the command post. The author joined them at 1:00 PM. Officer Alper and Hurtado were assigned to the apartment. Officers Dailey and Thompson operated the van. The decoys for this operation were Officers Conry and Alwill. The decoys were to operate from the Jay Center.

Dailey parked the van on Clarkson Avenue approximately forty feet east of the corner of Bedford Avenue. Equipped with a 500-mm. zoom lens camera, he planned to take pictures of all persons who fit the description of the suspect. Later, SCRU investigators would attempt to match these pictures with photos of criminals who have been arrested for crimes against the elderly. Once positive identifications are made, SCRU administrators will request the court's permission to detain for questioning those persons who are considered to be likely suspects.

At 12:45 PM, Alwill left the Jay Center, crossed the street to Waldbaum's, and shopped for groceries. After making some purchases, she walked to the apartment. At 1:31 PM, Conry repeated the procedure.

The difference between today's procedures and the previous ones is that the decoys stayed out on the street for a longer period. Nothing seemed to work. Sergeant Byrnes terminated the team's activities at 2:20 PM.

Later in the day, the author discussed the suspect and his possible motives for committing these crimes with some street-experienced officers. In response to the author's questions one officer said (and others agreed):

This fellow and others like him want gold in addition to money, because local fences have placed a high priority on it.

There is a diamond exchange in uptown Manhattan, some of whose members will buy such gold jewelry as watches, chains, rings, bracelets, and anything else that is made of gold. The gold from this type of property is then melted and can no longer be traced. The criminal receives a good price for his merchandise and has little chance of being apprehended. The exchange merchants ask no questions.

In addition to the Manhattan Exchange, there are some local exchanges in Brooklyn, some of whose members will also buy stolen goods. They also melt the gold so that it can't be traced.

We get this information from informers. It is very difficult to catch these guys; they have a pretty good system.

The irony in this entire crime situation is that the criminal is being encouraged into this type of crime by the supposedly honest businessman — the guy for whom we put our lives on the line.

This so-called *honest* businessman would rather buy gold from the criminal than in the open market. To him, it's a matter of economics. The price of gold in the open market is very high. This means he has a very low margin of profit. The gold he gets from the criminal comes at a very low price, therefore, he has a very high margin of profit.

So, the *honest* businessman and the criminal profit from crime, while the elderly are beaten and robbed — and we run into brick walls in trying to catch the bastards.

The author asked the officer if the police could, in any way, induce the exchange merchants to cooperate with them. He replied:

No. It would not serve their interests to cooperate with us. There are several reasons for this, but I'll give you the most important ones. First, if they cooperate, they will become involved in the crime, and this could lead to a lot of trouble. Second, they are not about to blow their sources of low-priced gold. We don't expect it to happen, and we haven't been disappointed.[3]

The conversation ended at this point because some of the officers were ready to leave for the second tour of the day. It was difficult to determine how the knowledge of these facts affected the team members. Judging by their attitudes, however, it did not appear to have effect at all.

On Thursday, June 21, 1979, Lieutenant Coles and Sergeant Byrnes decided that the team would conduct a surveillance of the target area. This meant that the decoys were not to make any plays.

Sergeant Byrnes and Officer Lohse took their positions at the command post. Officers Alper and Alwill were assigned to the apartment. Officer Hurtado was assigned to operate the van. He was to continue taking pictures of persons who fit the description of the suspect. Officer Conry was the decoy for today's activities and was to operate from the Jay Center. The author, hooked up with a radio transmitter and dressed as a decoy, joined Conry at the center.

The team moved into position at 11:30 AM. Officer Conry and the author took a position by a stained glass window of the Jay Center. This selected vantage point afforded the team an excellent view of the front entrance of Waldbaum's and of the west corner of Clarkson and Bedford avenues.

After an hour of observing young boys loitering near the entrance of the store, Sergeant Byrnes ordered Conry to make a surveillance run to the apartment. At 12:35 PM Conry left the center and walked to the corner of Clarkson and Bedford avenues. At the corner, Conry asked Byrnes if she should enter Waldbaum's. He instructed her to proceed to the apartment. On her way to the building two youths who had been loitering outside the store watched her as she walked on Clarkson Avenue. They did not follow her. Conry arrived at the apartment at 12:45 PM. She remained there for fifteen minutes and returned to the Jay Center at 1:11 PM.

At 1:35 PM, Conry and the author left the Jay Center for a surveillance run to the apartment. The team walked to the east corner of Clarkson and Bedford avenues. They crossed to the west corner, stopped by Waldbaum's, and then proceeded to the apartment. On the way, the same boys watched them until they reached the building. The team arrived at the apartment at 1:48 PM.

At 2:30 PM, Sergeant Byrnes ordered the apartment closed for the day. Hurtado moved to the command post. Alper and Alwill went to the van. Conry and the author returned to the Jay Center.

The team continued its surveillance activities for the remainder of the afternoon. The operation was called off at 2:30 PM.

On Friday, June 22, 1979, Lieutenant Coles and Sergeant Byrnes decided that the team would use the three decoys for a number of reasons: (1) The apartment was to be occupied by only one officer because of a shortage of personnel; (2) when a decoy moved from the street to the apartment she would double as a backup for the next decoy run; and (3) three decoys on the street would reduce the chances of having the operation or one of the decoys uncovered by the suspect or other streetwise youths.

Officer Lohse directed this day's operation from the command post. Officer Alper, joined by a backup decoy, as mentioned earlier, occupied the apartment. Officers Meehan and Dailey operated the van. The decoys, Thompson, Alwill, and Conry, worked out of the Jay Center. The author joined Lohse at the command post. The team moved into position at 12:25 PM.

The director decided not to send out decoys unless a person is sighted who matches the description of the suspect. Team members were instructed to contact the command post when such a person is sighted. Officer Lohse was to issue any orders for sending out a decoy or for securing a picture of the possible criminal.

At 1:45 PM, Meehan reported that a youth matching the description of the suspect was walking west on Clarkson Avenue. Lohse ordered Conry out. Under Lohse's direction, the decoy was able to time her approach to the corner of Bedford and Clarkson avenues to coincide with the arrival of the youth. She made her play, but the youth ignored her and continued on his way. Lohse told Conry to go to Waldbaum's and shop for gorceries. She left the store fifteen minutes later and returned to the Jay Center.

At approximately 2:05 PM Lohse directed the author's attention to two men who were leaning against a building railing next to the stakeout apartment building. One of the men was the Waldbaum security guard, and the other was not identified. Lohse said, "They are smoking marijuana."[4] Officer Alper who was much closer to the two men confirmed Lohse's suspicion. He also reported that three young boys who were sitting at the curb in front of 60 Clarkson Avenue were drinking wine out of a bottle.

At 2:15 PM, Alper reported that a young man matching the description of the suspect was walking east on Clarkson Avenue. Lohse ordered Alwill out. The youth entered Waldbaum's, and the decoy entered the store a few minutes later. At 2:45 PM, she told Lohse that the youth was employed at the store. Lohse told her to return to the Jay Center.

During the afternoon a number of incidents occurred that led SCRU supervisors to conclude that the location of the stakeout apartment might have to be changed.

First, the building superintendent, without prior notice, entered the apartment with a prospective tenant. At the moment of entry, Alper was in contact with the command post and did not have the opportunity to secure the police equipment. Then three girls came to the apartment and asked for the superintendent. Officer Hurtado, who had joined Alper earlier, told them that he was a telephone repairman, and that he did not know where they could locate him. The girls appeared to be annoyed by this answer but they left the area. Finally, the superintendent came to the apartment a second time and asked for police assistance. He told Alper and Hurtado that when the girls could not find him, they broke into a mailbox and removed its contents. Then they returned to his apartment and urinated in the hall outside his door.

Hurtado left the apartment to verify the damage. Upon his return he made contact with the command post and told Lohse what had occurred. Lohse called the seventy-first precinct and asked for a uniformed police patrol unit. He was told that a unit would be sent to the scene as soon as possible. He suspended decoy operations until uniformed police could complete their investigation.

Finally, Hurtado told Lohse that when he went to investigate the mailbox incident he noticed a group of teenagers loitering in the lobby. He said, "These are the same guys who were hanging around Waldbaum's earlier today."[5] He also told Lohse that he believed the team had been recognized by the youths.

Lohse called SCRU headquarters and explained the situation at the stakeout apartment to Sergeant Fitzpatrick. Although it was not certain that the team had been recognized, Sergeant Fitzpatrick decided to end the operation for the day. Because of the possible recognition of the team, SCRU administrators decided to move to a new location as soon as possible. The current apartment would be used until another one could be located.

On Monday, June 25, 1979, the team learned that the stakeout apartment had been rented. This new and unexpected situation caused SCRU supervisors to make some temporary changes in strategy. No decoy operations were to be used until a new apartment could be found. In the meantime, the decoys were to be assigned to surveillance duties. An unmarked squad car is to be added to the street surveillance unit, and the officer is to cruise in the target area. If he should see anyone who matches the description of the suspect, he is to notify the director. The director may order the van team to take a picture of the youth. Except for the van team and the squad car operator all teams will be limited to surveillance activities. In addition to taking pictures of persons who match the description of the suspect, the van team will double as the primary pursuit team in the event that an elderly person is in danger of attack. Finally, the operator of the squad car will double as the backup for the van team.

Sergeant Fitzpatrick was the director of this day's operation. He will be assisted by Officers W. Lohse and J. Alper. Officers Thompson and Conry worked out of the Jay Center. Officer J. Lohse operated the unmarked squad car. Officers Meehan and Dailey will operate the observation van. The author joined the van team for the day's activities.

The van in use was an enclosed vehicle. It provides for a driver and passenger in front; the rear area is curtained off and is twelve feet long. There is a sliding door for a quick exit on the right side, and there are four observation windows — two at the rear and one on each side.

This area also contains the following equipment: (a) a portable, magnetic-based, red dome light; (b) a siren; (c) a shotgun rack for three guns; (d) three leather bucket seat swivel chairs; (e) a desk; (f) a digi-alarm system (this system will be discussed below); (g) a **PBBS** base radio; and (h) two receiver/transmitters.

Except for a carpet, the van has no covering or insulation on the sides or the ceiling. When the blowers and the air conditioning system are turned off it gets very hot and uncomfortable in this area.

Dailey parked the vehicle on Bedford Avenue, south of Waldbaum's, with the rear of the vehicle facing north. This position will provide the team with an unobstructed view of the store. Dailey moved to the rear of the van. The blowers and air conditioning systems were turned off because of the vibration. The reason for this procedure is that the vibration caused by the systems will affect the quality of the pictures, because the hand camera cannot be held in a perfectly still position. As he entered the rear section Dailey turned on the PBBS base radio. At that precise moment, the operator reported that a man armed with a .44 caliber magnum pistol had just robbed a store on Flatbush Avenue, and that all police units in the area are responding. The director ordered the van to remain at its station.

Dailey sat by the rear windows and began to take pictures of suitable subjects. Meehan, who had been sitting in the front section, moved to the rear area in order to assist Dailey. After two hours at this station, the director ordered the team to cruise in the target area. During the surveillance of the area, Meehan, who had remained in the rear section, took three pictures. At 2:22 PM the director ordered the team to the Clarkson Avenue station, east of the Waldbaum store.

Upon arriving at Clarkson Avenue, Dailey moved to the rear observation windows. Meehan sat in the front section. Whenever he spotted a suitable subject, he would tell Dailey to take a picture of the youth at one of the side observation windows. Later, Meehan moved to the rear section and relieved Dailey.

During a slow period in the day's activities, the author commented to Dailey that this particular van appeared to be an unusual vehicle and not the type that is usually operated by SCRU personnel. Dailey agreed. He said that this van is normally used by the robbery assault team (RAT) — a unit of the PBBS task force. The vehicle is known as the RAT van.

The RAT unit is composed of four plainclothes policemen — three officers and a sergeant. As the name implies, it is an action-oriented team. Its members are equipped with shotguns and heavy-duty bulletproof vests.

The team is assigned to protect seven business establishments that are located within a specified target area. At the beginning of an eight-hour tour, the team proceeds to a strategically located station in the area and begins its watch. Once the team is on station no one is allowed to leave the van. The only time the sliding door on the right side of the van is opened is when the team moves into action. The sergeant is the driver of the vehicle, and he does not carry a shotgun.

Above the desk, taped to the side of the van, is a chart that identifies, among other things, the stores that are under the protection of the unit, the location of each store, and the time, date, and other pertinent data about previous robberies. The stores were identified as follows:

116 — Red — Bodega — 3721 Flatbush Avenue
123 — Brown — Cleaners — 2830 Flatbush Avenue
118 — Red — Drug — 3318 Flatbush Avenue
135 — Blue — Drug — 1619 Nostrand Avenue
103 — Green — Pizza — 2820 Bedford Avenue
121 — Brown — Meat Market — 3102 Bedford Avenue
106 — Green — Chinese Restaurant — 3610 Flatbush Avenue

The digi-alarm system is located at the desk. Each store has an alarm system that puts it into direct contact with the RAT van. Thus, when a robbery is in progress and an alarm is sounded, the RAT van receives it first and is able to respond immediately.

The PBBS base also receives the alarm; however, its personnel are not able to immediately respond because they must be contacted and given the location of the store. The RAT team, on the other hand, knows exactly when and where the robbery is taking place just as the alarm is sounded. For example, if the Chinese Restaurant is being robbed and the owner sounds the alarm, the color green is flashed on the ID color scheme indicator, and the number 106 is registered on the digital ID indicator. This is one of the several specialized teams utilized by the New York City Police Department in its never-ending effort to control crime.[6]

The director ended the day's operation at 3:45 PM. The team was able to take fourteen pictures during this period.

On Thursday morning, June 26, 1979, the team learned that the new stakeout apartment, located in Apartment 2B, fourth floor, 566 Parkside Avenue, was ready for use.

Officer Lohse also told team members that the alleged suspect had robbed two elderly women on the previous day, both of whom had been shopping at the Key Foods Store at Flatbush Avenue and Lenox Road.

At 4:10 PM, he had robbed a widow, Ruby Blackner, white, sixty-nine years old, of 58 Linden Boulevard, two blocks from the stakeout apartment. Her assailant followed the victim into the elevator and had left with her at the sixth floor. As soon as Mrs. Blackner had opened the door to her apartment, he pushed her inside and dragged her into a bedroom. In the bedroom, he tied her to a chair and began choking her, forcing her to tell where she hid her money. He took thirteen dollars and a ring from her finger. She described him as a black male, about twenty-two years old, and six feet tall.

At approximately 5:30 PM he robbed Irene Bromberg, a widow, white, seventy-two years old, in her apartment at 548 Ocean Avenue. As Mrs. Bromberg was entering her apartment, her assailant pushed her inside, dragged her into a bedroom, and tied her to a chair with scarves from her dresser. He beat and choked her until she revealed where she hid her money. He ransacked the apartment and forced her to write him a check. He took ten dollars, and he also cut the telephone wires before he fled.

The victim described him as follows: male, black, light-skinned, twenty-one years old, about five feet eight inches tall, and clean shaven, wearing a light blue shirt and dark trousers. This attack occurred three blocks from the stakeout.

Sergeant Fitzpatrick called a meeting at 10:45 AM. During the meeting, the team discussed strategy and deployment. Some thought that more unit members should be out on the street. Fitzpatrick suggested that two member teams might operate as anti-crime units in the Waldbaum and Key Foods stores. The teams, according to Fitzpatrick, could follow elderly women. If anyone matching the description of the suspect follows an elderly person, the team could then keep them both under surveillance. The suggestion was discussed at length, but it was finally ruled out.

It was decided that the team would resume Operation Silk Stocking at the new location on Parkside Avenue. The building is directly across the street from Public School 92. The task force commander called a senior member of the board of education, who agreed to allow a plainclothes officer to use a room in the school as an observation post.

The team on this day felt extreme frustration. They wanted to arrest the attacker and were annoyed when he continued to elude them. Fitzpatrick said, "This fellow is a smart one. He hasn't made any mistakes yet. He hasn't left us a neat set of prints. Something more. He varies the dates and the months of his attacks. In other words, he doesn't hit on the same day of each month. This fellow doesn't hit when the checks are in either; he is interested in cash and in jewelry."[7]

Officer W. Lohse directed the operation from the command post on Casey's roof. Officers Alper and Hurtado occupied the apartment. Officer Meehan operated the unmarked squad car and provided backup support for the apartment team. Officer Conry is the decoy for today, and she worked out of the squad car. Officer J. Lohse worked out of Public School 92 and provided backup support for the apartment team. Officer Dailey operated the van, and the author joined Officer Dailey.

Meehan parked the squad car facing north on Bedford Avenue. Dailey parked the van at its normal post on Clarkson Avenue. The team moved into position at 12:02 PM.

After Dailey parked the van, he began taking pictures of suitable suspects from the rear observation windows while the author assisted by using the observation windows at the sides. When he spotted a suitable subject, Dailey would come to the window and take the subject's picture.

At 1:28 PM, Conry advised Lohse that Meehan spotted a person who might match the description of the alleged suspect. The man had tried to get into the building next to the stakeout apartment, but the door was locked. He was walking west on Parkside Avenue with Meehan following in order to get a better look at him. Several minutes later he called to report that the man was not the suspect.

There was very little activity on this day, and the decoy was sent out only one time. During the remainder of the day, she stayed in the apartment while Meehan cruised in the target area. The van remained on station during the entire tour. Sergeant Fitzpatrick terminated the day's activities at 4:15 PM.

The only action of the day occurred on the return to the SCRU office. At that time, Dailey was driving the van on Flatbush Avenue. As he neared a MacDonald's restaurant he spotted a task force narcotics agent crossing the street and walking directly toward the restaurant. Three men were standing at the front entrance. Instinctively, Dailey slowed the vehicle and moved it toward the curb. He turned to the author and said, "Get ready for some action. Take the wheel when I get out!"[8]

As the agent crossed the street he held his shield in his left hand and his revolver, pointed at the three men, in the other hand. At the same time he gave them the familiar police command, "Police, don't move!" As he neared the curb, the man in the middle of the trio shouted, "Don't shoot. I'm okay. I give respect!" The agent ordered him to lie on his stomach. In the meantime, Dailey parked the van at the curb and proceeded to assist the agent. As Dailey handcuffed the suspect, the agent ordered the other two men to leave the area.

At that moment the agent's partner, who had been delayed by traffic at the intersection, arrived at the scene. The two agents, after acknowledging Dailey's assistance, took the suspect into custody. The entire action took less than sixty seconds.

On the trip to the SCRU office Dailey told the author that the arrest was set up by the narcotics agents. He explained that one of the other two men involved in the action was an undercover narcotics agent. He said that the narcotics people, either through their own efforts or through the use of informers, are able to penetrate the system and to identify drug dealers or pushers. Once a dealer or pusher is identified, undercover agents will work on him until he makes the sale to "customer." As in this day's case, the customer was an undercover policeman.

The author asked Dailey which of the two men was the undercover agent in today's arrest. He replied, "I thought you might have
picked him out! It was the black fellow. The one with the torn denim
shorts."[9]

On Wednesday morning, June 27, 1979, Lieutenant Coles held a
meeting with the Silk Stocking team. He told the members that a recent review of police crime reports disclosed that the alleged suspect
had changed his tactics to some extent.

> First, he has changed the time of his attacks. Prior to the last two rob-
> beries, he normally hit his victims from 12:00 PM to 4:00 PM. Lately, he
> has attacked his victim's after 4:00 PM. Second, he now attacks his victims
> on Wednesdays and Thursdays; in the past, he worked only on Mondays,
> Tuesdays, and Fridays. Third, he is not concentrating on the Waldbaum
> store, as in the past. It appears that he is staked out in a central area. From
> this area the suspect is able to spot his victims entering or leaving
> Waldbaum's, Key Foods, or Courtesy Drugs.
>
> As in the past, once he spots his victim he will follow her home. This
> fellow is strictly a push-in robber. He wants more than just the few dollars
> he can get out of a purse snatch or a vestibule robbery. And, as is his
> custom, he selects only the very old — the one's who offer the least
> resistance.[10]

Lieutenant Coles also informed the team that the Jay Center had
been closed. Coles continued his instructions to the team:

> As of today, decoys will work out of unmarked squad cars until further
> notice.
>
> Officer W. Lohse will direct today's operation from the command post
> on Casey's roof. Officers Alper and Conry will occupy the apartment.
> Officer J. Lohse will be stationed at Public School 92. Officer Dailey will
> operate the RAT van. Officer Thompson is the decoy for today's opera-
> tion. Officer Hurtado will operate an unmarked squad car. (The author
> joined W. Lohse at the command post.)
>
> The procedure for today is as follows: (1) Thompson will park the un-
> marked squad car a short distance behind the observation van, which will
> be parked at its usual station on Clarkson Avenue; (2) if W. Lohse spots a
> suitable subject he will contact Thompson. The decoy will then move into
> position and make a play. Hurtado will be parked on Lenox Road near the
> corner of Flatbush Avenue. From this selected vantage point he will have
> an excellent view of the Key Foods store. In the event that he spots a
> suitable subject the same procedure will be followed. Dailey will continue
> to take pictures from the van.
>
> The decoy phase of the operation will continue until 4:00 PM. At that
> time, Dailey will return the van to the RAT unit. He will return to the
> area and will assume command of the unmarked squad car parked on
> Clarkson Avenue. From that moment the decoy phase of the operation

will cease and the anti-crime phase will begin. The anti-crime phase will consist of a stakeout of business establishments from which victims have been spotted by the suspect.

These tactics will be in effect until Friday, June Twenty-ninth. If the suspect is not apprehended by that date, decoy operations will be discontinued. On Monday, July Second, a reinforced team will continue the anti-crime phase of the operation for at least another week.[11]

The team moved into position at 12:28 PM.

At the command post, W. Lohse asked the author to operate the radio while he conducted a surveillance of the area. There was very little activity on the streets this day. Lohse decided that he would not send the decoy out unless a suitable subject was spotted. Before this, if a suitable subject was not spotted, he would send the decoy out to do surveillance. The decoy phase of the operation was over at 4:05 PM. The anti-crime phase began at 4:20 PM.

Officer W. Lohse and the author joined Hurtado at his station near the Key Foods store. Alper, Conry, and J. Lohse joined Thompson at her station near the Waldbaum store.

As Lohse and Hurtado discussed a plan of operation, three youths passed by the squad car. One youth stared at Lohse for awhile, and then turned to speak to the other two. They crossed the street and continued to look toward the squad car. Lohse said to Hurtado, "Let's get out of here. That mutt recognized me. I put him away a couple of months ago."[12]

As the team cruised in the target area, Lohse and Hurtado discussed the possibility of obtaining a second stakeout apartment. Hurtado parked the car near the building at 55 Linden Boulevard. He suggested that the building was strategically located within the target area, and an apartment here would be ideal for use as an observation post. Lohse agreed. Hurtado located the building superintendent and discussed the possibility of obtaining an apartment. The superintendent told him that he did not have an apartment available at the moment. He wrote Hurtado's name and the SCRU telephone number on a memo pad and promised to call when one became available.

As the team cruised on Flatbush Avenue, Lohse noticed that a number of buildings, housing various business establishments, had low, flat roofs, one of which could be used as an observation post. Lohse discussed this possibility with the owner of the R. J. Porter Bootery, who was also owner of the building. Mr. Porter told him that there was no way to reach any of the roofs in the block since all exits and entrances had been cemented shut because of many robberies after hours. Mr. Porter offered his store, however, as an observation post or for other police activities.

Lohse ruled out a storefront observation post because it would not provide the security that the team required to order to conduct its operations. As he was canvassing merchants on the opposite side of the avenue, Hurtado and the author studied a spot map of the target area. After identifying the locations of the suspect's latest crimes, Hurtado said, "We're right in the middle of his hit area. We should try to find an apartment and an observation post right here. I don't think that we should use the Parkside apartment because it is not in his operating area."[13] Several minutes later Lohse returned to the squad car. He told Hurtado that all the roofs on both sides of the street were sealed in the same manner. After canvassing a few more merchants on the north side of Flatbush Avenue, Lohse ended the operation at 5:30 PM.

When the team members returned to SCRU headquarters, Sergeant Fitzpatrick told them, "Our guy hit again. This time he hit a woman on Lenox Road. Early reports on the case indicate that he got her at approximately 12:30 PM. She had been shopping at Waldbaum's. Noblin said that the victim reported the suspect to be about twenty-one years old, dark skinned, and with close-cropped hair. He was wearing a white, long-sleeved sweat shirt and dark pants. He had a gold chain around his neck."[14]

Alper said that the suspect matched the description of a person he spotted in the vicinity of Waldbaum's at 5:10 PM. Thompson, J. Lohse, and Conry also saw the person. They asked Sergeant Fitzpatrick if they could return to the target area and conduct a search for him. Fitzpatrick discussed the matter with Lieutenant Coles. Coles decided against another deployment at this hour. He preferred to concentrate on the investigation phase of the case. Fitzpatrick told him that in addition to Noblin, Sergeant Byrnes, Detective De Angelo, and Investigator Rainone were at the scene.

Lohse sat on the edge of a desk and said, "Ain't that a bitch? We were on post at 1228 hours. We must have missed him by a few minutes."[15]

The latest victim, Lillian Holtzman, a seventy-nine-year-old widow, told Noblin that she had gone shopping at Waldbaum's. On her return, she walked south on Bedford Avenue and then west on Lenox Road. As she entered her apartment building a tenant, Jimmy Sims, held the doors open for her. As she entered the lobby the suspect passed her and used the stairway to go upstairs. She did not pay much attention to him. After checking for her mail, she took the elevator to the fourth floor.

As she opened the door to her apartment, the suspect seized her and pushed her inside. He put one hand on her mouth and seized her by the throat with the other. He warned her, "Don't say anything, or I'll kill you! Come with me!" He pushed her into the dining room, took a chair and, still holding her by the throat, moved her into the bedroom. During this time, he repeatedly demanded where she hid her money. Finally she said, "I'll show you where it is." Clutching her throat with his hand, the assailant shoved Mrs. Holtzman into the living room, where she took thirty dollars from a hiding place. After counting the money, he threw it on the floor saying, "I need a hundred dollars, I have to make a plane." He continued applying pressure on her throat until she revealed another hiding place where she kept fifty dollars. After he was satisfied that she did not have any more hiding places, he searched her pocketbook and removed another thirteen dollars.[16]

The assailant then dragged Mrs. Holtzman into the bedroom and tied her to the chair with pantyhose and scarves. He put a nylon stocking around her neck, tied it into a slipknot, and began to choke her. He asked her where she hid her jewelry and other valuables. When Mrs. Holtzman did not respond, he choked and slapped her. He found a watch, a gold-plated chain, and two mink coats in the bedroom.

The man then left the bedroom to search the living room. During his absence, she began to stamp her feet on the floor in an attempt to attract the attention of the tenant below. The man came in and asked, "What are you doing?" He slapped her on the face several times and tightened the stocking around her neck. Then he turned on the television set and pulled the shades down.

After he searched the other rooms, the robber returned to the bedroom. He put on a pair of tan woolen gloves and searched the dressers. During his search he asked Mrs. Holtzman for her bankbooks. She told him that she was on social security, and that she did not have any savings. She told the police that he spoke to her only when he wanted something. If she tried to speak to him he would tighten the stocking around her neck. Finally, the suspect told her, "I'm coming back. I have my car, and I want your television set." As he left the bedroom he told her that he was going to make was going to make a long-distance telephone call.[17]

Upon assuring herself that he was no longer in the apartment, Mrs. Holtzman was able to loosen one of the scarfs that bound her arms. With some effort, she reached the telephone and called the police.

During the interview, Noblin called the Crime Scene Division. Detective Manning, a fingerprint expert, arrived at the apartment shortly thereafter and conducted a search for physical evidence. He told Noblin that a number of fingerprint impressions were lifted, and that Noblin would be notified by the latent fingerprint section as to the value of the prints.

Later in the evening Noblin interviewed the witness, Jimmy Sims. Sims said that he did not know the robber, but he had encountered him in the area a few times. He said that on one occasion he saw him loitering in the lobby. On another he saw him looking at the names on the building directory. Sims viewed a number of pictures from the SCRU photo file, but he could not identify the man. He also told Noblin that he might have some difficulty in identifying the man, but that he will cooperate with the police.[18]

The complainant (Mrs. Holtzman) described the subject as follows: male; black; 20-21 years old; five feet ten inches tall; and slender — about 150 pounds. He has tight, short hair and is dark skinned. He was wearing a white, long-sleeved sweat shirt, white sneakers, and dark pants. He wore a gold necklace with a small charm round his neck.

Jimmy Sims, the only person who saw the assailant on several occasions, gave the police the following description: male; black; twenty years old; five feet ten inches tall; slim; short, cropped hair brushed forward to create a wavy look; and he is dark complexioned. He was wearing dark pants and a dark shirt.

The victim and the witness agreed on some of the identifying characteristics of the suspect. The differences between the two identifications are as follows: (1) The victim said he had tight short hair. The witness said he had short cropped hair brushed forward to create a wavy look; (2) the victim said that the suspect was wearing a white, long-sleeved shirt. The witness said that he was wearing a dark shirt. He did not mention the sleeve length; (3) the victim said that the suspect was wearing white sneakers. The witness did not mention the suspect's footwear; and (4) the victim said that the suspect wore a gold chain around his neck. The witness did not mention the chain.

Another interesting, if not significant, factor is that the witness was willing and apparently able to assist the police in obtaining a positive identification of the suspect. Although Mrs. Holtzman saw him only during the time of the robbery and under extremely stressful conditions, she was certain that she could identify him. On the other hand, Jimmy Sims admitted that he saw the suspect on at least three occasions. Yet he told the police that he might have difficulty in recognizing him.

In discussing this aspect of the case with the author, Noblin said, "It is possible that Sims knows the suspect and is trying to protect him. Then again, it is possible that he fears retaliation from the suspect if he talks too much."[19]

On July 3, 1979, Noblin received a report from the latent fingerprint section advising him that the prints lifted at the scene of the Holtzman robbery were of no value.

At the briefing of Thursday, June 28, 1979, Sergeant Byrnes told the team that the anti-crime phase of the operation would be continued at least for the next few days. On this day, W. Lohse would direct today's operations from the command car. He was to be assisted by Officers Thompson and Conry. Officers Dailey and Hurtado would operate from the observation van, and Officers J. Lohse and Alper would operate from an unmarked squad car. The three teams would cruise in the target area concentrating, as directed by W. Lohse, on Waldbaum's supermarket at Clarkson and Bedford avenues, Key Foods store at Lenox Road and Flatbush Avenue, Courtesy Drugs at Flatbush Avenue and Linden Boulevard, the bank at Flatbush and Caton avenues, the bank at Ocean and Church avenues, and the intersection of Bedford Avenue and Linden Boulevard.

If any of the teams were to spot a suspect, one of the decoys will give him a play. If the suspect followed her, she would proceed to the apartment. The backup team nearest to the apartment building would go to that location. One man would occupy the apartment;

the other would cover the lobby and stairs. The other teams would proceed to the apartment building and enter after the suspect is inside.

If, on the other hand, the suspect followed an elderly person, the teams would deploy and follow him. After he entered the building, the teams would converge at that location and attempt to arrest him.

The teams moved into position at 11:45 AM.

Lohse parked the command car near the intersection of Linden Boulevard and Flatbush Avenue. This location is diagonally across from the Courtesy Drug store. Seven elderly persons were robbed recently after leaving this store. From the selected vantage point the team was able to observe any activity on the left side of Linden Boulevard. The police believe that the man they are looking for has committed a robbery in each building on this side of Linden Boulevard.

At 1:05 PM, Lohse decided to move to a new location. He notified the other teams that he was going to park near the intersection of Bedford Avenue and Linden Boulevard. On the way to the new station he stopped for a red light. Two boys riding bicycles stopped by the car. They spotted the decoys in the rear of the car. One of them yelled, "Hello, lady cop!" The other yelled, "Church Avenue is a hot spot!" After they made a few more remarks Lohse turned to one of them and said, "How would you like your jaw broken?" The boys rode away.

Lohse parked the command car on Bedford Avenue near the corner of Linden Boulevard. To the right, across the street, is number 77 Linden where the alleged suspect is said to have robbed at least two elderly women in the past month.

Police regulations require that the police base radio must be kept on when a vehicle is in use. Today, as previously, the dispatcher has been on the air almost continuously to report crimes committed or in progress. Police crime statistics indicate that in New York City a crime is committed every two minutes.

At 1:37 PM, a man matching the description of the alleged suspect followed an elderly woman into the building at 55 Linden Boulevard. Thompson and Conry left the command car and proceeded directly to the building. All units moved into position on either side of the building, and Lohse moved the command car near the entrance and made contact with the decoys.

At 1:42 PM, Thompson reported that the man was waiting near the stairway. There were some tenants in the lobby waiting for the mail. At 1:48 PM, Thompson reported that the mailman had left the building, and that the suspect entered the elevator with some of the tenants. The decoys were searching the building and were unable to locate the suspect. At 1:50 PM, Alper asked Thompson if she had noticed the floor at which the elevator stopped. She reported that it had stopped at the fifth floor. The decoys were now working on the fourth and fifth floors. At 1:55 PM, Thompson asked Lohse to send one of the backup people to meet her on the third floor. She said that she hears loud voices and a person crying. She said, "It sounds like a man beating a child, but we must make certain."[20]

Alper moved into the building at 1:56 PM and joined Thompson on the third floor.

Lohse told all the officers that the suspect entered the building empty-handed. "If he emerges with a package, or a bag, or anything, we'll have to arrest him."[21]

At 2:00 PM, neither the decoys nor Alper have made contact with the command car, but at 2:01 PM, Alper reported that he is in contact with Thompson. Conry was on the seventh floor. At 2:03 PM, Lohse called the SCRU office, asking Sergeant Fitzpatrick for more men. At 2:05 PM, Thompson reported that she was on the sixth floor. She had heard someone from one of the apartments command, "Get up!" "Lie down!" She was trying to locate the specific apartment. At 2:06 PM Lohse ordered J. Lohse into the building. There are four SCRU people in the building. At 2:08 PM, Conry reported that the man suspected came out of the Apartment 5E and left the building by the rear exit. At 2:09 PM, Alper reported that he had spoken to the building superintendent who told him that the man was a tenant. Lohse told Alper to get the man's name, age, place of employment, and any other pertinent information.

At 2:11 PM, Lohse saw the suspect walking on Bedford Avenue and, calling Dailey, told him to take a picture. Dailey reported that the camera was not working, but that Hurtado had gone for another. At 2:20 PM, the suspect turned a corner and disappeared. J. Lohse continued to search for him.

At 2:29 PM, Sergeant Fitzpatrick and Noblin caught up with the command car on Linden Boulevard. Lohse walked to Fitzpatrick's car where he and Fitzpatrick talked to a woman seated in the backseat. Noblin told the author that it was Lillian Holtzman, who was viewing photos from SCRU files, when Lohse called. They had taken her along in the hope that she could identify the suspect. At 2:40 PM, J. Lohse reported that he could not locate the suspect, and Fitzpatrick told him to remain in the area. At 2:45 PM, the decoys returned to the command car, and Alper rejoined J. Lohse. At 2:48 PM, Fitzpatrick and Noblin returned to SCRU headquarters. At 3:00 PM, Lohse parked the command car on Flatbush Avenue approximately sixty feet from the Key Foods store, and at 3:15 PM, Thompson went to the Key Foods store. Leaving the store at 3:25 PM, she went to the apartment. At 3:28 PM, Conry went into the store, which she left at 3:35 PM, proceeding to the apartment. Both decoys arrived at the apartment without incident and were met by Dailey and Hurtado.

The decoys returned to the command car at 3:50 PM. Lohse proceeded to Linden Boulevard and Flatbush Avenue. The team remained at this station until the operation was ended at 5:35 PM.

On Friday, June 29, 1979, W. Lohse directed operations from the observation van, assisted by Officer Hurtado. Officers Alper and Conry operated from an unmarked squad car, and Officer J. Lohse operated from a second command car, where he was joined by the author.

The team moved into position at 11:45 AM. W. Lohse parked the van on Bedford Avenue near the corner of Linden Boulevard, and Alper parked the squad car on Lenox near the corner of Flatbush Avenue. This station is near the Key Foods store. Officer J. Lohse decided to cruise in the target area.

At 12:01 PM, W. Lohse called J. Lohse to tell him that a person matching the description of the suspect had been spotted walking north on Bedford Avenue toward Clarkson. The suspect was wearing a red, short-sleeved shirt, green trousers, and blue running shoes. Officer J. Lohse proceeded to the area and spotted the youth walking west on Clarkson Avenue. He called W. Lohse and told him that the youth was not the suspect.

Next, J. Lohse decided to conduct surveillance in an area known as the "Bermuda Triangle," an area bordering the sixty-seventh, seventieth, and seventy-first precincts. This area is heavily populated by elderly citizens, and it has been designated as a high-crime area by police administrators. As Lohse was driving east on Linden

Boulevard at 12:35 PM, the base dispatcher notified all field units that a dead man was reported to be in a portable garbage-disposal bin on the corner of Linden and Forty-third Street. Proceeding to the area, Lohse parked the squad car on Linden Boulevard. The dump bin was on the north side of Forty-third Street. Lohse did not leave the squad car. He just sat there studying some men who were standing on the east side of the street. After a few minutes, the author asked him if he was going to verify the dispatcher's report. He said "No. Sometimes these things are booby-trapped. A guy could get his hands or head blown off." At that moment a uniformed police unit arrived. Lohse spoke to one of the officers for a few minutes and then left the scene. On the return to the Bermuda Triangle, he told the author, "They won't touch it, either. I think they're going to call for the bomb squad."[22]

Lohse parked the squad car on Caton Avenue near the corner of Linden Boulevard. From this vantage point he could keep a watch on four apartment buildings on Linden Boulevard and two on Caton Avenue. Elderly tenants of these buildings had been recent victims of robberies.

During this particular stakeout, base radio reported the following crimes:

12:55 PM: Bicycle stolen at knife point, Carroll Street and Bedford Avenue. Uniformed police patrol is investigating the incident.

12:57 PM: Man in store with shotgun. 2318 Newkirk Avenue. All available police units responding.

12:58 PM: Beer truck being held-up, McDonald and Ditmas avenues. All available units responding.

1:01 PM: Purse snatch on Albemarle Road and Nostrand Avenue. SCRU notified. Uniformed police patrol is at scene.

1:03 PM: Auto stripping in progress, 1979 Cougar. Rutland Road and Albany Avenue. Uniformed police patrol responding.

1:05 PM: Cola truck stolen while driver was making a delivery, Coney Island Avenue and Beverly Road. Uniformed police patrol responding.

At 1:45 PM, Lohse decided to cruise in the target area. After an hour, he parked the squad car on Linden Boulevard near the corner of Bedford Avenue. From this vantage point he could watch the apartment complexes on Linden Boulevard and on Canton and Bedford avenues. In addition, he was in a position to respond to a call for assistance by the team stationed in the Waldbaum store area. Lohse remained at this station until the operation ended at 5:25 PM.

On Tuesday, July 3, 1979, Sergeant Byrnes notified the team that Operation Silk Stocking was going to be closed down before the end of the week. Most of the members were unhappy with the decision. They wanted the operation to continue for at least another week. Officer Dailey, speaking for the team, said, "We feel that we are close to an arrest. To call it off at this time would be discouraging to all of us."[23]

Byrnes told the team members that the decision was out of his hands. He said that the administrators understood, from their discussions with Lieutenant Coles, that the team would prefer to continue searching for the suspect. They, too, would have preferred to continue the search, but were confronted by a man-hour problem. Several hundred man-hours had been expended in the search for the suspect with few tangible results. Moreover, the transfer of personnel to this operation had resulted in the neglect of other high-crime areas. He said that he would try to obtain permission to extend the operation for another week.[24]

Sergeant Byrnes then discussed the plans for the day's operation. First, the team would use four vehicles: two unmarked squad cars and two vans. Second, the decoys would wear regular civilian clothes and not make any plays. Finally, the team would concentrate on following elderly persons. It was hoped that the suspect would follow a likely victim, and that a team would be in position to intercept him.

Officer J. Lohse was named director for the day's operation. He and Officer Alwill operated from the command car. The author joined Officer Conry, who drove the second unmarked squad car. Officer Dailey and Meehan operated the RAT van, and Officers Hurtado and Alper operated the robbery van. The team moved into position at 11:00 AM. Conry parked the squad car on Flatbush Avenue near the corner of Lenox Road. From this vantage point she was in a position to observe the approaches to the Key Foods store.

During the surveillance of the store, Conry and the author discussed some questions about Operation Silk Stocking. She was of the opinion that the suspect was working with an accomplice. She said, "I think he has a spotter, who loiters in stores like Waldbaum's or Courtesy Drugs. When he spots an old lady he tells his accomplice where she is and what she looks like; the suspect will take it from there."[25]

Conry also suggested that if he did not have an accomplice, then he must live in the area. The reason for this assumption, according to Conry, is that he appears to have some knowledge of each of his victims. In every instance there was no one at home when he pushed his victim into her apartment. Furthermore, he has had plenty of time to ransack the apartment, and he almost always gets a women with money and jewelry. "The law of averages," Conroy said, "dictates that someone should be at home."[26]

Opinions similar to this have been voiced by almost every member of the team.

At 1:40 PM, Conry decided to conduct surveillance of the Courtesy Drugstore. As she neared the store, she spotted a young boy following an elderly woman. Conry followed the pair for six blocks, and then, for no apparent reason, the boy turned and walked away.

At 3:20 PM, Conry moved the squad car to Flatbush and Caton avenues, and she remained at this station until the operation ended at 5:10 PM.

On Thursday, July 5, 1979, the team learned that the alleged suspect robbed another elderly woman on Tuesday. The victim, Irene Selzman, an eighty-year-old widow, lived at 182 Linden Boulevard, Apartment 4F.

Mrs. Selzman told Detective Dattolico that she had visited her doctor on Tuesday morning. She left his office at 9:45 AM and took the Nostrand Avenue bus to Church Avenue. She went to a hosiery shop on Church Avenue, where she made a purchase. Afterward she had a cup of coffee and a doughnut in a coffee shop on Nostrand Avenue and then walked to her apartment.

Mrs. Selzman said that she had not observed anyone following her on the street, and there was no one in the lobby when she entered the building. When she entered the elevator she met her neighbor, Mr. Roberts, as he was leaving. As she walked along the hall to her fourth-floor apartment she had heard someone walking up the stairs, but she had not payed much attention. Within a few seconds, the robber had walked to the apartment directly across from hers, and as she opened her door he put his arm around her neck and pushed her inside.

The suspect then dragged her into the bedroom and said, "Give me your money, or I'll kill you!" She gave him four dollars. He became very angry and said, "That's not enough!" Mrs. Selzman told him she had more money hidden in the kitchen. The robber released his hold and allowed her to enter the kitchen. She retrieved 150 dollars from a hiding place under the sink and gave it to him.[27] She had the money hidden in a box of Brillo®.

The suspect then pushed her into the bedroom and forced her to lie on the floor, whereupon he searched inside her clothing for more money. Finding none, he tied her to a chair with wire and scarves. He also tied a scarf over her eyes. As he did this, she noticed that he was wearing woolen gloves. The robber turned the television set on and then proceeded to ransack the apartment.

Detective Dattolico located Mr. Roberts. He verified that he had encountered Mrs. Selzman in the lobby, but he did not recall seeing anyone else in the building at that time. He was not able to offer any further assistance.[28]

Mrs. Selzman told Investigator Noblin that the robber had continued to ask her for money. On one occasion he said, "I have to catch a plane. Give me more money, or I'll kill you!" On another occasion he told her, "Hurry up, I have my car double-parked."[29]

The robber cut the telephone wires before he left the apartment. Mrs. Selzman remained tied to the chair for almost five hours. She was finally able to loosen her blindfold and the gag from her mouth. Her scream brought a neighbor to her assistance. In this instance, the suspect did not close the door to the apartment.[30]

Under further questioning she told Noblin that the robber told her that he was going to make a long-distance phone call. She also told Noblin that she did not have a set routine when she left the apartment. When asked if she could identify the suspect, she said that she might be able to do so after she has had a rest.

There was some concern among the members of the team. This was the eighteenth recorded robbery with the same pattern. Hurtado voiced the sentiments of the team when he said, "Nothing seems to work against this guy. He's still out there, and we can't find him."[31]

J. Lohse assisted by Officer Conry directed the day's activities.

Officers Gibbons and Alper will operate the second unmarked squad car, and Officers Dailey and Hurtado will operate the observation van. The author joined Gibbons and Alper.

No decoy activity was planned for this day. Sergeant Byrnes wanted the three teams to cruise in the target area and to maintain constant contact with each other to avoid having two teams working in the same area.

The teams arrived in the target area at 11:20 AM. Officer Gibbons decided to cruise in the Bermuda Triangle, because, as he said, the perpetrator had not made a hit in this area lately, and he felt that he (the robber) might return that day. After cruising in the area for an hour, Gibbons parked the squad car on Linden Boulevard near the corner of Bedford Avenue. From this vantage point the two officers began a thirty-minute surveillance of three apartment house complexes. Next, Gibbons contacted Lohse to report that he was going to move to the Waldbaum area. Lohse suggested that it would be better if he moved to Lenox Road and Flatbush Avenue, near the Key Foods store. He told Gibbons that the van team had just moved into the Waldbaum area, and that he and Conry would be moving to the Bermuda Triangle.

At the Key Foods store area Gibbons and Alper agreed to concentrate on following elderly women rather than attempting to spot suitable suspects. This decision appeared to be a good one because within a few minutes Alper spotted an elderly woman being followed by a youth. It was apparent that the following was deliberate. He crossed the street and walked a little ahead of her and waited until she came up, then, for no obvious reason, he did not follow her when she turned the corner to walk to her apartment building.

The team followed four other elderly women who were either being followed or were walking alone during this surveillance period. In each instance, Gibbons made certain that the woman arrived home safely. On one occasion the team spotted a youth following an elderly woman who was pushing a shopping cart. The team lost sight of him when the woman approached the entrance to her building, and so Gibbons left the squad car and escorted the woman to her apartment.

At 2:30 PM, the team moved out of the Key Foods store area and began a general surveillance of the target area. During this time, the team checked bus stops, subway entrances and exits, senior citizen community centers, stores, and coffee shops. On one occasion, after inspecting an underground passageway, Gibbons said, "This son of a bitch is around here . . . but where?"

At 3:35 PM, the team moved to the intersection of Linden Boulevard and Bedford Avenue. Gibbons parked the squad car on Linden approximately forty feet from the corner of Bedford. He wanted to keep two apartment buildings under close surveillance. Several minutes later he noticed that Alper, the other police officer in the car, was staring at a black youth. Gibbons moved the squad car out of the area, immediately. He told Alper, "Quit looking at them! A white man in a black area doesn't look at them. He looks away from them because whites are supposed to be afraid of them. Only cops look!"[32]

The team continued to cruise in the target area until the day's activities were called off at 4:55 PM.

At SCRU headquarters some members of the team discussed the day's activities with the unit's investigators. Detective De Angelo suggested that additional investigators should be assigned to the operation. "The investigators," he said, "should go out and canvass the pawn shops. The suspect is undoubtedly selling some of the stolen property to these guys. We know that a lot of pawnbrokers are involved in illegal activities. They know that we can't do anything to them because we don't have the manpower. If we did, half of them would be out of business or in jail. They also know that we can make life very difficult for them. In other words, we should go out and 'rattle some cages.' We'll get the information we need!"[33]

The information that Detective De Angelo wanted was the name, address, and other identifying characteristics of the suspect.

Investigator Carbonaro said, "I know that it cannot be done, but I wish the court would allow us to bring in all known offenders for questioning. I have no doubt that our man will be caught in the dragnet.

"The trouble with the exclusionary rule is that it doesn't work in cases like Silk Stocking. The rulemakers must find something to replace it. I am certain that if these people really understood what we are up against, they would think differently. In other words, until you have experienced or witnessed the terror, then you just don't know."[34]

It should be noted that Carbonaro did not say that the police should be permitted to bring in all persons who match the description of the suspect. She limited the relaxation of the exclusionary rule only to *known* offenders.

When questioned on this point, she said, "If we brought everybody in, we would be violating the rights of some innocent people. I wouldn't want it to happen to me. Known offenders are a different story. These people are habitual criminals. Sooner or later the police will arrest them for other crimes. I know that what I have proposed may sound like I am an insensitive person. I am insensitive to the criminal but not to the victim. To me, solving a case like Silk Stocking outweighs the inconvenience of questioning a known offender without probable cause."[35]

Senior citizen robbert unit personnel recognize the need for some restraint on the discentionary powers of the police, but most feel that the rule is too restrictive. It does not allow for the reasonable use of police discretion when the situation requires it. The Silk Stocking case is one example of the negative aspects of the rule.

The Investigative Phase

As we reported earlier, police administrators had decided to terminate the decoy and anti-crime phases of the operation on July 6, 1979. On Monday, July 9, 1979, the decoy teams would resume normal operations. They would concentrate on the high-crime areas that were neglected during the past month. As directed by unit supervisors, the teams would also deploy in the areas in which the Silk Stocking robber had been most active. The investigative phase of the operation, however, would continue under the direction of Officer Noblin.

As a result of the impending termination of the street phase of the operation, the author asked to be allowed to work with Noblin on the investigation and joined him on the morning of July 9, 1979, as he was preparing a list of all victims assaulted since January 1979. The list was to serve as the basis for a pattern case file and for a new profile of the suspect. Noblin said that he also intended to establish a victim profile. From this profile he would be able to determine the approximate age, height, weight, and health of the typical victim selected by the suspect. Copies of the suspect and victim profiles would be supplied to all members of the unit.

Before leaving the office Noblin called several witnesses, all of whom agreed to see him that day.

At 12 PM, Noblin called at the apartment of Mrs. Ruby Blackner, who did not answer the door. She had told him earlier that she would be available to speak to him at noon.

At 12:20 PM, Noblin called at the apartment of Lillian Holtzman, who was not at home. Earlier, she had said that she would speak to him at anytime after the noon hour.

At 1:01 PM, Noblin called at the apartment of Molly Ratner, who agreed to be interviewed. She repeated essentially the same information she gave Detective De Angelo on June 11, 1979 (*see* Chap. 6). Mrs. Ratner said that she did not believe that she could identify the suspect. Noblin added this case to the crime pattern file.

At 2:05 PM, Noblin called at the apartment of Myra Rosen. She told him that she could not remember too much about the crime. After some gentle questioning by Noblin, she recalled that her assailant was a black male. He was in his early twenties and was approximately six feet tall. She told him that she did not see the suspect until she was entering her apartment. He came up to her and said, "I have a gun. Let me in, or I'll kill you." After he tied her to a chair with some scarves he said, "I am in a hurry. I have to catch a plane." Mrs. Rosen said that she would not be able to identify the subject.[36] Noblin added this case to the crime pattern file.

At 3:05 PM, Noblin returned to Mrs. Holtzman's apartment. She was at home and agreed to the interview. Mrs. Holtzman repeated the same information that she gave Noblin on June 27, 1979, but this time there was a marked change in her attitude. On that day she was willing to identify the suspect. As a matter of record, on June 20, 1979, she accompanied Sergeant Fitzpatrick and Noblin on a surveillance of the target area in an effort to locate and identify the suspect. Today she claimed that she did not get a good look at the suspect. She also refused to view photos of known criminals, and she told Noblin that she would not provide the police artist with a description of the suspect.[37]

When Noblin asked her if anyone had threatened her, she replied that she did not remember anything about her assailant. Later, Noblin told the author that Mrs. Holtzman has had time to think about her ordeal and is afraid of retaliation from the suspect or his friends. He did not believe that she had been threatened, and he added this case to the crime pattern file.

At 3:55 PM, Noblin called at the apartment of Sadie Epstein. Recalling the events before the robbery Mrs. Epstein told Noblin that she did not notice anyone following her on the street, nor did she see anyone in the lobby when she entered the building. Mrs. Epstein said that she was not aware of the suspect's presence until he seized her as she was entering the apartment. After he pushed her inside, he warned her that he would kill her if she screamed. The suspect then dragged her into the bedroom, tied her to a chair with some scarves, and pulled the shades down. He asked her for money on several occasions. The suspect left the bedroom three or four times. The first time he left the bedroom he went to the living room and turned the television set on. He returned only to search the bedroom and ask Mrs. Epstein for more money. Before he left the apartment the robber told her that he had his car parked downstairs.

Noblin asked Mrs. Epstein if she could assist the police in identifying the suspect. She said that she did not remember much about him. Noblin added this case to the crime pattern file.

On Monday, July 9, 1979, Noblin discussed his progress on the pattern cases with Lieutenant Coles and Sergeant Byrnes. He told them that he had established an index of cases for the crime pattern file and a questionnaire based on the *modus operandi* of the suspect. He said that he would also have a victim profile completed by Tuesday. Byrnes suggested and Coles agreed that the questionnaire and the victim profile should be made available to all police field units.

After the meeting, Noblin arranged interviews with Sara Lieberman and Mrs. Julia Beckel.

At 1:25 PM, Noblin called at the apartment of Mrs. Lieberman. At five feet six inches tall, Mrs. Lieberman was the tallest of the suspect's victims. The seventy-year-old widow told Noblin that the suspect seized her as she was entering her apartment, and after pushing her inside, he dragged her to the living room where he searched her clothes and purse for money. Not satisfied with the twelve dollars he found, he then searched her breast area. Mrs. Liberman said:

> He didn't find any money so he asked me for more. I remembered that I had about ten dollars in quarters in a drawer in the breakfront which is in the foyer. He took that and then he wanted more money.
>
> Then he tied me to a chair with some pantyhose. Then he took me into

the bedroom; my arms and waist were tied to the chair. At that point, he took the rings off my fingers. He took my diamond wedding band and a set of two gold rings.

In the bedroom he said, 'Now, where's the money?' I said, 'I have no money.' At that time, he had a noose around my neck, and he gagged me, and blindfolded me, and I said, 'but I haven't. . . .' He choked me so mercilessly that I thought it would be my last breath. I still don't know how I survived.

I did try to cooperate with him because I thought that there was no point in antagonizing him. I kept repeating that I had no money, which was the truth. Then he wanted to know where the gold was. I said, 'Anything I have is in that drawer.' So he went to the dresser drawer, and he took the pearls, another ring I had, two necklaces, and a watch.

Then he wanted to know when my husband was coming home. I told him that he was coming home late. He said, 'I'll wait for him. Maybe he's got money.' Then I thought better of it, and I said, 'There is no point in your waiting for my husband because he's dead.' And he came over to me, and he kept choking me repeatedly. He wanted to know 'where's the gold!' I said to him, 'All I have is in that drawer. The rest is in the safety deposit box in the bank.'

I was so anxious to get rid of him. I said him, 'Well, take the silver.' When he insisted on more money, I said, 'Well, I'll write you a check, that's all I can do. I have no more money.' He said 'I don't want your damn checks, lady.' Then he asked if I had a camera. I thought there was no point in denying it. I told him where it was. So he took the camera and a Bell and Howell projector that was in the closet. Then he went into the kitchen. He said, 'I'm going to make a phone call.'[38]

Noblin then asked Mrs. Lieberman the following series of questions:

OFFICER NOBLIN: "How long do you think the suspect was in the apartment?

MRS. LIEBERMAN: "About an hour-and-a-half."

OFFICER NOBLIN: "During this time did he mention anything about taking a plane or leaving the country?

MRS. LIEBERMAN: "Yes. He said he needed money to take the plane. I think he said to Trinidad."

OFFICER NOBLIN: "Did he mention anything about having a car downstairs?"

MRS. LIEBERMAN: "No."

OFFICER NOBLIN: "By any chance did he turn on any sort of appliances — for instance, a TV or a radio?"

MRS. LIEBERMAN: "No. Later, when I untied myself, I found that he cut the telephone wires. He cut them in the dining room and in the bedroom."

OFFICER NOBLIN: "By any chance did he alter in any way the curtains or shades in the apartment? For example, did he pull the shades down?"

MRS. LIEBERMAN: "No, he did not."

OFFICER NOBLIN: "By any chance did he wear gloves?"

MRS. LIEBERMAN: "Yes. He wore black gloves, a black hat, a black leather jacket. . . ."

OFFICER NOBLIN: "He had a hat on?"

MRS. LIEBERMAN: "Yes. You know, it was kind of a big cap with a brim. No, not a brim but a peak. A big one."

OFFICER NOBLIN: "Was he wearing any jewelry? For example, was he wearing any chains or medallions around his neck?"

MRS. LIEBERMAN: "No — at least I didn't see any. You know when he came in, the hallway was very dark. And the minute he came in he got right in back of me, and I have no idea what his face looks like. I don't know, my mind seems perfectly blank. It seems that it consciously blanked him out or what, I don't know."

OFFICER NOBLIN: "His type of voice. Do you think he might have been from the islands, or do you think he was an American black?"

MRS. LIEBERMAN: "No, I don't think he was an American black."

OFFICER NOBLIN: "Was he very soft spoken?"

MRS. LIEBERMAN: "Yes."

OFFICER NOBLIN: "Now, soft spoken, that is, natural speaking. I don't mean whispering."

MRS. LIEBERMAN: "No, he wasn't whispering. For instance, when he said, 'Are you going up?' And of course when he said, 'Don't make a sound, or I'll kill you,' it was very determined. It was really a command but it was not a coarse voice."

OFFICER NOBLIN: "Do you feel, personally, now I want your honest opinion. Do you feel he might have been from the islands, or that he might have been born in this country?"

MRS. LIEBERMAN: "I think he might have been from the islands."

OFFICER NOBLIN: "Do you have any idea where this man came from? Did you see anyone in the lobby when you entered?"

MRS. LIEBERMAN: "Usually when people go in before me I notice them. I met him when I got into the elevator. He might have been following me but I'm not sure."

OFFICER NOBLIN: "This happened some time ago. Let's go back a bit. This happened on a Friday. On Thursday, the day before, did you go shopping? Did you go to Waldbaum's or were you out in that neighborhood walking around? Basically, what I am trying to get down to is, do you have any sort of a routine?"

MRS. LIEBERMAN: "No, I don't have a regular routine of shopping, because I shop when I have the need. When I do go, I buy quite a number of things, and I don't have a regular routine."

OFFICER NOBLIN: "Do you shop only at Waldbaum's?"

MRS. LIEBERMAN: "No, I divide it between Waldbaum's and Discount City on Church Avenue."

OFFICER NOBLIN: "On that Friday were you out at any other time during the day?"

MRS. LIEBERMAN: "Yes. I had been out (pause). Where was I? I think I had been to the bank that day. I cannot remember a thing."

OFFICER NOBLIN: "We are trying to determine whether he followed you earlier on Friday or on Thursday, and that if he was to see you on the street he would know that you would enter into a particular building. He could then go into the building before you."

MRS. LIEBERMAN: "I think I had been to the bank that morning."

OFFICER NOBLIN: "Where do you bank?"

MRS. LIEBERMAN: "At Chemical, on the corner of Linden and Flatbush."

OFFICER NOBLIN: "Do you ever shop at Courtesy Drugs?"

MRS. LIEBERMAN: "Not very frequently."

OFFICER NOBLIN: "Sadie, when you are out on the street, are you a fast walker or a slow walker? Do you keep your head up when you are walking? Do you pay attention to what is going on?"

MRS. LIEBERMAN: "Yes, I think I do. I mean sometimes I get lost in thought. You know, I have certain problems and certain things to think about, and when I go walking (pause), I walk a lot. I am very fond of walking. I'm not a slow walker."

OFFICER NOBLIN: "Right now I see that you have a lot of jewelry on. Did you wear much jewelry that day?"

MRS. LIEBERMAN: "Yes. I always wear this gold chain and pendant. He didn't see it. I was wearing a pair of gold earrings which he didn't want either. He took another pair which he found on a table. He thought they were more expensive."

Noblin cautioned Mrs. Lieberman not to wear too much jewelry when she went shopping. He said that it could mean the difference between being robbed and being ignored by potential offenders. He also told her that the police have a good description of the robber, and that he might ask for her assistance if her assailant were captured. She replied, "I wish I could be more helpful in describing him, but I'll do what I can."[39]

The Lieberman robbery is of significance because it was the first case that enabled the police to determine the development of the crime pattern, and because it contained most of the essential elements in order for the police to identify the *modus operandi* of the suspect.

Noblin's next interview was with Mrs. Julia Beckel. On the way to her apartment, the base radio dispatcher at the base reported the presence of two suspicious black males in the lobby of the building at 40 Clarkson Avenue. This building is located next door to the former Silk Stocking stakeout apartment.

Noblin proceeded directly to 40 Clarkson Avenue. He gained entry into the building by pressing all the bell buttons on the west wall of the vestibule. Starting at the top floor, Noblin conducted a floor-by-floor search of the building. At the fourth floor, he met Gibbons and Alper who had entered the building and started a similar search from the lobby. In the meantime, Officer Thompson, aware that Gibbons and Alper were in the building, conducted a search of the basement area. The SCRU teams left the area when an uniformed police patrol arrived at the scene.

As we returned to the Beckel apartment, we heard these reports from the base radio dispatcher:

3:11 PM: A landlord is attacking a tenant with a machete. Uniformed police patrol responding.

3:14 PM: A woman having a heart attack near 1132 Bedford Avenue. Ambulance and police units responding.

3:17 PM: Man with a gun shot another person. No details.

3:20 PM: Child struck by an automobile, Linden and Rogers. Ambulance and police units responding.

3:23 PM: A man left a subway platform at the Fourth Avenue station and entered the track area. Transit police are not able to find him. Police department assistance requested. Uniformed police patrol responding.[40]

These notices give the background of ordinary police activity in one area in a fifteen-minute period.

Noblin arrived at the Beckel apartment at 3:27 PM. Mrs. Beckel was a willing and cooperative witness. The details of this interview are discussed in Chapter 5. Noblin added this case to the crime pattern file.

On Wednesday, July 11, 1979, Officer Noblin reviewed the SCRU file on known criminals. He selected three men from this file who matched the description of the suspect and told the author that he was going to try to locate these men. As he was preparing to leave, Officer DiCostanzo showed him a mug photo of an offender whom he had arrested about a year-and-a-half ago. DiCostanzo believed that this fellow, James Stevens, was the Silk Stocking Robber. Sergeant Fitzpatrick told Noblin to follow through on this lead.

Noblin checked Steven's file and learned that his last known address was 40 Clarkson Avenue. He proceeded to that address and located Steven's mother. She told him that her son had moved out three weeks before and is working at an engine repair shop on Third Avenue.

Noblin finally located Stevens at the repair shop. He decided that Stevens did not match the description of the suspect. As an added precaution, he asked the owner of the shop if he could check Steven's attendance records. A review of the records disclosed that the man was at work during the days that the crimes were committed.

Noblin decided not to attempt to locate the three known criminals whom he had selected from SCRU files earlier in the day. Instead, we were going to the sixty-seventh precinct to examine arrest records. He explained that no one resembling the described robber committed any robberies in the target area from April 9 through April 20, 1979. He thought that the man was either in the system (i.e. in jail) during this period, or that he struck in other areas. For this reason Noblin decided to review the arrest records of Precincts 67, 70, and 71 for the period in question. The names of all arrested persons will be recorded, their pictures will be obtained, and they will be compared with the description of the Silk Stocking Robber. Noblin feels that we may be able to identify him through this technique.

As he was examining the arrest records Noblin received a call from Officer Thomas Ackerman. Ackerman said that a criminal named Ranzano "Monsie" Campbell had been known to wear gloves during robberies. Noblin got his name and four mug photos from the Precinct 71 files. The man matched the general description of the suspect. He then went to the FAX room and asked the computer operator to run a check on Campbell. Within thirty minutes Noblin had a report on him: Campbell had a record of assaults against elderly persons, but the FAX data indicated that he was not the suspect.

Noblin returned to the SCRU office at 2:50 PM. As he was reviewing some arrest records, Sergeant Fitzpatrick told him that the Silk Stocking robber just robbed another victim. This time he assaulted Gertrude Kaplan, an eighty-year-old widow living at 306 Lenox Road. Noblin and the author went to that address. Noblin was admitted to the victim's apartment by Officer Schaars — the uniformed patrol officer who was first to arrive at the scene of the crime. Questioned, Mrs. Kaplan told Noblin that she had gone shopping with her sister early this afternoon. Later on her sister went to a beauty salon, and she returned to her apartment. As she entered the lobby of the building a young man and a young woman she had not seen before followed her inside. They walked quickly past her and took the stairs to the upper floors.

She said that she took no further notice of them. She checked for her mail and took the elevator to the fifth floor. As she opened her door, the robber appeared from nowhere, seized her by the neck, pushed her inside, and told her to be quiet. Once they were inside, the suspect tightened his grip on her throat and said, "I need money." She replied, "All right, don't choke me. I'll give you money. Let me sit down."[41]

The suspect dragged her into the kitchen and pushed her into a chair. He asked her to tell him where she hid her money. Mrs. Kaplan gave him her purse, which contained about five dollars. He became annoyed with her and told her that she was lying, and that he knew that she had more money. He seized her by the throat and took her into the bedroom. He then began searching the dressers. He returned to Mrs. Kaplan, grabbed her by the throat, and began to choke her. When she tried to hit and kick him he punched her in the stomach and ribs. As he continued to punch her she became dizzy and frightened. She finally told him where she hid her money and jewelry. At this point she fainted. After she regained consciousness, the suspect took her from room to room and demanded that she tell him where she hid her property. When she did not reply, he would tighten his grip on her throat.

He returned her to the kitchen and was searching in the living room when Mrs. Kaplan's neighbor and friend, Mrs. Saperstein, entered the apartment. The suspect quickly seized Mrs. Saperstein and then took both women into the bedroom. He tied Mrs. Kaplan to a chair with pantyhose and took Mrs. Saperstein out of the room.

Noblin then interviewed Mrs. Saperstein in her apartment. She is an eighty-eight-year-old widow who lives across the hall from Mrs. Kaplan. She told Noblin that as she entered her friend's apartment she saw a number of items scattered about the floor in the hallway area. Concerned for her friend, she walked toward the kitchen area. As she approached, Mrs. Kaplan cried out, "If you have any money, give it to him."[42] She saw Mrs. Kaplan sitting in a chair in a highly emotional condition. At the same moment, the suspect seized her by the throat. He took the two women into the bedroom, tied Mrs. Kaplan to a chair, and then took her to her own apartment, where the man seized her by the throat and asked where she hid her money. She told him, "Whatever I have is in that totebag." The suspect dumped the contents of the bag on the floor and retrieved seventeen dollars. He left the apartment without searching for more money or property. Mrs. Saperstein waited a few minutes and then went to the building superintendent's apartment for assistance.

She told Noblin that the man did not wear gloves during the time he was in her apartment. She described him as a black male in his early twenties. She said that he appeared to be about five feet nine inches tall, and that he was an American black. He wore a white shirt, dark pants, and brown shoes. Noblin returned to the Kaplan apartment to continue his interview.

Mrs. Kaplan complained of pains in the rib area and throat. She told Noblin that she was partially crippled and that she had a lung disorder and glaucoma.

Noblin asked her if she could tell him how much money she lost. After she examined the closet where she hid her money and jewelry, she told him that the robber had taken 500 dollars in cash and 2,500 dollars in jewelry. She gave him a list and description of the jewelry.

Asked to describe the suspect, she said that he was a black male, about seventeen or eighteen years old, about five feet nine inches tall, slender, with short hair, clean shaven, thin-lipped, and with a long, thin face. She added that he had a medium-to-dark complexion. He was wearing a zippered, body-fitting jacket and brown leather gloves. Noblin asked her if she would be willing to assist the police in identifying the suspect. She said that she would have difficulty in identifying him through photos but might be able to identify him in person.

After discussing the *modus operandi* of the suspect with Sergeant Fitzpatrick, Noblin added this case to the crime pattern file.

On Thursday, July 12, 1979, Noblin and the author reviewed all of the crime pattern cases. He noted the difference between the Kaplan and Saperstein descriptions for identification, and he put each in a separate folder. He explained that two identification folders were necessary at this time because of the conflicting descriptions of the robber given by the victims. In the next few days he will ask the department artist to sketch a composite drawing from the descriptions contained in these files.

At 1:05 PM, Sergeant Fitzpatrick called Noblin to his office to tell him that the Silk Stocking Robber assaulted another elderly woman. The victim was Mary Gross, an eighty-eight-year-old widow, who lived at 215 Lenox Road, Apartment C-11. Fitzpatrick told Noblin that SCRU investigators DiCostanzo and Carbonaro are on their way to the scene and will assist him in the initial investigation. Noblin and the author proceeded to the Gross apartment.

When Noblin arrived at the apartment, DiCostanzo told him that he had called for the crime scene unit — the fingerprint experts. Street crime unit personnel, uniformed police officers, and ambulance personnel were at the scene. Uniformed Police Officer Nicoll of the seventy-first precinct had responded to the citizen's complaint.

Noblin did not attempt to interview the victim at this time, because the ambulance attendants were preparing to move her to Kings County Hospital. The only information he had at the moment was that Mrs. Gross had been assaulted on July 11, 1979 (the previous afternoon), at about 1:00 PM. She had remained tied to her chair until 11:00 AM on the twelfth. Noblin decided to interview her at the hospital. As Mrs. Gross was being prepared for the trip to the hospital, a uniformed police officer, noting the bruises on her face, neck, and arms exclaimed, "If I catch this son of a bitch there's no way he makes it. . . !" His voice trailed off, and he walked away.[43] Mrs. Gross was transported to the hospital at 1:25 PM.

DiCostanzo and Carbonaro left the apartment to canvass the tenants of the building for information and for possible witnesses. Noblin remained in the apartment awaiting the arrival of the crime scene detectives. All other police officers left the scene.

Detectives J. Taylor and A. Roussine of the crime scene unit arrived at 2:15 PM. The two men began a search for physical evidence. After the search, Taylor informed Noblin that he was able to lift some prints. He was not certain of their value at this time. A report of his findings would be forwarded to Noblin as soon as possible.

After the detectives left, Noblin secured the apartment and went to Kings County Hospital. He found Mrs. Gross lying on a portable stretcher in the emergency room, waiting to be taken to a ward.

A doctor told Noblin that he had examined Mrs. Gross. He said that she had received multiple bruises and abrasions about the face, neck, arms, and body, and there was a possibility of internal injuries. He would know definitely when he received the X-ray report. Noblin asked him if he could interview her. The doctor said that she was awake and alert and that he did not believe that it would do any harm. He told Noblin that he could take her to a room across the hall.

Noblin asked Mrs. Gross if she was able to submit to an interview. She said that she was in some pain, but that she would speak to him. He pushed the stretcher into the room and began the interview. Mrs. Gross told him that she had gone to Waldbaum's to shop for groceries. After making a number of purchases, she returned to her residence. As she entered the vestibule, she encountered a youth who was attempting to gain entry into the building by ringing doorbells at random. She opened the inner door to the lobby, and he followed her inside. The youth entered the elevator with her and followed her when she got out at the third floor.

Mrs. Gross walked to her apartment, placed her packages on the floor, and started to turn the lock on the door to her apartment. In the meantime, the youth pretended to ring the doorbell to the adjacent apartment. As she opened the door, the youth seized her by the throat and pushed her inside. He slapped her on the mouth and told her to "shut-up."[44] He then pushed her into the bedroom and tied her to a chair using pantyhose and scarves. After he had tied her, he pulled the shades down and turned the radio on. He put a stocking around her neck and used it as a noose to choke her. He kept asking Mrs. Gross for money. When she told him that she did not have any money, he slapped and punched her about the face and body. She said that everytime she pleaded to be let alone he would punch and slap her. She told Noblin that he drank from a small bottle of liquor that he had brought with him. After he emptied its contents, he threw the bottle on the floor. At one point during the assault, he found a small hammer and threatened to hit her with it if she did not tell him where she hid the money. After removing five dollars from a dresser drawer, he left the apartment.

When Mrs. Gross was certain that the suspect was no longer in the apartment, she called for help. When no one responded she tried to move the chair nearer the door. Failing to do this, she attempted to untie herself, only to topple the chair and fall to the floor, where she remained until the next morning. She finally managed to untie some of the knots later in the morning. She then called her nephew who notified the police.[45]

The following dialogue, not to be found in the police report, was taped by the author during the interview.[46]

NOBLIN: "There's a small hammer on the bed. Did he bring it with him?"

MRS. GROSS: "No, it's mine."

NOBLIN: "Did he have any keys with him?"

MRS. GROSS: "No."

NOBLIN: "You only have those keys in the small brown purse?"

MRS. GROSS: "Yes. You have my keys?"

NOBLIN: "Yes. I put them in your shoe inside the bag. They're here. I will come to see you tomorrow. I want to get the scarves and the hammer. I'll return your keys. I locked up your apartment. I shut all the windows, and I locked the door with both locks."

MRS. GROSS: "You're very nice."

NOBLIN: "I called your nephew. He will call me at the office tomorrow. He wants to come and see you."

MRS. GROSS: "I would like to see him."

NOBLIN: "Mary, can you tell me if the fellow was dark? That is, his skin tone, was it dark or light?"

MRS. GROSS: "It is medium."

NOBLIN: "Another thing, Mary, do you walk slow or fast?"

MRS. GROSS: "I walk slow. You see, my legs hurt me."

NOBLIN: "Okay, Mary, I am going to leave my card with your keys. If you have any problems you can give me a call, and I'll come right down here.

Tomorrow, I'll bring you an application. We'll fill it out so that you will be covered for all of your medical expenses. You won't have to pay for anything."

MRS. GROSS: "Okay, you are a very nice man."

NOBLIN: "Mary, I put your keys in the small purse. Everything is in this bag."

MRS. GROSS: "I think you better take the keys with you."

NOBLIN: "You want me to hold on to the keys, and I'll bring them back to you tomorrow?"

MRS. GROSS: "Yes."

NOBLIN: "There were some detectives in your apartment. They dusted for fingerprints, so it's still a mess. When you come home and if I'm available, I'll take you home, and I'll help you clean up."

MRS. GROSS: "You're very sweet."

NOBLIN: "I'll see you tomorrow."

MRS. GROSS: "With Alan?" (her nephew)

NOBLIN: "Yes."

MRS. GROSS: "Watch my keys!"

NOBLIN: "I have them right here. I won't lose them. We're going to wheel you back to the other room."

MRS. GROSS: "Okay. Did I give you all the information?"

NOBLIN: "Yes. You were very good. Thank you. Don't worry about it anymore. Try to forget about it."

MRS. GROSS: "I can't forget about it. I can't, I just can't forget about it . . . because, to think he rang my neighbor's bell, and then he pushed me into the house."

NOBLIN: "You're safe now. You're in the hospital, and its all over."

MRS. GROSS: "My God, how could a man do anything like that to an old lady?"

NOBLIN: "We're going to try and catch this guy, Mary. Try not to worry about it."

MRS. GROSS: "Okay, I'll see you tomorrrow."

Earlier, Noblin had asked her if she could describe the robber. She said he was a medium-complexioned black man in his early twenties, about five feet ten inches tall. Mrs. Gross did not describe the suspect's outer wear, but she said he was wearing black gloves.

Noblin asked her if she could identify the man if she saw him. She told him that she was not certain because of her poor eyesight, but she would try to cooperate with the police. This case was added to the crime pattern file.

On Friday morning, July 13, 1979, Noblin went to Manhattan Central Division. He gave the detective at the latent fingerprint section a small plastic purse and two white envelopes. These items were found at the Gross apartment; the robber had searched them for money. The detective told him that he would call Noblin if he found prints that were of value.

On his return to Brooklyn South he went to visit Gertrude Kaplan. Noblin asked her how she was feeling and if she needed any assistance. Mrs. Kaplan told him that her ribs and throat still hurt her, but that she did not require assistance. Noblin suggested that she should go to the hospital for an examination, and she told him that she was going to visit her doctor later in the afternoon.

Mrs. Kaplan appeared to be more concerned with the loss of her jewelry than with her health. She asked Noblin if he could make a special effort to locate her late husband's watch and a silver necklace. She explained that her husband had been a watchmaker and had designed both items. She told him that they were of a great sentimental value to her. She said, "He (the robber) took everything that was dear to me. There's nothing left to live for anymore."[47]

Noblin told her that he was sorry about the loss of her jewelry. He promised to ask the robbery squad detectives to look into the matter. He said, "I'll stop by to see you whenever I get the chance. If I hear anything, I'll let you know. In the meantime, call me if you need any assistance."[48]

He then went to the building superintendent's apartment. On the day of the robbery, Mr. Harzani, the building superintendent, had told Noblin that he did not observe any suspicious persons loitering in or near the building. Today he admitted that he had seen Mrs. Kaplan enter the lobby and walk to the elevator. He also saw a black man and a black woman enter the lobby just before Mrs. Kaplan did. He said that they took the stairs to the upper floors. Mr.

Harzani believed that the young people, whom he had seen in the building on previous occasions, sometimes babysit for the tenant in Apartment 2E.[49] After discussing building security with the superintendent, Noblin went to Apartment 2E and rang the doorbell. Receiving no response, he returned to Mr. Harzani's apartment and got the tenant's name and telephone number.

Noblin then went to Kings County Hospital County Hospital to visit with Mrs. Gross. At the hospital he met Mr. Alan Gross, the victim's nephew. Mr. Gross told him that he was going to put his aunt in a nursing home in the borough of Manhattan. The home was near his apartment.

Mrs. Gross was resting comfortably and was in a good mood. He returned her keys and then helped her to complete some applications for medical and hospital services and for emergency financial aid. When the doctor arrived he told Noblin that she had suffered four broken ribs and some internal injuries, the extent not yet determined. He said that she was on the critical list, but explained that this was a routine procedure for people in her age bracket.

Noblin returned to SCRU headquarters at 4:20 PM.

On the morning of July 20, 1979, Noblin learned the Mrs. Mary Gross had died as a result of her injuries at Kings County Hospital on Thursday, July 19, 1979. The case was transferred to the twelfth homicide zone. Ordinarily, when the victim of a robbery dies, homicide detectives will assume responsibility for the conduct of the investigation. In this instance, because the SCRU has been involved in Operation Silk Stocking (also known as SCRU pattern case number one), Noblin will coordinate his activities with the detective squad.

At the twelfth homicide zone, Noblin discussed the Gross case with Lieutenant Ralph Feminella, Sergeant Shea, and Detective Kohler. Lieutenant Feminella informed Noblin that a task force would be established for SCRU pattern case number one, and that he would be assigned to work with the task force. Operation Silk Stocking was now a homicide investigation. The twelfth homicide detective squad assumed overall responsibility for the investigation. The SCRU continued its decoy and anti-crime activities, and Noblin would coordinate his investigative activities with twelfth zone detectives. Later in the day, Kohler reported that the Gross case was the third homicide committed by the Silk Stocking Robber.

On Wednesday, July 25, 1979, Lieutenant Feminella told Noblin that he had decided to bring the robbery and burglary detective squads into the task force. He thought that the robber had fenced at least some of the stolen property, and he wants to utilize the expertness of these detectives.

The detectives were supplied with a list and with sketches of all the property known to have been stolen by the robber. They would contact informers and visit known fence establishments in an effort to trace the property. They were aware, however, that they have little chance in locating any of the items, because, by this time, they have either been melted down or reconstructed. The primary purpose here was to identify the robber.

In the meantime, Sergeant Byrnes and Noblin focused on the forty-one-day period during which no robberies were reported in Brooklyn South, which fitted the *modus operandi* of the Silk Stocking Robber. The officers wanted to find out whether the robber was in the system, or whether he had committed robberies in other areas of the city during this time. On Monday, July 23, 1979, Noblin called the Bronx SCRU, Brooklyn North SCRU, and Manhattan South SCRU. He supplied these units with the descriptions and the *modus operandi* of the Silk Stocking Robber. On Tuesday, July 24, 1979, these commands reported no cases similar in nature to those under investigation in SCRU pattern case number one.

On this morning, the author accompanied Officer Noblin to the Queens SCRU, which is located in the one hundred and tenth police precinct. He conferred with SCRU Investigator Buonincontri, who told him that there had been a number of similar push-in, tie-up robberies committed in the Queens area during the past few months.

One case in particular contained most of the elements of the Silk Stocking Robber's *modus operandi* and a similar description of the suspect. For example, the victim was pushed into the apartment and tied to a chair in the bedroom area. The attacker used pantyhose to tie the victim, and he turned the television set on. He also told the victim that he had to catch a plane.[50]

This robbery had occurred on March 20, 1979, at approximately 2:15 PM. The victim was Nina Towers, a seventy-year-old widow who lived at 3534 Seventy-fifth Street, in Jackson Heights, borough of Queens. This case was being carried under 110 Precinct UF 61, No. 4003, Queens SCRU no. 125.

Noblin reviewed the crime pattern case file and found that the Silk Stocking suspect had not committed robbery in Brooklyn South from March third to April ninth, a period of thirty-seven days. The Queens SCRU case files for this period were added to SCRU pattern case number one.

Buonincontri supplied Noblin with photos and names of possible suspects whom he was investigating in connection with these particular robberies. He also gave him a photo and the name and address of the criminal who was arrested for the Towers robbery. The offender, one Anthony Clifford, proved not to be the Silk Stocking Robber.

Buonincontri told Noblin that there was another man, a Joel Jackson, male, black, twenty-seven years old, 49-26 Ninety-fifth Street, Jackson Heights, Queens, NYSIIS No. 3829437K; last arrest February 3, 1975, 114 Precinct. Noblin decided to try to obtain a "wet photo" (an expeditious method of obtaining required photos) from Manhattan central. He planned to show the photo to Brooklyn South victims.

At 12:45 PM, the author accompanied Noblin to Manhattan Central Division. He told the author that he wanted to accomplish the following at the division: (1) obtain a wet photo of Jackson; (2) visit the stolen property identification section (SPIS); (3) visit the latent fingerprint section; and (4) visit the department artist.

The wet photos were ready when he arrived at the photo section. After studying the photo, Noblin said that he did not believe that they would be helpful to the investigation, but he took them anyway.

Noblin then proceeded to SPIS and gave the officer in charge of recording stolen property a list of Gertrude Kaplan's property. The description of each item and other pertinent data was recorded on a jewelry card, P.D. 530-101, commonly called a "squeal" card. If the jewelry is sold at a pawnshop, the pawnbroker, as required by law, will identify the property and send a description of it along with the number of the pawn ticket to SPIS. The item is then matched with the description contained in the squeal card. Over the years a number of cases have been solved through the use of this technique.

Having been told earlier that a good set of prints were lifted at the Mary Gross apartment, Noblin went to the latent fingerprint section where the fingerprint experts were working on them. The supervisor told him that it was too early to tell whether they were of any value.

He said that Mary Gross' fingerprints had not been sent to this section yet, and the fingerprints might be hers.

Noblin wanted to know from the supervisor if fingerprint experts could work with partial prints (fingerprints or palms), which are considered to be of no value. A few words of explanation will clarify this point. The term *partial print* includes only fingertip prints or palmprints. It does not include, for example, partials of thumbprints or index fingerprints because these prints are considered to be of value.

Learning that the experts could work with partial prints, Noblin told the supervisor that he would send some fingertip prints lifted from apartments in Brooklyn South.

Finally, Noblin went to see the department artist. He told the artist that he would bring Gertrude Kaplan to him on Monday to describe certain unique jewelry to him so that the investigators may have a better description of her assailant. The artist will sketch a composite drawing of the man, and copies of the drawing will be distributed to all commands.[51]

On the return to SCRU headquarters Noblin told the author that the fingertip prints may be of significance to this investigation. At the SCRU office he proposed to Sergeant Byrnes that the fingertip prints he will send to the latent fingerprint section should be maintained in its files for at least the duration of Operation Silk Stocking. In addition, all criminals who are arrested for crimes committed against the elderly should have their fingertip prints and palmprints taken along with their regular prints. Byrnes agreed to the proposal. He discussed the matter with Lieutenant Feminella, who then told central booking personnel of this added requirement.

On the morning of July 26, 1979, Sergeant Byrnes told Noblin that the Silk Stocking Robber committed another robbery the previous night. He also informed Noblin that a review of the crime pattern case file had disclosed that the victim, Irene Selzman, had been assaulted and robbed earlier this month by the man who police administrators believe is the Silk Stocking Robber.

Noblin called Mrs. Selzman and asked her if she would consent to an interview. At first she told him that she was tired and upset, and that she did not want to discuss the incident with anyone. After he assured her that whatever she told him would remain confidential, she agreed to the interview. Investigator DiCostanzo accompanied Noblin to the victim's apartment. She told the two officers that at approximately 8:45 PM on Wednesday, the suspect rang her doorbell and, from outside the locked door to the apartment, informed her that water was leaking from her apartment to the apartment below. He asked to be admitted to her apartment in order to locate the source of the leak.

When she opened the door, the suspect pushed her back and seized her by the throat. He said, "If you don't tell me where your money is, I'll kill you."[52] Fearful for her life, she directed him to the kitchen area and told him that she had fifteen dollars in her pocketbook.

After he removed the money, he picked up a knife from the countertop and, tightening his grip on her throat, demanded more money. When she did not respond, he threatened her with the knife. Mrs. Selzman then told him where she had hidden an additional one hundred dollars in the bathroom.

The suspect then pushed her into the bedroom and tied her to a chair with stockings and scarves. He searched through the dressers for a few minutes. He returned to his victim and placed a scarf over her eyes and resumed his search of the bedroom. At one point during the search he told her, "I have to take a plane. You better give me more money, or I'll kill you."[53] She told him that she did not have any more money. The suspect left the bedroom area, searched the apartment for approximately twenty minutes, and left.

She described her assailant as a black male in his early twenties, approximately five feet eight inches tall, light-skinned, long thin face, clean shaven, and he spoke with a soft but clear voice. She thought that he was an American black.

Reminding Mrs. Selzman that the suspect operated in the same manner as the person who robbed her on July 3, 1979, Noblin asked her if she thought that he was the same man. She replied that she could not identify the man either from photographs or in person, and she expressed a desire not to cooperate with the police in the future.[54] Sergeant Byrnes and the author met with Noblin and DiCostanzo at the sixty-seventh precinct. Noblin and DiCostanzo told Byrnes that the woman was afraid of the robber, and that they believed that she could be of no further assistance in this investigation. After a brief discussion of the *modus operandi* of the suspect, Byrnes decided to add the case to the criminal pattern file.

Noblin asked Byrnes for permission to use the police computer-ized identification system. He explained that he wanted to run a composite description of the suspect through the system. The infor-mation received from the system might, according to Noblin, nar-row the scope of the search to one or two known criminals. Byrnes agreed to the use of this search technique and told him to oversee the computer search.

Computer-Assisted Terminal Criminal Hunt — CATCH

The computer-assisted terminal criminal hunt (CATCH) system was developed to assist the police in the identification of possible suspects to crimes based on the descriptions provided to them by vic-tims and/or witnesses.

In conducting the search for the criminal, the police will inter-rogate the system by supplying it with a description of the suspect. The data will include but not be limited to the suspect's age, height, weight, and facial and physical characteristics. Included in the inter-rogation will be the types of crimes committed by the suspects and the police precincts within which the crimes were committed.

An electronic search of the vast amount of data stored in the system will then begin. The search will continue until all known criminals who fit the description of the criminal and who have com-mitted the types of crimes specified in the designated precincts are located. The police can usually have this information — the New York State identification number of the criminals — in less than an hour.

Knowledge of the criminals identification number serves two im-portant purposes in the search for the suspect. First, with it the police can get photos of the criminal, which can be compared to the composite sketches of the criminal. Second, the police will be able to obtain the complete history of the criminal through an interrogation of the FAX system. As a minimum, the FAX data will provide the police with the incarceration record of the criminal. This informa-tion will allow the police to find out if the criminal was on the streets when the crimes were committed; the types of crimes committed; the time, date, and place of each crime; whether the criminal is still in the system, on probation, or on parole; what aliases or nicknames he uses; and what was his last known address.

Noblin has applied these techniques to the SCRU crime pattern cases. His purpose was to interrogate the computer with a composite description of the suspect taken from the Brooklyn South SCRU files and from the Queens area SCRU files. He wanted to find out whether the suspect who committed the Brooklyn South crimes was the same person who committed the Queens area crimes. If it was the same person, he could account for the lack of criminal activity in Brooklyn South and the corresponding increase in the Queens area. On the other hand, if he cannot determine that one man was responsible for these crimes, then the SCRU will be confronted with a search for two criminals who are using the same *modus operandi* instead of one as assumed by police administrators.[55]

Although Noblin believed that one man was responsible for the Silk Stocking felonies, he did not rule out the possibility that two men might be involved in the same type of criminal activity.

Noblin requested the Brooklyn South CATCH computer operator to interrogate the system with the following data: (1) male, black; (2) eighteen to twenty years old; (3) 5′8″ to 5′11′ tall; (4) 145 to 150 lbs; (5) short hair; (6) dark complexion; (7) clean shaven; and (8) arrested for robbery of elderly persons in any of five precincts, 70, 71, 67, 110, and 114, (70, 71, and 67 are located in Brooklyn South; the 110 and 114 are located in the Queens area).

This information was transmitted to the main terminal center, which is located at Number 1 Police Plaza in the borough of Manhattan.

Within thirty minutes Manhattan CATCH responded as follows (*see* Fig. 8-5):

There are 00008 respondents to your query.
Place X in appropriate line.
_____ No further information required.
_____ Send back list of respondents.

Brooklyn South CATCH requested back the list of respondents.

In less than forty-five minutes the respondents list was transmitted to the Brooklyn South CATCH computer. After reviewing the data, Byrnes and Noblin agreed that a FAX systems report would be required to supplement the information contained in the CATCH reports. Noblin made arrangements to obtain wet photos

```
C.A.T.C.H. SEARCH
                YEAR BORN 61     AGE RANGE 04
SEX M      RACE B  EYE COLOR BR   HEIGHT 5 FT 10 IN    HT RANGE 02 IN
WEIGHT 150         WT RANGE 05    HAIR COLOR BK         FOREIGN BORN?    DRUGS?
DEFORM TIES/PECULIARITIES (USE CODING SHEET)
         MARK TYP        MARK LOC        MARK TYP       MARK LOC        HAIR TYPE
         HAIRSTYLE CR    PART BALD?      OBV WIG?       DYED HAIR?      SIDEBURNS?
         MUSTACHE?       BEARD?          FRECKLED?      POCKED?         PIMPLED?
         COMPLXN DK      RUDDY?          S/C COMP?      GLASSES?        EYES?
         HEAR AID?       EARS?           NOSE?          TEETH?          TRACKS?
         ARM/HAND?       LEFTY?          LIMP?          LEG?            POSTURE?
         SPEECH?
10:
         IMP P.O.?       IMP FEMLE?      IMP OTHER?     HOMOSEXL?       TEAM?
         YOUTH GNG?      GUN USED?       KNIFE?
VEHICLE USED?           COLOR           MAKE           YEAR
NICKNAME                        CHARGE  PL 160.00
SEARCH:ENTER UP TO 7 PCTS 067 070 071 114 110

                        RESPONSE TO CATCH QUERY
REEL#   FRAME/CRIMINAL#
  015     1893 4083266Z
  033     2094 4150863N
  039     1396 3762417P   2396 3768107K
  041     1503 3818367P
  047     0296 4184417H
  049     1679 4179063M
  061     0551 4259532Z
SEARCH COMPLETED, OPERATOR K59    DATE 00792
```

Figure 8-5. This is what a copy of the initial interrogation of the CATCH system looks like, as requested by Officer Noblin. The upper portion shows the interrogation by Brooklyn South CATCH. The lower portion shows the response by Manhattan CATCH.

and FAX systems reports.

As Byrnes was studying some mug photos from the Queens SCRU, Noblin showed him the wet photos of Joel Jackson. The two officers agreed that he did not fit the description of the assailant, but they wanted to be more certain. Earlier, Byrnes learned from Officer Buonincontri, of the Queens SCRU, that the building superintendent, of 4926 Ninety-fifth Street in Jackson Heights, Queens, knew Jackson and that he was willing to identify him. The author accompanied Byrnes and Noblin to that address.

The officers located the superintendent, Mr. Marco Sanchez. After viewing the photo of Jackson, Sanchz said that he knew the man, and that he looks identical to the photo.

Joel Jackson's name was deleted from the list of possible suspects in the continuing investigation of the Silk Stocking case.[56]

After the officers returned to Brooklyn South, they went to a liquor store on Bedford Avenue. Earlier, Noblin obtained the federal stamp tax number (B6829 177/1970) from the empty pint bottle of Canadian Club® whiskey that the criminal left at the Gross apartment. Byrnes and Noblin were trying through the liquor tax stamp number to trace the bottle to the store from which it was purchased. They thought that if they could locate the store, then they might be able to obtain some information that would lead to the identification of the criminal.

They learned that the last four digits in the stamp tax number indicated the year that the whiskey went into bond. It is then kept in bond for six years, and this particular bottle came out of bond in 1976. It may, therefore, have been on the shelf of a Brooklyn South Liquor Store for three years. It was obvious to Byrnes and Noblin that they had to canvass small neighborhood liquor stores with a low turnover. The store they visited first had pints of Canadian Club whiskey that went into bond in 1973. Byrnes decided to assign two SCRU investigative teams to canvass all small liquor stores in the Brooklyn South area.

Byrnes and Noblin then decided to visit Mrs. Lillian Holtzman. Noblin wanted her to view some mug photos from the SCRU files. Mrs. Holtzman could not identify any of the suspects. Byrnes asked her if she was willing to accompany him or Noblin to Manhattan central in order to view more photos. She replied, "I wouldn't even consider it." Noblin asked her if she would be willing to identify the suspect from a police lineup. Again, the answer was, "No!"[57] Byrnes spoke to her about the robbery for a few minutes, then he asked her if she would be willing, with the advice of her physician, to visit a department hypnotist. He told her that he was a certified hypnotist and that he might be able to help her to remember some of the facial features and characteristics of the robber. She replied, "I won't even consider it. Furthermore, I'm not going to help you or the department in identifying the robber."[58]

Noblin tried to reason with Mrs. Holtzman. He told her that the police and the SCAN people were concerned for her safety. He gave her his card and asked her to call him if she needed assistance. As the officer prepared to leave the apartment, she turned to Byrnes and said, "Why haven't you caught him yet?" Byrnes replied, "Lillian, we have been hunting for this fellow for more than a month. We want him off the streets as much as you do, and sooner or later we'll get him. I know how you feel, and I'm not angry with you. I just wish that you would help us catch him."[59] She did not reply.

After they left the apartment, Byrnes told Noblin that he should visit Mrs. Holtzman whenever he got the opportunity. Byrnes thought that someone might have threatened her, or that she had spent some time thinking about her ordeal and was consequently living in fear of the criminal.

At the SCRU headquarters Byrnes and Noblin discussed the events of the day. Byrnes assigned two investigators to each SCRU zone. On Friday, July 27, 1979, the investigators were to begin canvassing liquor stores in an effort to trace the pint bottle of Canadian Club whiskey.

At 2:55 PM, the author accompanied Detective Knox and Investigator DiCostanzo to the seventieth precinct where Knox and DiCostanzo interrogated two burglars, Antoine Pearson, sixteen years old, and Wanda Latimer, seventeen years old. The pair had been captured burglarizing an apartment on Bedford Avenue.

The teenagers were taken to separate rooms for the interrogation. As the questioning progressed it became evident to Knox and DiCostanzo that the Pearson boy was the more experienced and streetwise of the pair. Other than telling the police that it was the girl's idea to burglarize the apartment, he said little else. Knox and DiCostanzo decided to concentrate their efforts on the Latimer girl. She denied Pearson's charges and said that this was her first burglary. Knox asked her if she ever robbed any elderly women or if she knew anyone who did. The girl replied that she never robbed anyone. She repeated her claim that this was her first venture into crime. Knox left to question Pearson.

DiCostanzo told the girl that he knew that she was lying. He told her that Pearson was concerned only for himself, and that it did not matter to him if she went to jail. He said, "The best thing that you could do is to cooperate with us. If you do, we will tell the district attorney that you were cooperative. I can't promise you anything, but it might help you."[60]

DiCostanzo then directed his questioning to fences and pawnshops. He asked her if she know where her friend, Pearson, sold his goods. After a moment of hesitation, she identified a pawnshop on Fifth and Atlantic avenues, a disco record shop on Nostrand Avenue and Martense Street, and a private house at 95 East Twenty-second

Street. (The record shop has a trap door at the rear, and stolen goods are pushed through this door immediately upon receipt.) She told DiCostanzo that all the people she knows fence their stolen goods at any one of the three drops. They usually trade the good for marijuana or cocaine; sometimes they receive money. She said, "When we can't get rid of the goods at the disco or the pawnshop, we go to the house. We see a guy named Paul. He takes care of us. He gives us grass or coke. If we want money, he gives it to us."[61]

Knox and DiCostanzo recorded the names and addresses of the establishments identified by Latimer. Knox is going to ask Lieutenant Feminella to place these drops under surveillance.

After the interrogation was completed, the prisoners were escorted to central booking by the arresting officers.

On the morning of July 27, 1979, the author accompanied Noblin to the sixty-seventh precinct, where Noblin reviewed the CATCH systems data and the FAX systems data on the eight criminals who were selected from the suspect description file.

He was aware, from the previous day's study of the CATCH data, that none of the criminals was arrested for robbery in the Queens area. This knowledge, and the earlier elimination of Anthony Clifford and Joel Jackson as suspects, led him to reconsider the one-suspect theory.

Noblin arranged to have the fingerprint records of the criminals sent to the latent fingerprint section for a possible match with prints that were lifted from the apartments of crime pattern case victims.

He considered the possibility of asking for a warrant in order to locate these people and bring them in for fingertip print and palmprint impressions. He said, "I wish that it could be done, but I know that they will be back in the system before long. We just have to wait until they come back in. We'll run a CATCH interrogation on them every so often."[62]

After he completed his study of the data, Noblin obtained a crime victim's compensation form for Mrs. Gertrude Kaplan. Before leaving for her residence he called and told her that he was going to bring the form to her. On the way to the Kaplan apartment, he stopped at a small disco record shop on Roger's Avenue. He gave the proprietor a description of the Silk Stocking criminal and asked the man to call him if he spotted the man or if he hears anything about him. The proprietor agreed to cooperate with him.

Later, Noblin told the author that informers are a necessary evil in police work. They provide the police with much valuable information, and in turn, the police will allow them, within certain limits, to operate without interference. The proprietor is one of his sources of information. He said, "He gives us information when we need it. If he don't, then we'll bust his chops, and he knows it."[68]

Noblin called on Mrs. Kaplan and gave her the victim's compensation form. After she completed it, he placed the form in an envelope and told her that he would mail it to the Crime Victim's Compensation Board. He spoke with her for several minutes and then left the apartment.

Noblin then went to Apartment 2E. He wanted to talk to the tenant about the babysitters. When he rang the doorbell he heard movement inside the apartment, but no one came to the door. After waiting for a few minutes, he left the building and went to the twelfth homicide detective zone office, where he briefed Lieutenant Feminella on the results of his CATCH and FAX inquiries. He gave the lieutenant the list of criminals whose fingerprint records he sent to the latent fingerprint section and a list of the latest Silk Stocking cases.

Lieutenant Feminella asked Noblin if he had had the opportunity to interview the tenant in Apartment 2E. Noblin told him that he had gone to the apartment on two occasions and received no response. Feminella told him that he would send a detective to the apartment on Monday.

When Noblin returned to the SCRU office, Byrnes told him that his vacation would begin, as planned, on Monday, July 30, 1979. Byrnes informed the author that he (Byrnes) would work with Officer DiCostanzo during Noblin's absence. The author joined this team.

On Monday morning, July 30, 1979, DiCostanzo asked the author to assist him in a review of the crime pattern case file. The purpose of the review was to identify and to remove from the file all cases in which the criminal does not fit the description of the suspect. Three such cases were found and removed.

At 11:30 AM, Detective John Breslin of the property recovery squad, missing person unit visited the SCRU office. He conferred with Byrnes and DiCostanzo on the problem of identifying and tracing the property that was taken by the suspect. He explained that once the property is listed and identified by its physical characteristics, it could be traced, for example, through a serial number, a code designation, a warranty, or by an insurance number.

After the property is identified, investigators will conduct a canvass of all pawnshops and secondhand dealers located in Brooklyn. An examination of all records and transactions may lead to the identification of the suspect through his signature, driver's license, social security number, or through some other form of identification. Upon learning that the SCRU did not have a list of the property, Breslin suggested that it should be established as soon as possible. Thus, for the second time in one day the team conducted a review of the crime pattern case file. The results of the review are as follows:

Case 320	June 11, 1979	Molly Ratner
		359 Ocean Ave., 3A
		Property Taken
		2 mink jackets
Case 350	June 27, 1979	Lillian Holtzman
		70 Lenox Road, 4D
		Property taken
		2 mink coats
Case 281	May 18, 1979	Etta Weinstein
		49 Linden Blvd., 2B
		Property Taken
		Jewelry and 2 radios
Case 367	July 3, 1979	Irene Selzman
		182 Linden Blvd., 4F
		Property Taken
		Jewelry
Case 384	July 11, 1979	Gertrude Kaplan
		306 Lenox Road, 5C
		Property Taken
		Jewelry
		Sterling silver flatware
		Movie camera and projector
		Mink jacket
		Navy blue cashmere coat
		Mink coat

Case 304	June 4, 1979	Hilda Rossman
		223 Lenox Road, 6B
		Property Taken
		Jewelry
Case 348	June 25, 1979	Ruby Blackner
		58 Linden Blvd., 6B
		Property Taken
		Jewelry
Case 349	June 25, 1979	Irene Bromberg
		548 Ocean Avenue, 3C
		Property Taken
		Jewelry
Case 129	February 23, 1979	Esther Baker
		85 Clarkson Avenue, 6G
		Property Taken
		Jewelry
Case 257	May 4, 1979	Myra Rosen
		310 Lenox Road, 5A
		Property Taken
		Sony TV
Case 165	March 9, 1979	Sara Lieberman
		40 Linden Blvd., 4F
		Property Taken
		Jewelry
		Movie camera and projector

The list was submitted to Sergeant Byrnes for his evaluation. Breslin told him that he required a detailed description of the property. He suggested that the victims should be reinterviewed for this purpose, and Byrnes agreed. DiCostanzo and Detective McManus were assigned to conduct the reinterviews.

Breslin gave each officer a list of *things to do* when conducting interviews with victims or other persons who may be familiar with the property. The list is designed to explain the type of information that is required for a detailed description of the property.

Things to Do

Property

1. Reinterview victims or families of deceased. Try to obtain a

more complete and detailed description of property taken.
EXAMPLE:

Watches: lady's or man's; color — yellow or white gold; stainless steel back; white face or black; type of numerals — Roman numerals or dots; any diamonds; type of band — leather, expandable metal, color; make — Benrus, Bulova, etc; obtain, if possible, the case number, movement number, and model number; ask if the watch was insured; where purchased (Is there a warranty on watch?); value of watch; anything unique about watch — was it repaired (if so, by who); for jewelers scratch mark file check for any inscriptions (names, dates); is it a calendar (date, month); second sweep hand.

Furs: type of fur (mink, sable etc.); color — autumn haze, brown; length of fur — full-length coat, 3/4 jacket, stole; type of lining — initials or name in lining; inquire where purchased; interview manufacturer — he may have registered in dye each skin that makes up the coat.

Rings: man's, lady's; type of metal — gold, silver; color — yellow, white gold; type of setting (mounting) — signet, gypsie, tiffany, band; type of stones — diamond, ruby, emerald; shape of stones — round, pear, marquise; size of stones — 1 carat, 2 carats, 55 points; manufacturer logo in shank of ring; 14 or 18 karat gold; inscriptions — names, dates; jeweler purchased from; was it appraised? insured? was ring unique (one of a kind) or a stock item?

Bracelets, Pendants, Chains, Charms: from whom purchased; amount of charms on bracelet; description of them.

2. After information on property is obtained from victims, investigator should visit police headquarters, fourth floor and make sure that property containing serial and model numers are entered in the computer at NCIC. See Clint Hardy or Eddie Barr and use my name for help. Property that has no serial or model numbers should be entered on cards in the stolen property inquiry section. Example: charms, furs, bracelets, and diamonds. See Tom Padget and use my name for help.

3. A canvass of the Brooklyn pawnshops and various second-hand dealers should be conducted for the wanted property. A check should be made of their records for any suspects names that will show if they pawned or sold any of the wanted prop-

erty. It will divulge name, address, signature, and what seller gave as identification (driver's license, social security number, etc.).

Detective John Breslin
Missing Person Unit
233-4152 or 3
Home 737-6105

Pawnshops

Manhattan

Century Pawn	725 Eleventh Avenue	245-7321
Dollar Pawn	525 Lenox Avenue	862-2037
Edelstein Pawn	233 East Fourteenth Street	254-1638
S & G Gross	486 Eighth Avenue	736-6555
L. Harlan	608 Eighth Avenue	736-1690
Lowne Pawn	140 Ninth Avenue	243-0607
Lincoln Square Pawn	2672 Broadway	865-2360
Arthur Narquiles	150 Lasseu Street	268-2732
Second Avenue Pawn	120 Second Street	477-2555
J. Simpson	1200 Sixth Avenue	575-9500
W. Simpson-Ed Capriola	165 Church Street	243-2569
Sobel Brothers	605 Amsterdam Avenue	787-5907
Tri-Lex Pawn	104 East 125th Street	544-4950
United Pledge Society	860 Eighth Avenue	265-0730
Washington Pawn	1952 Amsterdam Avenue	244-0437
Gramerey Pawn	338 Third Avenue	472-6170
Paramount Pawn	933 Eighth Avenue	765-4943
Royal Loan Model		

Bronx

Bronx Pawn	1917 Washington Avenue	731-5801
Lenox Collateral	307 East Fordham Road	367-7644
Edelstein Pawn	428 East 149th Street	699-1055
Maxies	3822 Third Avenue	294-5200

Brooklyn

Fulton Pawn	1543 Fulton Street	778-4050
Heaney-Koski	214 Atlantic Avenue	624-3182
Pitkin Pawn	1730 Pitkin Avenue	496-5074
John Savor	1305 Fulton Street	783-5081

| Gen. Pawn | 12 Fourth Avenue | 624-2961 |
| Reliable Pawn | 657 Fulton Street | 855-6881 |

Queens

Boulevard Loan	147-13 Jamaica Avenue	526-8680
J.J. Friel	171-03 Jamaica Avenue	739-1696
Jamaica Loan (Cohen-Weaver)	91-13 Herrick Boulevard	297-1129

In an effort to enlist the assistance of field personnel in Brooklyn and in Queens, Sergeant Byrnes sent a flyer to thirty-eight police precincts located in these boroughs. The flyer contained a description of the criminal and his *modus operandi*. The information contained in the flyer was to be read at twenty-one consecutive roll calls in each precinct. In discussing the roll call procedure with the author, Byrnes said, "There will be a total of 456 six roll calls. The chances are that at least one cop will remember an offender with whom he has come into contact who fits the description of the suspect or who used the same *modus operandi*."[64]

On Tuesday, July 31, 1979, Lieutenant Coles, task force commander, Brooklyn South, and Detective Lieutenant Feminella, twelfth homicide zone, designated the following personnel as the prime investigating team for SCRU pattern case number one:

Sergeant Byrnes — SCRU
Officer DiCostanzo — SCRU
Detective Knox — twelfth homicide zone
Detective Rango — twelfth homicide zone
Detective McManus — robbery squad

On Wednesday, August 1, 1979, the team reviewed all SCRU cases of 1979 in which robberies were committed of the elderly and which were not in the crime pattern case file. The purpose of the review was to find out if any case in this group belonged in the file.

The team found and added to the file six additional possible crime pattern cases. While the review was going on, McManus called the Brooklyn South Narcotics Squad to ask for information about the fences identified by Wanda Latimer. The detective who took the call said that he would look into the matter and would call back later. Sergeant Byrnes said that if the narcotics people did not have any information, then Lieutenant Coles or Lieutenant Feminella would call the narcotics squad lieutenant and request that he assign an undercover agent to this area. The agent would then purchase marijuana from the disco record shop proprietor; with the evidence in hand, the task force commander would ask the court for a search warrant, which would include a list of stolen property. The team would move in with the narcotics people when they make the arrest.

At 2:45 PM, Officer Albert Guorineri (Lieutenant Coles' driver) called SCRU headquarters to report that he had been placed on temporary cruise patrol in the target area. During this time he spotted an elderly woman, and he decided to follow her, but he broke off his surveillance in order to respond to a robbery call.

At 2:40 PM, he received a citizen complaint from the 911 police emergency call number, and Guorineri responded to this call. When he arrived at the victim's apartment, he found that it was the same woman that he had been following earlier in the day. The victim of the latest robbery is Ruth Margolin, eighty-six years old, of 191 Lenox Road. The team went to the victim's apartment, where DiCostanzo interviewed Mrs. Margolin. Earlier that day Mrs. Margolin's neighbor had taken her to Kings County Hospital emergency room because she was feeling ill. After an examination, the doctor gave her some medicine and released her. She took a cab to her apartment, arriving at 1:05 PM. She had been in her apartment about ten minutes when someone rang the doorbell. She went to the door and looked through the peephole to identify the caller. A man called to her and said, "I'm Pete's son. There's a leak in your bathroom; I have to fix it." Mrs. Margolin knew that Pete was the handyman for the building, but she did not know if he had a son. To make certain of the caller's identity she said, "Step back so that I can see you." He replied, "Is the water still flooding the bathroom?"[65] Mrs. Margolin, having had problems with water leaks on an earlier occasion, opened the door to admit him.

The man seized her by the throat and said, "Where's the money? Do you want to die?" He tightened his grip on her throat and dragged her into the bedroom. Mrs. Margolin told DiCostanzo that she lost consciousness at this time. When she became conscious again she was lying on the floor. The offender helped her to her feet and then tied her to a chair with pantyhose and scarves.

After searching the bedroom the assailant returned to Mrs. Margolin and, seizing her by the throat, demanded to know where she hid her money. She told him that she had five dollars in her purse. He searched the purse and removed the money. After approximately twenty minutes, the robber left the bedroom and did not return. When she was certain that he was no longer in the apartment, Mrs. Margolin untied herself and called for assistance.

During the interview, members of the team canvassed her neighbors and other tenants. The police were not able to obtain any information from the persons they had questioned.

DiCostanzo added this case to the crime pattern case file.

On Thursday, August 2, 1979, McManus reported that a narcotics squad undercover agent had visited the disco record shop. He reported that there was no activity at that establishment. The squad would continue its surveillance for a few days.

At 11:30 AM, a citizen complaint was received from the seventieth precinct dispatcher. Although the information was incomplete, the team learned that the Silk Stocking Robber had robbed another elderly woman living at 191 Lenox Road, the same building in which Mrs. Margolin was assaulted the day before. The victim, Mrs. Mary Bailey, a ninety-two-year-old widow, lived in Apartment C-3, a few steps down the hall from Mrs. Margolin's apartment. The team also learned that Mrs. Bailey was similarly assaulted on May 5, 1979.

At the Bailey apartment, Byrnes and DiCostanzo conducted the interview. Mrs. Bailey told them at about noon she went downstairs to check for her mail. On her return as she opened the door to her apartment, her assailant seized her by the throat and pushed her inside. The suspect threw her to the floor and demanded money. When she did not respond, he pulled her to her feet. He then put his hand on her throat and took her into the bedroom, where he tied her to a chair with some scarves.

As the interview proceeded, Officer Ellen Alwill asked Mrs. Bailey if she needed something to drink. She replied, "Yes, I'll have a beer."[66] Sergeant Byrnes gave Alwill five dollars and told her to buy a six pack.

DiCostanzo resumed the questioning. He asked her if she had fainted at any time during the assault. She said that she had not fainted. Byrnes asked her if the suspect spoke to her. She said that he tightened his grip on her throat and demanded money. At one point he said, "Be quiet, or I'll kill you. Where is your money?"[67] She told him that she had some money in one of the dresser drawers. The suspect searched the drawers and took twenty-five dollars.

Mrs. Bailey said that the robber pulled the shades in the bedroom. On two occasions, he closed the door to the bedroom and searched the other rooms. She did not remember when he left the apartment. DiCostanzo asked her if she could describe the suspect. She told him that she could not because she had poor vision.

Mrs. Bailey remained tied to the chair until 11:00 AM on Thursday. She called for help during the night, but no one responded. She was discovered by Dolly Baker, the building superintendent. Mrs. Baker said that she was passing through the hall when she noticed that Mrs. Bailey's door was ajar. Entering the apartment to investigate, she found Mrs. Bailey tied to the chair in the bedroom. She cut her bonds and called the police.

Lieutenant Coles and Sergeant Byrnes reasoned that she could have been tied up during the time the team was investigating the Margolin robbery. It is also possible that the suspect may have been in the apartment during that time. The police cannot be certain of this, because Mrs. Bailey did not remember when the suspect left the apartment.

It is known, however, that Officer Bounincontri and the author called at Mrs. Bailey's apartment. When there was no response, Buonincontri tried the door but found it locked. Later, DiCostanzo also called at the Bailey apartment and received no response. On the next morning, however, at about 11:00 AM, the superintendent found the door ajar.

DiCostanzo added this case to the crime pattern case file.

At 3:00 PM, DiCostanzo and Alwill escorted Mrs. Margolin to Manhattan central. The eighty-six-year-old woman gave the department artist the description of the suspect.

On Friday, August 3, 1979, Lieutenant Coles and Sergeant Byrnes assigned to surveillance duty in the target area all available personnel as follows: observation van — W. Lohse and T. Meehan; unmarked squad car — J. Lohse and A. Gourineri; on foot — E. Thompson, E. Alwill, A. Hurtado, and J. Martinez; stationed in Mrs. Gertrude Kaplan's apartment — C. Conry; command car — Lieutenant R. Coles, Sergeant T. Byrnes, and the author.

Lieutenant Coles and Sergeant Byrnes planned this day's strategy carefully, as shown in the following dialogue excerpted from the author's tapes:[68]

BYRNES: "I want to run two vehicles — the van and the squad car. I want the van right here (pointing to the intersection of Bedford and Clarkson avenues). This will be his post. And run the squad car, this post (pointing to the intersection of Nostrand and Parkside avenues). Rogers Avenue will be their common avenue. They will be responsible for the side streets.

"We'll run two girl's together, Eileen Thompson and Ellen Alwill. They'll cover Lenox to Nostrand on foot.

"Abe Hurtado and Julio Martinez will cover Linden Boulevard, from Bedford to Nostrand avenues."

COLES: "You say that you are going to run the two girls. Are you going to run them as decoys?"

BYRNES: "No, straight. They'll work the opposite sides of the street. I would prefer that they work on opposite sides of the street."

COLES: "In this way, they'll be in sight of each other at all times? They should be no farther than a block apart."

BYRNES: "Yes."

COLES: "How are you going to handle communcations?"

BYRNES: "They'll all have portables. We'll direct from the command car."

COLES: "You're going to have four on foot and four in vehicles. Why do you want to go up Clarkson?"

BYRNES: "Because we've had at least three hits on Clarkson. When he's been hitting and dodging, this is what he does. He hits about a block out. He hits Lenox, then he goes to Clarkson. He hits Linden and then he goes to Clarkson. Then he goes the other way; he goes down to Linden."

COLES: "Where does Kaplan live?"

BYRNES: "306 Lenox. Now what I want to do with her is to put Carol (Conry) inside. I want Carol to stay with the woman.

"The alternative to the Rogers Avenue common denominator is to switch the vehicles to Lenox Avenue."

COLES: "No. Leave it the way you have it. The two girls will be walking on Lenox.

"How are you going to cover the area between Flatbush and Bedford avenues?"

BYRNES: "We only have a few hits in this area; nothing like Clarkson. The surveillance teams can provide adequate coverage. They will be responsible for those streets."

COLES: "Okay. Let's brief them and get them out there."

Byrnes assembled the teams in the operations room and briefed them on the day's activities. Coles told the team, "We have a theory that this fellow is beginning to double back on his victims. He's come back on two so far, and we think that he'll be hitting a few more. We did some checking, and we believe that he might come back to the Kaplan apartment. That's why Carol is going in there.

"I also have a gut feeling that this guy may be using the mailmen along the route as some sort of an indicator as to when the elderly will leave their apartments. They seem to have a habit of meeting the mailman for their checks or for letters from relatives. I have a feeling that he is hitting these people a few minutes before the mailman gets to the building. You can usually set your watch by some of them. So when you are out on the street and you see a mailman in the neighborhood, keep an eye on him. Our guy may be in the vicinity.

"Keep in mind what he did to the Bailey woman. She went shopping and returned to her apartment. He didn't follow her into the building. He went into the building between the time she came home and the time the mailman got there. Later, Mrs. Bailey came down and met the mailman. He came in behind her when she returned to her apartment."[69]

Byrnes said, "I have two other things. Eileen this is for you. The mailman gets to 181 Lenox about 12:30 PM. He usually finishes about 12:55 PM. He may vary his time by five minutes, so you can judge just about where he will be at that time. We don't have a schedule on Linden, so you'll have to play it by ear."[70]

Coles said, "I did a time check on Lenox Road and Linden Boulevard with Sergeant Fitzpatrick yesterday. On Lenox Road your prime time is between noon and 1:00 PM; most of the hits there have been at this time. He's hit on Linden Boulevard a little later, but not much."

Byrnes said, "Also, if the 10-20 does come over, we don't want you to respond to the signal. We'll give you the information over the radio, switch to channel one, and we'll get everything over. It makes no sense to have everybody on the scene trying to pick up bits of information when the guy is escaping.

"Have enough smarts to stay out there, pick up the description, and start looking for people out on the perimeter. If he hits somewhere on Lenox or Linden, he's not going to stick around, he's going to get out of there."

Coles told the team, "I left orders with the task force this morning that if a 10-20 occurs in that area, at least one of the cars (uniformed patrol) assigned to the seventy-first must respond to the location, and we'll give out the description.

"As the sergeant said, if it does go down, don't go flocking to the location because you will do us no good there. If we need a search of the building we'll call you. You have to hit the perimeter. Go to some of the streets and to some of the places that you think he may be.[71]

Sergeant Byrnes said, "Keep in mind he might be changing clothes. He's not going to keep the same shirt on. He might take it off, change it, or go barechested, or whatever. A 250 is definitely in order at that particular point; we've heightened your reasonable cause to believe that a crime has been committed, so there's no problem. That's it, I don't have anything else. I would like to get them out there."[72]

The teams moved into position at 11:45 AM.

At 1:15 PM, Thompson spotted a youth who fit the description of the Silk Stocking Robber. At the time she spotted the man, Thompson was on the roof of 181 Lenox. Alwill was at the other end of Lenox and could not continue the surveillance. As he moved out of Thompson's area, J. Lohse, and A. Gourineri made contact and kept him in sight until he entered a building at 99 Ocean Avenue. In the meantime, Lieutenant Coles and Sergeant Byrnes moved to the vicinity of the building. After the youth entered, Sergeant Byrnes and the author went in after him. Byrnes made a floor-to-floor search of the building and spoke to several of the tenants, showing them a sketch of the suspect. They were not able to identify him.

During the search, Lieutenant Coles had a view of the front entrance to the building; J. Lohse and his partner were parked near the rear entrance. After thirty minutes Coles told Byrnes to discontinue the search.

At 1:28 PM, Alwill spotted a youth who matched the general description of the Silk Stocking Robber. She followed him for several blocks. He entered the building at 1271 Nostrand Avenue.

Thompson joined her at the front entrance of the building. The two officers entered the building and began a floor-to-floor search for the youth. Thompson rang some doorbells but received no response. At one apartment, Number 3-C, no one answered, but she heard noises inside. Coles told Thompson to keep the apartment under surveillance.

At 2:00 PM, Hurtado called Lieutenant Coles and reported that he spotted a youth running from 227 Linden Boulevard and got into a waiting Gypsy cab, license 693 ZAT. Hurtado told Coles that some apartments in the building have the blinds drawn. Coles directed Hurtado to continue on his surveillance of the area and told him that he was going to send a uniformed police patrol unit from the seventy-first precinct to check the building.

At 2:40 PM, the base radio dispatcher reported that two suspicious males were in the building at 181 Lenox Road. Byrnes asked for a confirmation. After he received it he asked if SCRU people were at the scene, and the dispatcher reported that SCRU people were there. Byrnes proceeded to the building. On the way to the scene, Detective Knox, who was on surveillance duty in the area, spotted the command car. He called Lieutenant Coles and told him that no further action was required at 181 Linden. He explained that he had responded to the call along with other members of the SCRU team. A tenant told them that the suspects left the area before the police arrived.

At 3:05 PM, Byrnes parked the command car approximately forty feet from the entrance to Kings County Hospital. From this vantage point they could observe people leaving and entering the premises. Coles reasoned that the suspect could have some connection with the hospital. A person having access to hospital records could easily obtain names, addresses, apartment numbers, and other information about potential victims. The surveillance produced no results, and Lieuteant Coles terminated operations at 4:17 PM.

At SCRU headquarters, Coles, Byrnes, and Fitzpatrick conducted a thorough review of each team's activities during the course of this day's surveillance. Lieutenant Feminella conducted a similar review of the twelfth zone detectives activities. On Monday, Coles and Feminella would confer with police administrators regarding the next course of action to be taken in the continuing search for the Silk Stocking Robber.

This day also marked the conclusion of the author's *On The Spot* study of the senior citizen robbery unit. On Monday, August 6, 1979, preparations were completed for the return trip to Minnesota. All subsequent information and data have been made available to the author by Sergeant Byrnes and Officer Noblin.

Because of the lack of necessary manpower, and because of the continuing need for police surveillance in Brooklyn South's other high-crime areas, police administrators decided to discontinue the active decoy and anti-crime activities of the search. On Monday, August 6, 1979, therefore, the decoy teams were to resume normal operations. The street phase of the search was to be conducted as part of the teams' routine activities in the affected precincts.

The investigative phase of the search, however, was to be continued. Noblin and DiCostanzo were to remain on assignment with the twelfth detective zone. Sergeant Byrnes was to divide his activities between the SCRU and the twelfth detective zone.

Officer DiCostanzo and Detective Rango continued their efforts to trace the pint bottle of Canadian Club whiskey through its liquor tax stamp number. After failing to obtain any information from several local distributors, they contacted Agent D. Hatcher of the Alcohol, Tobacco, and Firearms Bureau for assistance. A few days later Agent Hatcher telephoned Rango and told him that the whiskey was bottled in Canada, and that after it came out of bond it could have been sent to anyone of seventeen distributors, none of which was in the New York City area. The nearest distributor was in Pennsylvania.

Although the whiskey bottle was retained as evidence in the crime pattern case file, the attempt to identify the store where it was purchased was not actively pursued after August, 6, 1979.

As part of the continuing investigation of the crime pattern cases, Lieutenant Coles and Sergeant Byrnes instructed the team to review the SCRU case file on all push-in robberies that had been committed since the inception of the unit. They reasoned that if the robber had been active in the area during recent years, he might have used the same *modus operandi*, or he might have been arrested after committing a similar robbery.

During the review of the 1978 and 1977 cases, DiCostanzo recalled that he had arrested two criminals who had committed push-in robberies in the Brooklyn South area. A review of cases for the year 1977 disclosed that DiCostanzo arrested Fred Medford and James Rollins for a number of robberies committed against elderly citizens. An associate of these criminals, Frank Downing, was arrested by SCRU Investigator Fitzgerald for the commission of similar crimes.

A subsequent investigation by Detectives Knox, McManus, and Rango, and Officer DiCostanzo disclosed the following:

1. The *modus operandi* used by these criminals is the same as that which is being used by the Silk Stocking Robber.
2. The three men lived in an apartment, with a possible fourth unknown suspect, at 38 Saint Francis Place in Brooklyn.
3. Two of the three arrested were charged by the Brooklyn Grand Jury with forty-three counts of robbery, seventeen counts of burglary, and fourteen counts of grand larceny. All of these crimes were committed against the elderly citizens.
4. All are incarcerated at present.[74]

Upon receiving this information, Lieutenant Coles told the team members to concentrate their efforts on locating the possible fourth unknown suspect.

On Thursday, August 9, 1979, Detective Knox went to the Atlantic House of Detention in Brooklyn to interview James Rollins. Rollins told Knox that he knew the person being sought by the police. He gave Knox a description of the man and said, "I told that stupid bastard to stop a long time ago!"[75] Rollins then declined to divulge any further information without advice of counsel.

Later that afternoon Sergeant Byrnes and the team were informed by Assistant District Attorney Fogelson that Rollins was serving a five- to fifteen-year term and was awaiting additional sentencing for robbing senior citizens.

Mr. Fogelson told Rollins' attorney, Mr. Ira Drezner, that his client had made certain statements to the police.

On August 13, 1979, Detective Rango received a phone call from Mr. Paul Beltram, the attorney for Alvin Boland, a suspect Rango had wanted to interview. Mr. Beltram wanted to know the reason why he wanted to speak to his client and whether Boland was the subject of a police investigation. After being assured that his client was not under investigation, he agreed to the interview.

On August 14, 1979, Rango and DiCostanzo interviewed Boland

in the office of his attorney, Mr. Beltram. Boland told the officers that he had no knowledge of the push-in robberies in the Flatbush section of Brooklyn, that he seldom frequents the area, and that he did not have any friends there. Although the officers were not convinced that Boland was telling the truth, they were satisfied with the interview because they had gotten a good look at Boland, and they agreed that he fitted the general description of the Silk Stocking robber.

On August 17, 1979, Rango received a call from James Rollins. He asked Rango to contact his minister, Mr. Jesse Jordan, at 349-4629. He told Rango that Mr. Jordan operates the Freedom House at 714 Twenty-fifth Street in Brooklyn, and that he, Rollins, wanted to participate in Mr. Jordan's program.

Rango told Rollins that he could not comply with his request because he had already been sentenced to prison. He asked Rollins if he was willing to reveal the name of the suspect who had been committing the push-in robberies in Brooklyn South. He also asked Rollins why he was so certain that he knew the identity of the suspect. Rollins replied, "I've seen him in action, and I know how he operates. If you people don't help me, I'll have to do my time and jail, and I'll take the information you want upstate with me!"[76]

It was obvious that Rollins wanted to trade the information for his freedom or for a lesser sentence, but Rango knew that he could not offer such concessions.

On August 20, 1979, Rango and DiCostanzo visited Mr. Jordan at the Freedom House. The officers informed him that James Rollins had called them and asked that they speak with him. Rango told Mr. Jordan that James was withholding certain information from the police and that he would release it only if he were allowed to participate in the Freedom House program. DiCostanzo asked Mr. Jordan if he was willing to assist the police in obtaining the needed information. He told him that if Rollins cooperated, the police and the district attorney will help him to adjust to his life in prison. Mr. Jordan said that he was not feeling well at the moment, but that he would try to visit with Rollins next week. He promised to discuss the matter with Rollins.[77]

On Wednesday, August 22, 1979, Detective McManus called the Greenhaven State Prison officials and asked them to find out whether Mr. Frank Downing would agreed to be interviewed. He did agree. McManus and Noblin arrived at the Greenhaven Correctional Facility at approximately 12:00 M. Downing is serving eight to twenty-five years for robbery. All of the crimes were committed against elderly persons.

McManus asked Downing if he could identify the person with whom he, Rollins, and Medford shared an apartment at 38 Saint Francis Place in Brooklyn. Downing told him that he knew a person named John Motts, who lived with them during the time Rollins and Medford were committing push-in robberies in Brooklyn. When McManus asked him if Motts was involved in any of these crimes or if he had ever been arrested, Downing refused to comment.[78]

On the return trip to Brooklyn, McManus and Noblin decided to initiate a search for John Motts. Later that afternoon they discussed the Downing interview with DiCostanzo and Rango. The officers agreed that an effort should be made to locate Motts.

On Thursday, August 23, 1979, DiCostanzo and Rango went to the Brooklyn Supreme Court to meet with Rhoda Siegal, the attorney for Frank Downing. Mrs. Siegel was not able to meet with them because of previous court committments. She did leave word with her secretary, however, that she would call Rango later in the day. At approximately 3:30 PM, Mrs. Siegal reached Rango at the SCRU office to tell him that John Motts was Alvin Boland.[79]

Although the police now knew the identity of the possible fourth suspect in the 1977 push-in robberies, they could not assume without physical evidence or eyewitness testimony that he was directly involved in these crimes or that he was the suspect in the crime pattern cases.

The mere fact that Boland lived with the three criminals who are at present incarcerated for committing the 1977 push-in robberies is insufficient evidence to allow the police to detain him for questioning. To obtain a warrant for his arrest was not possible at this time because of the probable cause restrictions of the Fourth Amendment. The only physical evidence in the possession of the police that could link Boland to the crime pattern cases were the two sets of no value palmprints and a set of fingertip prints. The police could only wait until the suspect either makes a mistake or for a victim to identify him.

One factor that led the police to focus on Boland as a prime suspect in the present investigation was that he had lied to Rango and DiCostanzo during the interview on August 14, 1979. At that time, he told them that he seldom visited the Flatbush section of Brooklyn and had no friends in the area. This, and the fact that Downing said that Boland lived with them during the 1977 robberies,[80] suggests that he did know the area well and was familiar with the *modus operandi* of the perpertrators.

In some instances, Fourth Amendment protections tend to restrict the effectiveness of police work, in that a prime suspect to an investigation may not be detained except for probable cause. The following cases and events serve to illustrate this proposition.

On Tuesday, September 4, 1979, DiCostanzo and Rango went to 97 Ocean Avenue, Apartment 3C, to interview Cora Mitchell. Mrs. Mitchell was the victim of a crime committed on April 25, 1979, in which Alvin Boland is the subject under investigation. Mrs. Mitchell told the officers that at approximately 6:30 PM, a man rang the doorbell to her apartment. She approached the door and asked the caller to identify himself. The man said he was the plumber. He told her that he was there to repair the plumbing in the bathroom. Having had problems with the plumbing on an earlier occasion, she did not bother to look through the peephole so that she could make a positive identification. As she opened the door, a masked gunman forced his way inside and demanded money. She gave him all the money she had in her pocketbook. He said to her, "If you want to live, tell me where the rest of your money is!"[81] He then told her that he knew she had more money in the drawers, because he saw her put it there as he watched through the peephole.[82]

After she gave him the rest of her money, he ordered her to undress. He told her that he had to have sex with her "before catching a plane."[83] After she undressed, he put a blindfold over her eyes and told her to lie on the bed. At that moment someone rang the doorbell. As the suspect moved toward the door, Mrs. Mitchell began to scream. The suspect opened the door and ran out of the apartment. He took the stairway to the lobby.

As he ran to the front entrance of the building, the building security guard, Mr. Lawrence Hackwork, spotted him. Mr. Hackwork told the investigating officers that he knew the man. Alvin Boland was arrested by the seventy-first precinct detectives on July 22, 1979. He was charged with first-degree robbery, first-degree burglary, and attempted rape. He was able to post bond and was released on bail on July 23, 1979.

This case was not reported to SCRU because Mrs. Mitchell was thirty-five years old at the time of the assault. The unit does not assume jurisdiction in robbery cases unless the victim is a senior citizen. As a result, SCRU administrators were not aware of Boland's arrest or of his subsequent release.

In the meantime, the SCRU/twelfth detective zone teams that were assigned to the investigation of the crime pattern cases were encountering difficulties in their efforts to locate Boland. The investigators canvassed the tenants at the Saint Francis Place building and interviewed Boland's friends without success. On September 6, 1979, Rango and DiCostanzo called on Mrs. Dolly Baker and Mr. Judd Patterson, the superintendent and the handyman of the building at 191 Lenox Road. In separate interviews the officers asked them to view a lineup photo that included Alvin Boland, neither Mrs. Baker nor Mr. Patterson were able to identify him.[84]

It should be observed that 191 Lenox Road is the building in which Mary Bailey was robbed on May 9, 1979, and in which Mrs. Bailey and Mrs. Ruth Margolin were assaulted and robbed in separate incidents on August 2, 1979.

Of further interest is the fact that from the time Alvin Boland was released on bail on July 23, 1979, to the time he was remanded for trial on December 6, 1979, seven robberies against the elderly citizens, including the Bailey and Margolin assaults, were committed in the Brooklyn South area by an offender who used the same *modus operandi* as the Silk Stocking suspect. These cases, all of which were added to the crime pattern case file, are as follows (*see* Table 8-I).

In the Katz robbery, the victim was able to provide the police with a description of the suspect.

On Tuesday, October 30, 1979, SCRU administrators received information from seventy-first precinct detectives that a young black male, matching the description of the Silk Stocking robber, accosted and robbed a woman in the lobby of the building located at 109 Linden Boulevard.

On Wednesday, October 31, 1979, Noblin and McManus went to 115 Linden Boulevard to interview the victim, a black, thirty-year-old woman named Anjane Powell. McManus told Mrs. Powell that the investigation of her case was being conducted by the sev-

TABLE 8-I

CRIME PATTERN CASE FILE

Date	Day	Time	Victim	Location	Precinct	Precinct Complaint	SCRU No.
July 24	Tues.	1630	Harriet Loesser	252 Sterling St	78	4495	405
July 25	Wed.	2045	Irene Selzman	182 Linden Blvd.	67	7257	408
Aug. 21	Tues.	1330	Rose Bernstein	2701 Dorchester	70	9421	448
Oct. 8	Mon.	1400	Ida Kurtz	372 E. 17th St.	70	11577	538
Oct. 22	Mon.	1665	Lillian Katz	1781 Newkirk Ave.	70	12018	559

enty-first precinct detective squad. The purpose of this visit, he explained, was to obtain a detailed description of her assailant.

After reviewing some of the details of the robber, Mrs. Powell described the suspect as a dark-complexioned American black, approximately twenty to twenty-five years old, and about five feet eleven inches tall. She also recalled that he had close-cropped hair and that he was wearing a black leather jacket, black turtleneck sweater, and dark trousers. She told the officers that she was certain that she could identify the suspect either from photos or from a police lineup. After further questioning she told them that a friend of hers, named Melanie, was approached, apparently by the same person, in the lobby of her building on Friday, October 26, 1979. She said that Melanie had told her that a man fitting the description of her assailant spoke to her for a few minutes and then had tried to rob her.

Her friend had fled and returned to her apartment several hours later. She had not reported the incident to the police. When Noblin asked Mrs. Powell if she could provide him with some additional information about her friend, she said that she knew her only by the name Melanie and that she lived at 130 Lenox Road.

Later in the day, Noblin and McManus went to 152 Lenox Road to interview Miss Bettina Cumberbatch, a twenty-two-year-old black woman, regarding an attempted robbery.

Miss Cumberbatch told the officers that as she approached the fifth-floor landing in the building located at 130 Lenox Road, a man in his early twenties tried to rob her pocketbook. He fled when a tenant heard her screams and came out of his apartment. She said that the incident occurred at approximately 7:25 PM on October 25, 1979. She described her assailant as an American black, about five feet nine inches tall, thin oval face, dark skin, and slim in build. He was wearing a dark cap, dark jacket, and dark trousers.

She agreed to provide the department artist with a description of her assailant; on November 1, 1979, she accompanied the officers to Manhattan central for that purpose. The artist's sketch of the suspect is illustrated in Figure 8-6.

On Tuesday, November 6, 1979, Noblin and McManus went to 130 Lenox Road in an attempt to locate Mrs. Powell's friend, Melanie. After canvassing several tenants they located Melanie Krebs who lived in Apartment 5B. Visiting Mrs. Krebs at the time of the interview was her friend Dorothy Gilbert. Mrs. Gilbert lived at 231 Hawthorne Street.

Mrs. Gilbert told the officers of an incident that occurred on Friday, October 20, 1979, at approximately 7:30 PM. She recalled that as she walked through the lobby of 130 Lenox Road, an unidentified black man stopped her near the door and spoke to her for a few moments. She then continued out of the building and waited for her friend, Mrs. Krebs. The two women planned to go shopping.

Upon returning to the building a short time later, they found the police in the process of investigating the robbery of an elderly female. Mrs. Gilbert had not mentioned the incident to the police because she did not connect the young man to the robbery. Noblin asked her to view a number of photos and sketches. She selected sketches numbered 376 and 377 as fitting the description of the man who spoke to her that evening. This is the same person who was described by Miss Cumberbatch as the man who tried to rob her at that address on October 25, 1979.

Noblin and McManus then went to 103 Linden Boulevard to interview Mr. Romuald Carson in connection with the Anjane Powell robbery. Mr. Carson told officers that on the night of the robbery he was standing outside his residence when he observed the suspect coming from the direction of Mrs. Powell's building. After describing the suspect, Noblin showed him a number of photos and sketches. Mr. Carson chose sketches numbered 376 and 377 as fitting the description of the person he saw that evening.

THE ABOVE IS A SKETCH RESEMBLING A SUSPECT, SOUGHT FOR ATTEMPTED
ROBBERY IN THE 71ST PRECINCT ON OCTOBER 25th 1979 AT APPOX 1925
HOURS. SUBJECT ALSO WANTED FOR QUESTIONING IN CONNECTION WITH
PUSH-IN ROBBERIES OF SENIOR CITIZEN'S IN THE 67TH & 71ST PCT'S

THIS SKETCH IS BASED ON A DESCRIPTION, SUPPLIED BY A WITNESS
DESCRIPTION AS FOLLOWS.
Male/black/5'8 - 5"10"/150-160 Lbs./22-25yrs old/dark complexion
black short croped hair/small narrow eyes/stud earring in right
ear/pencil type mustache/slight bags under eyes.

ANYONE WITH ANY INFORMATION PLEASE CONTACT; PO ROBERT NOBLIN
OR PO JOSEPH DICOSTANZO - SENIOR CITIZEN ROBBERY UNIT, BKLYN
SOUTH-UF 61 # 17933 & PATTERN CASE # 1 TELEPHONE # 627-6643.

POLICE DEPT.
CITY OF NEW YORK

Figure 8-6. This department sketch of the Silk Stocking Robber was given to the artist by Miss Cumberbatch — a victim of the robber.

Noblin and McManus discussed their findings with Sergeant Byrnes, and the three officers agreed that man might be the Silk Stocking Robber. The files on the cases were set aside for further review.[84]

On December 6, 1979, Boland surrendered himself for trial in Superior Court, Brooklyn. On December 7, 1979, he was found guilty of robbery, burglary, and of the attempted rape of Cora Mitchell.

Boland was remanded to the Atlantic House of Detention in Brooklyn. While awaiting sentencing he appealed his conviction on the grounds that his attorney was incompetent. On this appeal he was released on January 8, 1980, pending a new trial. Some of the police officers involved in this investigation had doubts that Boland would ever be brought to trial on these charges again. They did know, however, that there were no reported push-in robberies in which the offender used the same *modus operandi* as the Silk Stocking Robber while Boland was in jail.

Even more frustrating to the police was the fact that Boland disappeared completely as soon as he was released.

On February 15, 1980, Margaret Shapley an eighty-one-year old widow was the victim of a push-in robbery. An investigation of this crime revealed that the offender used the same *modus operandi* as the Silk Stocking Robber.

On March 14, 1980, another elderly woman, Harriet Saffer, was robbed of 120 dollars and of a gold chain that contained six diamonds. An investigation of this crime disclosed that, once more, the offender used the same *modus operandi* as the Silk Stocking Robber.

During this period Noblin and McManus, as well as other members of the team, continued the search for the suspect. At one point during the search, Noblin and McManus contacted Boland's lawyer. The officers told him that they had not been able to contact his client and asked for his assistance in this matter. According to Noblin, the lawyer was not very cooperative. His answers to their questions were vague and evasive. Finally, he told them that Boland lived at 610 Stone Avenue. This information proved to be false. A canvass of the tenants of that building by Noblin and McManus disclosed that the suspect had never lived there.

Perhaps because of a mental lapse, however, the lawyer did provide them with the information they needed. During the interview he told them that his clients had been able to find occasional odd jobs at various hamburger establishments in Brooklyn and in Manhattan. Then, in discussing some other places where Boland had been employed, he mentioned that he had worked in a nursing home in Manhattan.

Noblin and McManus decided to concentrate their efforts on a canvass of nursing homes in that borough. After several days they visited the Hudson View Manor, a nursing home at 1403 Riverside Drive. The owner and operator of the home, Mr. Joseph Stender, verified Boland's being a former employee.

Noblin asked Mr. Stender to notify the SCRU office immediately if Boland contacted him. Two days later Boland visited the nursing home and asked Stender for a job. Stender told him that a position might be available in the next few days, but that he was not certain of it yet. Boland said that he would return. After he left, Stender called Sergeant Fitzpatrick and told him what had happened. Fitzpatrick asked him to hire Boland, and Stender agreed to cooperate.

Fitzpatrick asked Stender to let him know when Boland returned. On Monday, May 19, 1980, Boland appeared at the nursing home office. He filled out an application for employment, had his photograph and fingerprints taken, and was told to report to work the next morning. On Tuesday morning, May, 20, 1980, Alvin Boland was arrested by Officer DiCostanzo and other team members outside the Hudson View Manor nursing home on Riverside Drive. He was taken to the office of the Brooklyn District Attorney for the purpose of a corporal identification. At the district attorney's office Boland's palmprint was taken, and he was then moved to the lineup room. At the subsequent lineup, Margaret Shapley, one of Boland's most recent victims, could not make a positive identification of the prisoner.[85]

Officer Hagenlocker of the latent fingerprint unit made a positive identification of Alvin Boland. The palmprint taken May 20, 1980, matched the palmprint that was found on the refrigerator door in the apartment of Harriet Loesser. Mrs. Loesser had been assaulted and robbed on July 24, 1979. As a result of this positive identification, Boland was charged with the crimes of robbery, burglary, assault, unlawful imprisonment, and criminal possession of stolen property, on the complaint of Harriet Loesser, of 1979, of the seventy-eighth precinct, SCRU case number 405.[86]

At the time of his arrest Boland was wearing a gold chain containing six diamonds. This jewelry was positively identified by Mrs. Harriet Saffer as taken from her on March 14, 1980. Boland also had on his person a business card from Jayson Jewelers, located at Seventh Avenue and West Forty-third Street, Manhattan. On Monday, May 26, 1980, DiCostanzo interviewed the proprietor of Jayson Jewelers, Mr. Claude Schecter. He told DiCostanzo that Boland had been a regular customer at his establishment for more than a year.

He said that Boland would come into his establishment two or three times a week either to sell or to buy jewelry. Schecter described him as a big spender, the type who would buy twelve gold chains valued at 250 to 300 dollars each. Schecter also admitted that he had altered jewelry for Boland. On several occasions he had cleaned off old engravings on some jewelry and etched new inscriptions on them. Approximately four weeks ago Boland had tried to sell him a gold chain containing six diamonds. Schecter did not tell DiCostanzo why he did not buy the chain.[87]

On May 29, 1980, Boland, while in custody, was arrested by DiCostanzo for criminal possession of stolen property in connection with the Harriet Saffer robbery of March 14, 1980. Mrs. Saffer was unable to identify Boland in a second lineup, which was held at the district attorney's office on June 19, 1980.[88]

On August 29, 1980, Officer Hagenlocker of the latent fingerprint unit informed DiCostanzo that he had made a positive identification of Boland's prints with those found on the outer panel of the door to Mary Bailey's apartment. Although the evidence in the various cases might seem to be utterly convincing, the fingerprint identification could not be used as evidence against Boland because they were found on the outer panel of the door. Mary Bailey was not able to make a photo identification of the suspect. At the time of this inquiry, the ninety-two-year-old woman was in a nursing home and was not capable of attending a lineup. The district attorney advised DiCostanzo not to arrest Boland for the Bailey push-in robberies.

The Mary Bailey cases, U.F. 61 #7494, 1979, 71 Precinct, SCRU case #266, and U.F. #61 12721, 1979, 71 Precinct, SCRU case #419 were marked closed on August 29, 1980.[89]

On February 16, 1981, Alvin Boland went to trial in the Supreme

Court of Kings County in the borough of Brooklyn. He was convicted, upon verdict after trial, of the following charges:

Robbery, first-degree.
Sentence: twelve-and-one-half years to twenty-five years.
Burglary, second-degree.
Sentence: seven-and-one-half years to fifteen years.
Assault, second-degree.
Sentence: three-and-one-half years to seven years.
Unlawful imprisonment, first-degree.
Sentence: two years to four years.
Criminal possession of a weapon, fourth-degree.
Sentence: one year (maximum).

The sentences were to be served consecutively, and, therefore, Boland must serve a minimum of seventeen years in prison before he may apply for a parole hearing.

NOTES

1. Author's notes, June 15, 1979.
2. Author's notes, June 20, 1979.
3. *Ibid.*, June 20, 1979.
4. Author's notes, June 22, 1979.
5. *Ibid.*, June 22, 1979.
6. Author's notes, June 25, 1979.
7. Author's notes, June 26, 1979.
8. *Ibid.*, June 26, 1979.
9. *Ibid.*, June 26, 1979.
10. Author's notes, June 27, 1979, Lieutenant Coles — Interview.
11. *Ibid.*, June 27, 1979, Lieutenant Coles — Interview.
12. *Ibid.*, June 27, 1979.
13. *Ibid.*, June 27, 1979.
14. *Ibid.*, June 27, 1979.
15. *Ibid.*, June 27, 1979.
16. New York Police Department Report, Form P.D. 313-081a, Precinct 71, Complaint No. 10753, June 27, 1979, p. 1.
17. *Ibid.*, p. 1.
18. *Ibid.*, p. 2.
19. Author's notes, June 27, 1979.
20. Author's notes, June 28, 1979.
21. *Ibid.*, June 28, 1979.
22. Author's notes, June 29, 1979.
23. Author's notes, July 3, 1979.

24. *Ibid.*, July 3, 1979.
25. *Ibid.*, July 3, 1979.
26. *Ibid.*, July 3, 1979.
27. New York Police Department Report, Form P.D. 313-081a, Precinct 67, Complaint No. 6383, July 3, 1979, Dattolico.
28. New York City P.D. Complaint No. 6383, Dattolico Interview, p. 1.
29. New York City P.D., Complaint No. 6383, July 3, 1979, Noblin Interview, July 9, 1979, p. 2.
30. Author's notes, July 5, 1979.
31. *Ibid.*, July 5, 1979.
32. *Ibid.*, July 5, 1979.
33. *Ibid.*, July 5, 1979.
34. *Ibid.*, July 5, 1979.
35. *Ibid.*, July 5, 1979.
36. Author's notes, July 6, 1979.
37. *Ibid.*, July 6, 1979.
38. Author's tapes, July 9, 1979.
39. *Ibid.*, July 9, 1979.
40. Author's notes, July 10, 1979.
41. New York City Police Department Report Form, P.D. 313-081a, Precinct 71, Complaint Nos. 11521, 11522, July 11, 1979, Noblin Interview, p. 1.
42. *Ibid.*, p. 2.
43. Author's notes, July 12, 1979.
44. New York City Police Department Report Form, P.D. 313-081a, Precinct 71, Complaint No. 11580, July 17, 1979, Noblin interview, p. 1.
45. *Ibid.*, p. 1.
46. Author's tapes, July 12, 1979.
47. Author's tapes, July 13, 1979.
48. *Ibid.*, July 13, 1979.
49. New York City Police Department Report Form, P.D. 313-081a, Precinct 71, Complaints Nos. 11521 and 11522, July 20, 1979, p. 1.
50. New York City Police Department Report Form, P.D. 313-081a, Precinct 71, Visit to Queens, SCRU, PBBS. SCRU, July 27, 1979, p. 1.
51. Author's notes, July 26, 1979.
52. New York City Police Department Report Form, P.D. 313-081a, Precinct 67, Complaint No. 7257, July 27, 1979, p. 1.
53. *Ibid.*, p. 1.
54. *Ibid.*, p. 1.
55. Author's notes, July 26, 1979.
56. New York City Police Department Report Form, P.D. 313-081a, PBBS-SCRU, Suspect Identification, July 27, 1979, p. 1.
57. Author's notes, July 26, 1979.
58. *Ibid.*, July 26, 1979.
59. *Ibid.*, July 26, 1979.
60. *Ibid.*, July 26, 1979.
61. *Ibid.*, July 26, 1979.

62. Author's notes, July 27, 1979.
63. *Ibid.*, July 27, 1979.
64. Author's notes, July 30, 1979.
65. Author's tapes, August 1, 1979.
66. Author's tapes, August 2, 1979.
67. *Ibid.*, tapes, August 2, 1979.
68. Author's tapes, August 3, 1979.
69. *Ibid.*, August 3, 1979.
70. *Ibid.*, August 3, 1979.
71. *Ibid.*, August 3, 1979.
72. *Ibid.*, August 3, 1979.
73. Author's notes, August 3, 1979.
74. New York City Police Department Report, Form P.D. 313-081a, Precinct 71, Complaint No. 3273, August 9, 1979, p. 1.
75. *Ibid.*, p. 1.
76. New York City Police Department Report, Form P.D. 313-081a, PBBS-SCRU, follow-up No. 57, August 20, 1979, p. 1.
77. *Ibid.*, p. 1.
78. New York City Police Department Report, Form P.D. 313-081a, PBBS-SCRU, follow-up No. 61, August 23, 1979, p. 1.
79. New York City Police Department Report, Form P.D. 313-081a, PBBS-SCRU, follow-up No. 62, August 24, 2979, p. 1.
80. New York City Police Department Report Form, P.D. 313-081a, PBBS-SCRU, DiCostanzo Report, August 1, 1980, p. 2.
81. New York City Police Department Report Form, P.D. 313-081a, follow-up No. 71, September 6, 1979, p. 1.
82. *Ibid.*, p. 1.
83. New York City Police Department Report, P.D. 313-081a, PBBS-SCRU, follow-up No. 74, September 6, 1979, p. 1.
84. New York City Police Department Report, P.D. 313-081a, PBBS-SCRU, follow-up 133, pp. 1-2.
85. DiCostanzo report, August 1, 1980, p. 1.
86. *Ibid.*, p. 1.
87. *Ibid.*, p. 3.
88. *Ibid.*, p. 1.
89. *Ibid.*, p. 1.

CHAPTER 9

CASE HISTORIES OF
SELECTED PERPETRATORS

$\mathbf{I}$N this chapter the author will discuss the criminal histories of twenty-five perpetrators who committed crimes against the elderly in the high-crime areas of Patrol Borough Brooklyn South from January 1977 through June 1981 and will develop from these records a profile of the typical area offender. The records of the criminals who are the subjects of this study were randomly selected by the author and Officer Robert Noblin from the files of the senior citizen robbery unit and from the Division of Criminal Justice Services (DCJS).

From this group, the author will take a random sample of fifteen criminal histories as a means of illustration. Among the factors to be examined are age, sex, and race of the offenders; age, race, and sex of the victims; crime or crimes committed; charges placed against the offenders; guilty pleas; convictions; sentences; and recidivism rates. Some of the data relating to the individual criminal's economic status, family history, and educational background were not made available to the author by the DCJS. The names and the New York State criminal identification (NYSID) numbers have been changed to protect the rights of the offenders. No other changes have been made in the crime data used in this study.

SELECTED CRIMINAL HISTORIES

Anthony Squires, Males, Black, 18 Years Old

NYSID: 4272446Z
Date of arrest: June 25, 1980
Crime: Robbery of female police decoy
Place of crime: Street

Charge(s): Personal grand larceny
            Criminal possession of stolen property
Date of birth: July 7, 1962
Place of birth: Brooklyn, New York
Occupation: Unemployed
Drug used: None
Modus operandi: Known to follow senior citizens
Handgun or other weapon involved: None
Relative notified: Mother
Complainant:
    Age:
    Sex: (Not applicable — police decoy)
    Race:

Criminal Record

Arrest Date (s) and Crime (s)	*Disposition*
August 21, 1979	
Robbery, second-degree	No disposition
Assault on non-participant during robbery	reported to Division of Criminal Justice Services
Criminal possession of stolen property	(DCJS).
	Corrections data: subject placed on probation on December 7, 1979. Discharged from probation on April 17, 1980.
April 9, 1980	
Attempted burglary, third-degree	Convicted upon a plea of guilty to the following charge: disorderly conduct.
	Date of sentence: April 9, 1980. Sentence: conditional discharge. Not arraigned on the following charge: attempted burglary, third-degree.
April 29, 1980	
Burglary, third-degree	Convicted upon a plea of
Grand larceny, third-degree	guilty of the following charge: disorderly conduct.

Date of Sentence: April 30, 1980.
Sentence: conditional discharge.

June 5, 1980
  Personal grand larceny, third-degree
  Possession of stolen property, third-degree

Convicted upon a plea of guilty to the following charge: attempted robbery, second-degree.
Date of sentence: November 13, 1980.
Sentence: probation (five years).
Maximum expiration date: November 12, 1985.

June 21, 1980
  Burglary, third-degree
  Possession of burglar tools

Court appearance: July 16, 1980.
Charges dismissed.

June 25, 1980
  Grand larceny, third-degree
  Possession of stolen property, third-degree

Convicted upon a plea of guilty to the following charge: petit larceny.
Date of sentence: July 16, 1980.
Sentence: 60 days (maximum).

December 3, 1980
  Personal grand larceny
  Grand larceny
  Possession of stolen property, second-degree
  Unauthorized use of vehicle
December 10, 1980
  Criminal trespass, second-degree
March 19, 1981
  Criminal trespass, third-degree

On February 23, 1981, a bench warrant for the subject's arrest was issued in criminal court, Kings County, Brooklyn.

No disposition reported to DCJS.

No disposition reported to DCJS.

Unlawful possession of
marijuana

A summary of Anthony Squires' criminal history is as follows:

Arrests — 9
Convictions — 5
Guilty pleas — 4
Dismissals — 1
Probation — 4
Prison sentences — 1
No dispositions reported — 3
Felonies — 12
Misdemeanors — 5
Other — 1

Ernest Bisset, Male, Black, 16 Years Old

Date of arrest: November 16, 1979
NYSID: 4681482J
Crime: Robbery of female police decoy
Place of crime: Vestibule in apartment building.
Charge(s): Personal grand larceny
            Criminal possession of stolen property
Date of birth: September 4, 1963
Place of birth: Port-au-Prince, Haiti
Occupation: Unemployed
Drug used: None
Modus operandi: None
Handgun or other weapon involved: None
Relative notified: Sister
Complainant:
    Age:
    Sex: (Not applicable — police decoy)
    Race:

Criminal Record

Arrest Date(s) and Crime(s)	*Disposition*
September 24, 1979	
Burglary, third-degree	These crimes were committed

Grand larceny, third-degree
Possession of stolen property,
second-degree

in Queens County, New York.
Bench warrant issued in criminal court, Queens County, December 3, 1979.

COMMENT: On March 12, 1981, the defendant was convicted in the Supreme Court, Queens County, upon a plea of guilty to the following charge: attempted burglary, third-degree. He was sentenced to serve from one to three years at the Elmira State Prison. This sentence was in full satisfaction of the following charges: burglary, third-degree; grand larceny, third-degree; and criminal mischief, fourth-degree. Bisset was admitted to the Elmira reception center on April 2, 1981.

November 16, 1979

Grand larceny, third-degree
Possession of stolen property,
third-degree

These crimes were committed in Kings County, Brooklyn.
Bench warrant issued in criminal court, Kings County.

COMMENT: On February 25, 1981, the defendant was convicted in criminal court, Kings County, upon a plea of guilty to the following charge: attempted grand larceny, third degree. He was sentenced to nine months imprisonment. This sentence was in full satisfaction of the following charge: criminal possession of stolen property, third-degree.

April 18, 1980

Reckless endangerment, second degree
Criminal possession of a weapon with intent to use
Disorderly conduct: fighting; violent behavior

These crimes were committed in Queens County. On April 21, 1980, he was convicted in criminal court, Queens County, upon a plea of guilty to the following charge: disorderly conduct: fighting, violent behavior. He was sentenced to serve ten days in jail. This sentence was in full satisfaction of the following charges: criminal possession of a weapon, fourth-degree;

resisting arrest; and menacing. He was not arraigned
for the following charge: reckless endangerment, second-
degree.

May 28, 1980
    Burglary, third-degree
    Possession of stolen property,
       second-degree
    Criminal mischief, fourth-
       degree

These crimes were committed
in Kings County, Brooklyn.
Bench warrant issued in criminal court, Kings County,
July 11, 1980.

COMMENT: On February 25, 1981, the defendant was convicted in criminal court, Kings County, upon a plea of guilty to
the following charge: possession of stolen property, third-degree.
He was sentenced to nine months imprisonment. This sentence
was in full satisfaction of the following charges: criminal mischief, fourth-degree.

October 10, 1980
    Attempted burglary, third-
       degree

This crime was committed in
Queen's County. This charge
was dismissed in criminal
court, Queens County, on
October 25, 1980.

October 21, 1980
    Petit larceny
    Possession of stolen property,
       third-degree

These crimes were comitted
in Bronx County, New York.
Bench warrant issued in criminal court, Bronx County,
November 8, 1980.

COMMENT: On February 11, 1981, the defendant was convicted in criminal court, Bronx County, upon a plea of guilty to
the following charges: attempted petit larceny and possession of
stolen property, third-degree. His sentence was limited to the
time he spent in jail while awaiting trial. This sentence was in full
satisfaction of the following charges: petit larceny and criminal
possession of stolen property, third-degree.

November 21, 1980
    Petit larceny

This crime was committed in

Newark, New Jersey. No disposition reported to DCJS.

February 4, 1981
  Theft of services

This crime was committed in Kings County, Brooklyn. On February 25, 1981, the defendant was convicted in criminal court, Kings County, upon a plea of guilty to the following charge: theft of services. He was sentenced to serve nine months in prison.

A summary of Ernest Bisset's criminal history is as follows:

Arrests — 8
Convictions — 6
Guilty pleas — 6
Dismissals — 1
Probation — 0
Prison sentences — 6
No disposition reported — 1
Felonies — 7
Misdemeanors — 8
Other — 2

James Dexter, Male, Black, 17 Years Old

Date of arrest: December 18, 1979
NYSID: 4495245H
Crime: Robbery of female police decoy
Place of crime: Street
Charges: Personal grand larceny, third-degree
        Criminal possession of stolen property, third-degree
        Resisting arrest
Date of birth: November 24, 1962
Place of birth: Trinidad
Occupation: Student
Drug used: Marijuana

Modus operandi: None
Relative notified: Mother
Complainant:
　　Age:
　　Sex:　(Not applicable — police decoy)
　　Race:

Criminal Record

Arrest Date(s) and Crime(s)　　　　　*Disposition*
December 18, 1979
　　Grand larceny, third-degree　　No disposition reported to
　　Resisting arrest　　　　　　　DCJS.
　　Possession of stolen property,　Corrections data: Dexter re-
　　　　third-degree　　　　　　ceived a sentence of 90 days
　　　　　　　　　　　　　　　　(maximum).

　　The following information represents a summary of the criminal history of James Dexter from December 18, 1979 to April 20, 1980:

　　Arrests — 1
　　Convictions — 1
　　Guilty pleas — 0
　　Dismissals — 0
　　Probation — 0
　　Prison sentences — 1
　　No disposition reported — 1
　　Felonies — 1
　　Misdemeanors — 2

Gregory Johnson, Male, Black, 20 Years Old

Date of arrest: October 1, 1980
NYSID: 3720102P
Crime: Attempted robbery — elderly citizen
Place of crime: Lobby of apartment building
Charges(s): Attempted robbery, third-degree
Date of birth: January 3, 1959
Place of birth: Spartanburg, South Carolina
Occupation: Unemployed

Drug used: None
Modus operandi: None
Handgun or other weapon involved: None
Relative notified: Mother
Complainant:
    Age: 72
    Sex: Male
    Race: Black

Criminal Record

Arrest Date(s) and Crime(s)   *Disposition*

January 10, 1975
    Attempted robbery, second-   Charge dismissed
        degree
January 23, 1975
    Forcible theft with use of   Subject was adjudicated a
        instrument   youthful offender. He was
    Criminal possession of a   convicted of the following
        weapon, fourth-degree   charges: robbery, first-degree;
    Possession of stolen property,   robbery, second-degree;
        third-degree   grand larceny, third-degree;
                                      criminal possession of a
                                      weapon, fourth-degree. No
                                      other information was avail-
                                      able from DCJS.

October 10, 1975
    Robbery, second-degree   Convicted upon a plea of
    Assault, second-degree   guilty to the following charge:
                                      harassment.
                                      Date of sentence: February 4,
                                      1976.
                                      No other information was
                                      available from DCJS.

April 26, 1980
    Menacing   No disposition reported to
    Harassment   DCJS.
    Disorderly conduct
October 1, 1980
    Attempted robbery,   Convicted on a plea of guilty

third-degree

to the following charge: harassment.
Sentence date: February 24, 1981.
Sentence: conditional discharge.

November 8, 1980
Robbery, first-degree
Criminal use of a firearm,
first-degree

The subject was not arraigned on the following charges: criminal use of a firearm, first-degree; criminal use of a firearm, second-degree.

April 24, 1981
Robbery, second-degree
Possession of stolen property,
third-degree

No disposition reported to DCJS.

May 5, 1981
Robbery, forcible theft with
deadly weapon
Assault with intent to cause
physical injury with
weapon
Criminal possession of a
weapon

No disposition reported to DCJS.

May 29, 1981
Robbery, second-degree
Assault, second-degree

No disposition reported to DCJS.

June 2, 1981
Robbery, second-degree

No disposition reported to DCJS.

The following is a summary of Gregory Johnson's criminal history from January 23, 1975 to June 2, 1981:

Arrests — 10
Convictions — 3
Guilty pleas — 2
Dismissals — 1
Probation — Not known
Prison sentences — Not known
No disposition reported -- 5

Felonies — 14
Misdemeanors — 4
Other — 2

Ramon Chacon, Male, Hispanic, 16 Years Old

Date of arrest: July 15, 1980
NYSID: 4309775N
Crime: Robbery of female police decoy
Place of crime: Street
Charge(s): Personal grand larceny
              Resisting arrest
Date of birth: June 6, 1964
Place of birth: Brooklyn, New York
Occupation: Student
Drug used: None
Modus operandi: None
Handgun or other weapon used: None
Relative notified: Mother
Complainant:
    Age:
    Sex: (Not applicable — police decoy)
    Race:

Criminal Record

Arrest Date(s) and Crime(s)	*Disposition*
Personal grand larceny, third-degree Resisting arrest	Convicted upon a plea of guilty to the following charge: attempted robbery, third-degree, July 21, 1980. Defendant was placed on probation for one year.

A summary of Ramon Chacon's criminal history is as follows:

Arrests — 1
Convictions — 1
Guilty pleas — 1
Probation — 1

Prison sentences — 0
No dispositions reported — 0
Felonies — 1
Misdemeanors — 1

Leonard Sipes, Male, Black, 17 Years Old

Date of Arrest: May 26, 1980
NYSID: 4416758Y
Crime: Robbery of an elderly male citizen
Place of crime: Lobby in apartment building
Charge(s): Robbery, second-degree
　　　　　　Assault, second-degree
Date of birth: December 8, 1962
Place of birth: Charleston, South Carolina
Occupation: Unemployed
Drug used: None
Modus operandi: None
Handgun or other weapon used: None
Relative notified: Mother
Complaint:
　Age:　85
　Sex:　Male
　Race: White

Criminal Record

Arrest Date(s) and Crime(s)
May 5, 1979
　Robbery, first-degree
　Burglary, first-degree
　Possession of stolen property,
　　second-degree
　Reckless endangerment, sec-
　　degree
　Resisting arrest
　Criminal mischief, fourth-
　　degree
　Criminal possession of a

Disposition

Conviction upon a plea of
guilty to unspecified charges.
May 8, 1979. Information on
charges and sentence received
not reported to DCJS. The
defendant was not arraigned
on the following charges: robbery, first-degree; burglary,
first-degree; and menacing.

weapon, fourth-degree
Menacing
January 25, 1980
Criminal possession of
weapon, third-degree
Possession of stolen property,
third-degree

Convicted upon a plea of guilty to an unspecified charge, January 30, 1980. Information on charge and sentence not reported to DCJS. The defendant was not arraigned on the following charges: criminal possession of a weapon, third-degree, and possession of stolen property, third-degree.

May 26, 1980
Robbery, second-degree
Assault, second-degree

No disposition reported to DCJS.

A summary of Leonard Sipes' criminal history is as follows:

Arrests — 3
Convictions — 2
Guilty pleas — 2
Probation — not known
Prison sentences — not known
No disposition reported — 3
Felonies — 4
Misdemeanors — 6

Laverne Davis, Female, Black, 16 Years Old

Date of Arrest: February 21, 1980
NYSID: 4428137R
Crime: Robbery of a female police decoy
Place of Crime: Vestibule in apartment building
Charges(s): Personal grand larceny
              Criminal possession of stolen property
Date of birth: October 25, 1963
Place of birth: Brooklyn, New York
Occupation: Student

Drug used: None
Modus operandi: None
Handgun or other weapon used: None
Relative notified: Sister
Complainant:
    Age:
    Sex: (Not applicable — police decoy)
    Race:

Criminal Record

Arrest Date(s) and Crime(s)	*Disposition*
February 21, 1980	
Personal grand larceny, third-degree Possession of stolen property, third-degree	The defendant was convicted upon a plea of guilty to the following charge: petit larceny on April 15, 1980. She was adjudicated a youthful offender and placed on probation for three years.
February 12, 1981	
Entered subway platform through open gate.	The defendant was caught by New York City Transit Authority Policeman. No disposition reported to DCJS.

A summary of Laverne Davis' criminal history is as follows:

Arrests — 2
Convictions — 1
Guilty pleas — 1
Probation — 1
Prison Sentences — 0
No disposition reported — 1
Felonies — 1
Misdemeanors — 1
Other — 1

Robert Santoro, Male, White, 26 Years Old

Date of arrest: March 10, 1980

NYSID: 3845078K
Crime: Robbery of elderly female citizen
Place of crime: Private residence
Charge(s): Robbery, first-degree
              Criminal possession of a weapon, fourth-degree
              Burglary, first-degree
Date of birth: September 30, 1953
Place of birth: New York, New York
Occupation: Unemployed
Drug used: Methadone
Modus operandi: None
Handgun or other weapon used: Revolver
Relative notified: Wife
Complainant:
    Age: 72
    Sex: Female
    Race: White

Criminal Record

Arrest Date(s) and Crime(s)	*Disposition*
November 18, 1972 Reckless damage to property	On January 15, 1973, the defendant was convicted upon a plea of guilty to the following charge: disorderly conduct. He was fined $50.
April 17, 1974 Criminal possession of controlled substance	On April 18, 1974, the defendant was convicted upon a plea of guilty to the following charge: disorderly conduct. The sentence was limited to time served in jail while awaiting trial.

March 10, 1980
    Robbery, first-degree
    Criminal possession of a
        weapon, fourth-degree
	No disposition reported to DCJS.

Burglary, first-degree

A summary of Robert Santoro's criminal history is as follows:

Arrests — 3
Convictions — 2
Guilty pleas — 2
Probation — 0
Prison sentences — Not known
No disposition reported — 1
Felonies — 2
Misdemeanors — 4

Thomas Samuels, Male, Black, 27 Years Old

Date of arrest: July 16, 1980
NYSID: 3186396
Crime: Criminal trespass
Place of crime: Private residence
Charge(s): Criminal trespass, second-degree
        Burglary, second-degree
        Criminal possession of weapon, fourth-degree
        Unlawful possession of marijuana
Date of birth: May 20, 1953
Place of Birth: Columbia, South Carolina
Occupation: Unemployed
Drug used: Cocaine
Modus operandi: None
Handgun or other weapon used: Gravity knife
Relative notified: Sister
Complainant:
    Age: 60
    Sex: Male
    Race: White

Criminal Record

Arrest Date(s) and Crime(s)	*Disposition*
July 25, 1969	
Break-in and entry, larceny	These crimes were committed in South Carolina. No dispo-

sition reported to DCJS.

November 11, 1969
  Burglary, third-degree

No disposition reported to DCJS.

April 22, 1970
  Burglary, third-degree

Charge was dismissed on October 15, 1970.

May 24, 1970
  Criminal possession of stolen property, second-degree

Charge was dismissed on May 27, 1970.

June 30, 1970
  Grand larceny, third-degree

On September 11, 1970, the defendant was convicted upon a plea of guilty on the following charge: grand larceny, third-degree. He was sentenced to serve three years (maximum) at Elmira State Prison. He was admitted to that institution on December 10, 1971.

November 15, 1971
  Burlgary, third-degree

On December 8, 1971, the defendant was convicted upon a plea of guilty to the following charge: criminal trespass, fourth-degree. His sentence was limited to the time served in jail while awaiting trial.

February 22, 1972
  Grand larceny auto, third-degree
  Possession of stolen property, first-degree
  Unauthorized use of a vehicle

On March 27, 1971, the defendant was convicted upon a plea of guilty to petit larceny. He was sentenced to serve six months (maximum) in prison.

May 23, 1973
  Robbery, first-degree

On June 6, 1973, the defendant was convicted upon a plea of guilty to the following charge: unspecified class D felony. He was sentenced to serve three years (maximum) in prison. He was admitted to Elmira State Prison on October 17, 1973. The prisoner was paroled on April 10, 1975.

August 7, 1973
Assault, second-degree

This crime was committed in Bronx County. The defendant was acquitted of this charge on December 4, 1973.

July 9, 1975
Grand larceny auto, third-degree
Criminal possession of stolen property, first-degree
Unauthorized use of a vehicle

On October 6, 1975, the defendant was convicted upon a plea of guilty to the following charge: robbery, third-degree. He was sentenced to serve two to four years in prison. Date of parole was not reported to DCJS.

July 30, 1975
Robbery, second-degree
Burglary, third-degree

No disposition reported to DCJS.

March 16, 1979
Grand larceny, third-degree
Possession of stolen property, third-degree

On September 11, 1979, the defendant was convicted upon a plea of guilty to the following charge: petit larceny. He was sentenced to serve nine months (maximum) in prison.

March 20, 1979
Burglary, third-degree
Petit larceny

On September 11, 1979, the defendant was convicted upon a plea of guilty to the following charge: petit larceny. He was sentenced to serve three months (maximum) in prison.

The prisoner was paroled on January 24, 1980.

May 16, 1980

Robbery, second-degree

Attempted robbery, second-degree

Assault, third-degree

Criminal possession of a controlled substance

No disposition reported to DCJS.

July 16, 1980

Burglary, second-degree

Criminal trespass, second-degree

Criminal possession of a weapon, fourth-degree

Unlawful possession of marijuana

No disposition reported to DCJS

A summary of Thomas Samuel's criminal history is as follows:

Arrests — 15
Convictions — 7
Guilty pleas — 7
Acquittals — 1
Probation — 0
Parole — 2
Prison sentences — 6
No disposition reported — 5
Felonies — 18
Misdemeanors — 7
Other — 1

Philip Thompson, Male, Black, 17 Years Old

Date of arrest: March 15, 1979
NYSID: 4493927J
Crime: Robbery of elderly female
Place of crime: Private residence
Charge(s): Robbery, first-degree
Burglary, second-degree
Grand larceny, third-degree

Date of birth: June 12, 1961
Place of birth: New York, New York
Occupation: Unemployed
Drug used: None
Modus operandi: None
Handgun or other weapon used: None
Relative notified: Mother
Complainant:
    Age: 78
    Sex: Female
    Race: White

Criminal Record

Arrest Date(s) and Crime(s)

March 14, 1979
    Robbery, first-degree
    Burglary, second-degree
    Criminal trespass, third-
        degree

Disposition

On June 22, 1979, the defendant was convicted upon a plea of guilty to the following charge: robbery, second-degree. He was sentenced to serve from 18 months to 54 months at Elmira State Prison. This sentence was in full satisfaction of the following crimes: burglary, second-degree; assault, second-degree; burglary, third-degree; grand larceny, third-degree; assault, third-degree; attempted petit larceny. He was taken to the Elmira reception center on July 12, 1979.

The defendant was not arraigned on the following charges: robbery, first-degree; and criminal trespass, third-degree.

March 15, 1979

Robbery, forcible theft with use of instrument
Burglary, second-degree
Grand larceny, third-degree

On June 22, 1979, the defendant was convicted upon a plea of guilty to the following charge: robbery, second-degree. He was sentenced to serve 2 to 6 years at Elmira State Prison. This sentence was in full satisfaction of the following charges: robbery, first-degree; burglary, second-degree; burglary, third-degree; and petit larceny. The defendant was not arraigned on the following charges: robbery, forcible theft with the use of instrument; burglary, second-degree; grand larceny, third-degree; and criminal possession of a weapon, fourth-degree.

A summary of Philip Thompson's criminal history is as follows:

Arrests — 2
Convictions — 2
Guilty pleas — 2
Probation — 0
Prison sentences — 2
No disposition reported — 0
Felonies — 5
Misdemeanors — 1

Edwina Windsor, Female, Black, 26 Years Old

Date of arrest: October 28, 1979
NYSID: 3319272Y
Crime: Robbery of elderly female
Place of crime: Street
Charge(s): Robbery, second-degree

Burglary, second-degree
Criminal possession of stolen property
Resisting arrest
Date of birth: November 26, 1953
Place of birth: Brooklyn, New York
Occupation: Unemployed
Drug used: None
Modus operandi: None
Handgun or other weapon used: None
Relative notified: Mother
Complainant:
  Age: 69
  Sex: Female
  Race: White

Criminal Record

Arrest Date(s) and Crime(s)	*Disposition*
October 6, 1971 Grand larceny, third-degree	No disposition reported to DCJS.
July 5, 1972 Petit larceny	On July 24, 1972, the defendant was acquitted of the following charge: petit larceny.

November 19, 1974
  Possession of a hypodermic
    instrument
  Disorderly conduct
	On November 11, 1974, the defendant was convicted upon a plea of guilty to the following charge: disorderly conduct. She was placed on probation for one year. This sentence was in full satisfaction of the following charge: possession of a hypodermic instrument.

November 16, 1976
  Assault, second-degree
  Resisting arrest
  Obstructing government
	A bench warrant was issued in criminal court, Kings County, on June 20, 1977.

administration
Disorderly conduct
October 28, 1979
　　Robbery, first-degree
　　Burglary, second-degree
　　Resisting arrest
　　Possession of stolen property,
　　　　third-degree

On October 31, 1979, the defendant was convicted upon a plea of guilty to the following charge: petit larceny. She was sentenced to a jail term of nine months (maximum). This sentence was in full satisfaction of the following charges: criminal trespass, second-degree, and resisting arrest. The defendant was not arraigned on the following charges: robbery, first-degree, and possession of stolen property, third-degree.

A summary of Edwina Windsor's criminal history is as follows:

Arrests — 5
Convictions — 2
Acquittals — 1
Guilty pleas — 2
Prison sentences — 0
Probations — 1
No dispositions reported — 1
Felonies — 4
Misdemeanors — 6
Other — 2

Mark Jackson, Male, Black, 19 Years Old

Date of arrest: April 3, 1979
NYSID: 4739028K
Crime: Robbery of elderly female
Place of crime: Lobby in apartment building
Charge(s): Robbery, second-degree
　　　　　Assault, third-degree
　　　　　Burglary, second-degree

Date of birth: June 28, 1959
Place of birth: Brooklyn, New York
Occupation: Unemployed
Drug used: None
Modus operandi: None
Handgun or other weapon involved: None
Relative notified: Brother
Complainant:
    Age: 60
    Sex: Female
    Race: White

Criminal Record

Arrest Date(s) and Crime(s)

November 19, 1976
    Robbery, second-degree
    Burglary, third-degree
    Petit larceny

April 3, 1979
    Robbery, second-degree
    Burglary, second-degree
    Assault, third-degree

Disposition

On December 9, 1976, the defendant was convicted upon a plea of guilty to the following charge: petit larceny. He was sentenced to serve a jail term of 6 months (maximum).

On October 17, 1979, trial was held in the Supreme Court, Kings County. The defendant was found guilty of assault, second-degree; robbery, second-degree; and burglary, second-degree. He was sentenced to a term of 28 months to 7 years for the assault, count and to terms of 4 to 12 years each for the robbery and burglary counts. The DCJS data did not indicate whether the sentences were to be served concurrently or consecutively. The following charge was dismissed: assault, third-degree.

A summary of Mark Jackson's criminal history is as follows:

Arrests — 2
Convictions — 2
Acquittals — 0
Dismissals — 1
Guilty pleas — 1
Prison sentences — 2
Probations — 0
No dispositions reported — 0
Felonies — 3
Misdemeanors — 2

Gary Chapman, Male, Black, 23 Years Old

Date of arrest: August 28, 1979
NYSID: 4608093L
Crime: Robbery of elderly female
Place of crime: Apartment of victim
Charge(s): Robbery, first-degree
  •   Burglary, second-degree
        Possession of stolen property, third-degree
Date of birth: August 15, 1956
Place of birth: Brooklyn, New York
Occupation: Unemployed
Drug used: None
Modus operandi: None
Handgun or other weapon involved: None
Relative notified: Mother
Complainant:
  Age: 69
  Sex: Female
  Race: White

Criminal Record

Arrest Date(s) and Crime(s)	*Disposition*
October 10, 1976	
Burglary, third-degree	On November 16, 1976, the
Possession of stolen property,	defendant was convicted upon
third-degree	a plea of guilty to the follow-

ing charges: trespass. He was placed on probation for one year. This sentence was in full satisfaction of the following charges: criminal possession of stolen property, third-degree and criminal trespass, third-degree.

July 27, 1979
    Burglary, third-degree
    Grand larceny, second-degree

A bench warrant was issued in criminal court, Kings County, on October 13, 1979.

August 28, 1979
    Robbery, first-degree
    Burglary, second-degree
    Possession of stolen property, third-degree

On October 31, 1979, the defendant was convicted upon a plea of guilty to the following charge: petit larceny. He was sentenced to serve a jail term of nine months (maximum). This sentence was in full satisfaction of the following charges: criminal trespass, second-degree, and resisting arrest.

He was not arraigned on the following charges: robbery, first-degree, and possession of stolen property, third-degree.

May 1, 1980
    Burglary, third-degree
    Grand larceny, third-degree

On May 22, 1980, the defendant was convicted upon a plea of guilty to the following charges: petit larceny. He was sentenced to a jail term of five months (maximum). This sentence was in full satisfaction of the following charge: criminal possession of stolen property, third-degree.

He was not arraigned on the

following charge: petit larceny.

May 4, 1981
    Robbery, third-degree   On May 16, 1981, the defen-
                                    dant was convicted upon a
                                    plea of guilty to the following
                                    charge: petit larceny. He was
                                    sentenced to serve a jail term
                                    of five months (maximum).

A summary of Gary Chapman's criminal history is as follows:

Arrests — 5
Convictions — 4
Dismissals — 0
Guilty pleas — 4
Prison sentences — 3
Probation — 1
No dispositions reported — 0
Felonies — 8
Misdemeanors — 2

Leroy Chisolm, Male, Black, 30 Years Old

Date of arrest: July 13, 1979
NYSID: 1384072H
Crime: Robbery of female police decoy
Place of crime: Vestibule in apartment building
Charge(s): Grand larceny, third-degree
           Possession of stolen property, third-degree
Date of birth: October 5, 1948
Place of birth: Charleston, South Carolina
Occupation: Unemployed
Drug used: None
Modus operandi: None
Handgun or other weapon involved: None
Relative notified: Sister
Complainant:
    Age:
    Sex: (Not applicable — police decoy)
    Race:

Criminal Record

Arrest Date(s) and Crime(s)	*Disposition*
January 13, 1967 Burglary	No disposition reported to DCJS.
February 3, 1967	No disposition reported to DCJS.
November 23, 1970 Burglary, third-degree Petit larceny	The defendant was not arraigned on the following charge: petit larceny. On December 16, 1970, the following charge was dismissed: burglary, third-degree.
February 29, 1972 Burglary, third-degree	The following charges were dismissed on November 11, 1972: criminal trespass, second-degree, and petit larceny.
May 3, 1973 Petit larceny	The defendant was acquitted of this charge on October 10, 1973.
August 7, 1973 Burglary, illegal entry with criminal intent	The following charges were dismissed on June 11, 1974: custodial interference, second-degree, and criminal trespass, second-degree.
December 15, 1974 Failure to pay for services: based on stealth. Public intoxication	On November 11, 1975, the defendant was convicted upon a plea of guilty to the following charge: attempt at misdemeanor. He was sentenced to serve a jail term of thirty days (maximum).

April 3, 1978

False alarm, third-degree

This charge was dismissed on May 1, 1978.

July 13, 1979

Grand larceny, third-degree
Possession of stolen property, third-degree

On November 15, 1979, the defendant was convicted upon a plea of guilty to the following charges: petit larceny, and possession of stolen property, third-degree. He was sentenced to thirty days (maximum) for each charge. The sentences were served concurrently.

February 16, 1981

Criminal trespass, second-degree

On February 16, 1981, the defendant was convicted on a plea of guilty to the following charge: trespass. The sentence was limited to time served while awaiting trial.

A summary of Leroy Chisolm's criminal history is as follows:

Arrests — 10
Convictions — 3
Dismissals — 4
Acquittals — 1
Guilty pleas — 3
Prison sentences — 2
No dispositions returned — 2
Repeat offences — 9
Felonies — 4
Misdemeanors — 5
Other — 1

Albert Hutmacher, Male, White, 17 Years Old

Date of arrest: February 8, 1979
NYSID: 4138708Q
Crime: Robbery of an elderly female

Place of crime: Lobby in apartment building
Charge(s): Grand larceny, third-degree
       Possession of stolen property, second-degree
Date of birth: February 2, 1962
Place of birth: Brooklyn, New York
Occupation: Unemployed
Drug used: None
Modus operandi: None
Handgun or other weapon involved: None
Relative notified: Mother
Complainant:
   Age: 63
   Sex: Female
   Race: White

Criminal Record

Arrest Date(s) and Crime(s)	*Disposition*
May 31, 1978	
Grand larceny, third-degree	These charges were dismissed
Possession of stolen property, second-degree	on June 22, 1979.
Unauthorized use of vehicle	
August 17, 1978	
Burglary, third-degree	On October 5, 1978, the defendant was convicted upon a plea of guilty to the following charge: criminal trespass, second-degree. He was placed on probation for three years.
December 18, 1978	
Criminal trespass, second-degree	The charge of criminal trespass was dismissed on December 18, 1978. The defendant was not arraigned on the charge of harassment.
Harassment	
February 8, 1979	
Grand larceny, third-degree	On April 10, 1979, the defendant was convicted upon a
Possession of stolen property,	

third-degree

plea of guilty to the following charge: petit larceny. He was sentenced to serve thirty days (maximum) at the New York City Correctional Institution for Men. This sentence was in full satisfaction for the charge of: criminal possession of stolen property, third-degree.

July 6, 1979

Burglary, third-degree
Grand larceny, second-degree
Possession of stolen property, first-degree
Criminal mischief, third-degree

On September 14, 1979, the defendant was convicted upon a plea of guilty to the following charge: petit larceny. He was sentenced to serve a nine-month (maximum) prison term. This sentence was in full satisfaction of the following charges: resisting arrest; criminal mischief, fourth-degree; criminal possession of stolen property, third-degree; and criminal trespass, third-degree.

August 3, 1979

Robbery, second-degree
Burglary, second-degree
Assault, second-degree

On August 13, 1979, the defendant was convicted upon a plea of guilty to the following charge: disorderly conduct. He was sentenced to a term of 100/15 (100 days maximum — 15 days minimum) days at the New York City Correctional Institution for Men. This sentence was in full satisfaction of the following charges: assault, third-degree; criminal trespass, sec-degree; and petit larceny.

September 24, 1980

Criminal possession of a weapon

Unspecified violation of local law

On September 24, 1979, the defendant was convicted upon a plea of guilty to the following charge: disorderly conduct. He was sentenced to a term of 100/30 (100 days maximum — 30 days minimum) days and an unspecified fine. This sentence was in full satisfaction of the following charge: criminal possession of a weapon, fourth-degree. He was not arraigned on the charge of: unspecified violation of local law.

May 5, 1981

Burglary, third-degree

Possession of burglar tools

No disposition reported to DCJS.

A summary of Albert Hutmacher's criminal history is as follows:

Arrests — 8
Convictions — 5
Dismissals — 2
Acquittals — 0
Guilty pleas — 5
Prison sentences — 5
No dispositions returned — 1
Felonies — 13
Misdemeanors — 3
Other — 2

A summary of the criminal histories of the twenty-five perpetrators selected for this study will serve as an example of the larger problems that exist in the high-crime areas of Brooklyn South. The summary is as follows:

Perpetrator:

Age: 18.5

Sex:

Male: 22
Female: 3
Race:
White: 3
American black: 18
West Indian black: 2
Hispanic: 2

Victim:
Age: 60-92
Sex:
Male: 6
Female: 13
Female Police Decoy: 6
Race:
White: 23
Black: 2
Hispanic: 0

Arrests: 193
Convictions: 101
Dismissals: 26
Bench warrants issued: 19
Number of criminals adjudicated as youthful offenders: 8
No disposition reported to Division of Criminal Justice
   Services: 39
Sentences imposed (including probations): 101
Probations: 23
Violations: 9
Paroles: 3
Violations: 3
Guilty pleas: 98
Number of persons who entered guilty pleas: 23
Recidivates: 23
Recidivism rate: 92 percent
Total felonies: 153
Total misdemeanors: 146
Other: 31

It should be noted that the total number of arrests (193) recorded
against the subjects of this study represents the number of arrests

made by units in more than one department command. As mentioned earlier, the sample for this study was taken from the files of the senior citizen robbery unit and, therefore, represents only twenty-five arrests made by unit personnel. It is not known how many more of the remaining arrests (168) were made by SCRU personnel, because the data obtained from the Division of Criminal Justice Services do not identify the units or commands responsible for them.

Another factor that limited the scope of this study is that the sample was restricted to criminals sixteen years old and older. For obvious reasons, New York State statutes restrict the use of crime data involving youthful offenders to law enforcement authorities and to specified groups or organizations.

In spite of these limitations, the author is of the opinion that the data that was developed from this study is a reasonably accurate indicator of the numbers and types of crimes that have been committed against the elderly in other high-crime areas of the city. Moreover, if similar studies were to be conducted in these areas, the only change that would occur in the data would be in the ethnicity of the criminals and of the victims.

The profile of the typical youthful offender who frequents the inner-city areas of Brooklyn South was developed from the sample taken from the files of the senior citizen robbery unit and from the supporting data obtained from the files of the Division of Criminal Justice Services. Additional information relating to the economic status, family history, and educational background of the individual offender was taken from police custodial interrogation reports and from SCRU investigative reports.

The area's typical youthful offender is an American black, approximately 18.5 years old. He is about five feet eight inches tall, slender, with short hair, clean shaven, and dresses neatly. He is a high school dropout who finds an occasional odd job, but is mostly unemployed. He comes from a matriarchal family and lives at home.

It should be observed that a study of police crime data indicate that the typical offender's age has been established at 17.5 years instead of the 18.5 reported by the author. The reason for this disparity may be explained by the fact that the police data included offenders of all ages, while the author's small sample was limited to youths sixteen years old or older.

The offender is a recidivist who may have committed a number of crimes — some of these against elderly persons — prior to reaching his sixteenth birthday. He knows the habits of the elderly and usually waits for his victim to emerge from a grocery store, a bank, or from some other business establishment. Sometimes he will rob his victim on the street. At other times, in an effort to avoid detection and possible capture by the police, he will follow his intended victim to her apartment building and will rob her after she has entered the vestibule or the lobby.

In vestibule or lobby robberies the offender usually does not harm his victim. He is content to take her purse or wallet and leave the scene as quickly as possible. In push-in robberies, however, he will beat his elderly victim until she tells him where she has hidden her money or valuables. Sometimes he may beat his victim for no apparent reason.

Comments

Juvenile crime in America is a serious social problem. Through the years, law enforcement authorities, criminologists, and sociologists have proposed a number of theories for its control or elimination. None has worked, and the problem is becoming unmanageable for the police. The question to be answered here is not can society afford to incapacitate the Squires, the Bissets, and the Hutmachers, but when will it begin to do so?

CHAPTER 10

THE USE OF HYPNOSIS AS A
TOOL IN CRIME INVESTIGATION

THIS chapter will contain a discussion on the use of hypnosis as a police investigative tool. The purpose here is to examine how this unorthodox technique may be used to assist the victim of a crime to recall information that he/she did not supply to the police through the normal questioning procedure.

Since the beginning of man's thinking about knowledge, the secrets of memory, which nature so reluctantly yields, have been pursued by philosophers, scientists, poets, artists — by all who wished to understand the world of living creatures.[1]

The Greeks, characterized by a passion to penetrate the ultimate nature of things, considered *Mnemosyne* the mother of all nine Muses. Thus they symbolized in their mythology their intuitive understanding that the creative arts owe their existence in part to man's capacity for memory. It is a profound riddle of human life that an event at a specific point in time influences an event at a later point in time or is revived in some form after a period of time has elapsed.[2]

It is this continuing search to penetrate the secrets of the mind that has led some present-day practitioners of hypnosis to assist the victim of crime to revive those events that are hidden in some part of the mind.

Attitudes

Hypnosis is not easily understood or readily accepted by many people. The average person, more often than not, associates the practice of hypnosis with the theatrical or even with the occult, rather than with the practice of psychology or psychiatry. What accounts for this attitude? Why is it that some people refuse to take the practice seriously, while others consider it to be dangerous?

Some find it difficult to understand why this attitude continues to persist in a society that has witnessed major advances in the fields of psychology and psychiatry in the past three decades. In a discussion on the attitude of the public toward the practice of hypnosis, Professor F. L. Marcuse provided some answers to these questions when he said:

> It reflects the fact that the general public is influenced by misinformation, half-truths, quarter-truths, near fiction, and even outright fiction about the nature of hypnosis. This situation is not surprising when one considers how the average person usually receives his first impression and knowledge about hypnosis. This information is generally obtained in the setting of a music hall, nightclub, radio programme, comic strip, or vaudeville act whose sole intention is to entertain. Other signs of a misinformed attitude are the frequently heard phrases: 'to be hypnotized you must be gullible,' 'you can't be hypnotized against your will,' 'to be hypnotized is a sign of low intelligence,' 'hypnosis is only of value if your disturbance is neurotic,' 'the hypnotist must be concentrating on hypnotizing you,' 'in hypnosis one cannot be made to act contrary to one's moral standards,' and so on. The existence of such misinformed attitudes facilitates attributing to hypnosis many occurences (sic) in which hypnosis plays no part whatsoever. Thus, for example, hypnosis may be said to be the cause for such diverse events as falling off a stool in a coffee shop, apparent pregnancies, or even still-births.[3]

Professor Marcuse makes it clear that hypnosis has its limitations as well as its values in both the experimental and the applied areas. "It is," he said, "a field in which there is much confusion and ignorance, and those interested in this area have an obligation to indicate what can and what cannot be done."[4]

Perhaps some of the confusion that exists in this field can be traced to the lack of agreement among practitioners and students on an acceptable definition of hypnosis.

In discussing the various theories of hypnosis, L. Chertok, the noted psychiatrist said, "It is difficult to find a satisfactory definition of hypnotism or hypnosis. These two terms have very similar meanings. The former was first used by Braid in 1843 and introduced into France a few years later. (Braid had replaced the term, *animal magnetism*, with hypnotism.) Littre' in 1863 defines it in his dictionary as follows: 'Hypnotism; physiological term. A kind of magnetic state induced by making someone look at a bright object held near the eyes.'

"It is difficult to say just when the word 'hypnosis' appeared. The *Grand Dictionnaire universel larousse* gives it for the first time in the 1865-90 edition (Vol. IX, H-K, 1873) with the following definition: 'sleep induced especially by prolonged fixation of bright objects.' We make no distinction between the two terms, although it must be pointed out that some writers do, regarding 'hypnosis' as a state, and 'hypnotism' as a collection of techniques for producing this state.

"Porot's (173) *Manuel alphabetique de Psychiatrie* (in 1952) gives the following definition: 'The name *hypnosis* is given to a state of incomplete sleep of a special, artificially induced kind.'

"The definition proposed by the committee of the British Medical Association is more elaborate. It states that hypnosis is: 'a temporary condition of altered attention in the subject which may be induced by another person and in which a variety of phenomena may appear spontaneously or in response to verbal or other stimuli. These phenomena include alterations in consciousness and memory, increased susceptibility to suggestion and the production in the subject of responses and ideas unfamiliar to him in his usual state of mind. Further, phenomena such as anaesthesia, paralysis and rigidity of muscles, and vasomotor changes can be produced and removed in the hypnotic state."[5]

Doctor Chertok did not find any of these definitions acceptable, because he concluded that each one merely reflected its author's idea of the nature of the phenomenon.

David A. Gouch, M.D., and Garland H. Fross, D.D.S., are in general agreement with the views expounded by Doctor Chertok, a decade earlier. In an article on the subjects of hypnosis and self-hypnosis they agreed that a clear definition is difficult to obtain, primarily because no one really knows for certain what goes on inside a person's head when he is in hypnosis. According to Gouch and Garland, the following facts are known about the hypnotic state:

> Our minds work on two levels — consciously and sub-consciously. We use our conscious mind as we go about our day-to-day business. We make decisions, we perform physical actions, we think, and so on with our conscious mind. Our sub-conscious mind, on the other hand, handles the bodily functions we don't have to think about, such as heartbeat, breathing, elimination, blinking our eyes, feeling pain, etc. It also handles our habits — the actions which are largely under voluntary control, but which we do without thinking. It is the sub-conscious mind that comes into play when hypnosis takes place.

> When a person is hypnotized, his conscious mind is somewhat subdued. It is not asleep at all, but merely less interested in what is happening. This allows the subconscious to become a little more active. When a hypnotist talks to a person who is in hypnosis, the sub-conscious mind more readily accepts what it is told and governs the body accordingly.

If the hypnotist tells a person's sub-conscious mind that the heartbeat is increasing, that part of the mind accepts the suggestion uncritically and the heartbeat may begin to speed up. If the hypnotist tells a subject that all of the feeling has left his hand, the subject may feel nothing when pinched.

In simple terms, hypnosis is merely a state of increased suggestibility — a state in which we are more likely to be able to accept the suggestions of another person than we are without the condition of hypnosis.

You are not asleep or unconscious when in hypnosis. Most persons new to hypnosis expect to go into some kind of "trance" from which they will awaken remembering nothing. This is a myth that has been perpetuated for many years by stage hypnotists, movies and stories. When you are in hypnosis, even in the deepest stages, you always hear the hypnotist's voice and may hear other sounds around you as well, such as the ticking of a clock, cars driving by outside, or voices in the next room. These sounds will seem rather unimportant to you and will not disturb you, but you will hear them nonetheless.

You may not 'feel' hypnotized at all. In fact, most people cannot tell the difference between a hypnotized state and a 'waking' state and will insist that hypnosis did not occur when it most definitely did. There is no "hypnotized feeling," so you will not know for certain whether or not you are in hypnosis unless certain subjective indications are pointed out to you by the hypnotist. Some people find that they feel relaxed and lethargic when in hypnosis, for example. Others have tingling feelings in their fingers, others feel detached, and so on.

Hypnosis is safe. A hypnotized person will do nothing that he or she would not agree to do through other methods of persuasion. A subject can hear the hypnotist at all times and will not accept a suggestion if he does not wish to. A subject will not answer any question that he does not wish to answer.

The sub-conscious mind contains certain "safeguards" that will not let you do anything or accept any suggestion that may be damaging to you. And you cannot remain in hypnosis for more than a few minutes without the presence of the hypnotist. Therefore, no one has ever been "stuck" in hypnosis. If left alone, a subject will awaken on his own after a few minutes or simply fall into a natural sleep from which he will awaken normally.

Contrary to many second and thirdhand stories that have found their way into print, hypnosis has never caused anyone to become mentally ill, has never forced a person into performing an immoral or illegal act he strongly did not wish to perform, and has never turned anyone into a "zombie" who must carry out every command of the hypnotist.

The induction of hypnosis takes many forms. Usually the hypnotist talks to you while you look at a spot on the wall or possibly at a revolving disc. Or you may merely sit comfortably with your eyes closed while the hypnotist helps you to relax completely, and gradually you merge into a state of hypnosis. In any event, you will not be given any drugs unless the hypnotist is a physician or a psychiatrist who feels that a relaxing agent may be of help. Do not accept drugs from other than these two kinds of practitioners.[6]

Although Gouch, Fross, and other practitioners have presented some logical arguments that should help to dispel some of the myths associated with hypnosis, the average person continues to view the practice with skepticism and suspicion.

Some Arguments Against the Use of Investigative Hypnosis

Most of the arguments against the use of investigative hypnosis have been proposed by medical experts and some civil libertarians. Medical experts are concerned with the potential for harm to the emotional well-being of the voluntary witness who is hypnotized by a person untrained either in medicine or in clinical psychology. Civil libertarians, on the other hand, are concerned with the invasion of individual rights through the use of investigative hypnosis.

The following case taken from R. W. Dellinger's article, "Investigative Hypnosis: Tapping our Cerebral Memory Banks," will serve to illustrate the differences of opinion that exist between medical experts who are opposed to investigative hypnosis, and psychologists and others who favor this unorthodox technique:

On January 7, 1974 two Los Angeles police investigators from the Wilshire Division — a police artist and a witness — paid a visit to Martin Reiser, the department's staff psychologist. (Dr. Reiser is Director of Behavior Sciences Services, Los Angeles Police Department, and the Director of the Law Enforcement Hypnosis Institute, Los Angeles.) The witness, a middle-aged woman, had been in her boyfriend's apartment on December 17, 1973, at 1:30 AM when he was murdered. But because she had been drinking and popping pills, she couldn't remember anything except seeing another man and hearing five gunshots being fired outside the front door. Her boyfriend's body was found on the doorstep.

The investigators wondered if hypnosis might help the witness remember something about the suspect. The psychologist, however, was skeptical — he felt that her original perceptions would be too fuzzy. But because the woman wanted desperately to help the police find the killer, Reiser agreed to go ahead with the procedure. Dr.

Reiser uses several techniques in enhancing recall. The one that he uses most often is the TV technique, which is used in this case.

TONIGHT'S FLICK. After the witness was put in a hypnotic state, she was told to see herself in her favorite rocking chair in front of her television. She was about to watch a special TV movie, one that could slow down, stop, and zero in on scenes or people. She would stay calm and detached, she was assured, because this was, of course, only a television show.

The woman was asked to see herself getting up and turning on the TV set and then going back to her rocking chair. While she was waiting for the set to warm up, she was told that tonights motion picture was a documentary about what happened at her boyfriend's place on December 17, 1973, from midnight until two in the morning. After being informed that the television screen was now bright, she was asked to describe what was happening on the tube.

In a low voice, the woman slowly began telling about how she and her boyfriend had been talking, dancing, and carrying on when a man knocked at the door, and her boyfriend let him in.

SLOW MOTION REPLAY. The film was stopped for a close-up of the intruder. The woman had no trouble describing him as a tall thin man in his early twenties. Then with the camera zoomed in on his face, she clicked off his race; the shape and size of his head, nose, and lips; and his hairstyle, including what his sideburns, mustache, and beard looked like. She also gave an exact account of what he had on, from the stripes on his pants to the dots on his tie.

The woman was told that the camera would go through the entire twenty minutes that it took the crime to unfold in slow motion. Obediently she recalled how her boyfriend had silently let the man in, as if he knew him, and how her boyfriend went out to the kitchen and came back with a gun in his back pocket. She remembered that both men then went outside on the front step, out of view, and that a little while later she heard the five shots.

After the investigators and the artist had a chance to ask the woman questions, Reiser informed her that she was now turning off the TV. She was told that she could remember whatever was comfortable for her and that she would awaken feeling refreshed and relaxed. The psychologist slowly went through the alphabet. On the letter E, the witness laughed and said that she felt fine.

CEREBRAL IMPRESSIONS. A few months later a man was identified in a police lineup as a dead ringer for the composite drawing. But as it turned out, he proved not to be the murderer. Two accomplices had been waiting outside, and one of them had shot the boyfriend. Both were subsequently apprehended.

"If you liken conscious perception to a camera, her lenses were all fogged up with booze and pills, and she wasn't aware of any auditory or visual input," says Reiser.* "But cerebrally — down at a subconscious level — she was recording this stuff, and we got it back through hypnosis."[7]

In discussing the use of hypnosis as an investigative tool, Dennis L. Breo offers some interesting comments by a number of experts on the subject. The comments, taken from his article, "Hypnosis in the Courtroom," are as follows[8]:

"Dr. Reiser's example sounds convincing to the uninitiated, but hypnosis experts challenge its basic premise. 'Human memory is productive, not reproductive,' says Stanford psychologist Ernest R. Hilgard, Ph.D. 'This means,' says Pennsylvania psychiatrist Martin Orne, M.D., Ph.D., 'that there is no such thing as a "tape" that can be retrieved and literally played back just the way things happened. Human memory is constantly changing and shifting and affected by new experiences. This is something that everyone doing research on human memory agrees upon. Memories are not simply bringing to mind a fixed memory trace. This is the basic error in Dr. Reiser's contentions.' "[9]

The medical experts warn that the absolute subjective conviction that a person may convey while under hypnosis can as easily relate to confabulation as to an actual memory and that hypnotists may unwittingly implant memories, so that hypnotized persons accept them as their own.

"Hypnosis has not been found reliable in obtaining truth from a reluctant witness," said Dr. Orne, professor of psychiatry at the University of Pennsylvania, past president of the Society for Clinical and Experimental Hypnosis, and editor since 1962 of the International Journal of Clinical and Experimental Hypnosis. Even if it were possible to induce hypnosis against one's will, it is well documented that the deeply hypnotized individual still can willfully lie.

"When dealing with voluntary hypnotized subjects there is an even greater concern that they may remember distorted versions of

---

*From R. W. Dellinger, Investigative Hypnosis — Tapping Our Cerebral Memory Banks, *Human Behavior* (Vol. 7, No. 4), April, 1978.

actual events and are themselves deceived. When recalled in hypnosis, such inaccurate or pseudomemories are accompanied by strong subjective conviction and outward signs of recall that are most compelling to almost any observer. Caution and independent verification are essential in such circumstances."

Dr. Reiser counters such warnings brusquely: "Hypnotechnicians," he said, "know from subsequent corroboration when they're obtaining useful information and when they're getting fantasy. Experts in therapeutic hypnosis are not necessarily experts in investigative hypnosis. We're just looking for facts. And we're dealing with volunteer witnesses who have very little motivation to lie."[10]

But Dr. Orne, who has been an expert witness across the country in cases involving hypnosis, can cite as many cases where hypnosis has played justice false as Dr. Reiser can cite success stories.

It was this concern that prompted Dr. Orne and Dr. Ernest Hilgard, co-director of the laboratory of hypnosis research at Stanford University, to file affidavits before the United States Supreme Court, calling for strict judicial controls on evidence introduced by witnesses who have been hypnotized.

In his affidavit to the Supreme Court, Dr. Orne cites several cases in which he was involved and in which hypnosis led to questionable or false testimony.

In one of these — a California murder trial — Dr. Orne testified that hypnosis clearly altered the nature of the witness. Instead of a previously uncertain, confused individual who gives an inconsistent description that she says may well be a dream, she has become a self-assured young girl who appears thoroughly convinced about what actually happened, including the fact that she was hit on the head and could not remember what happened until she woke up.

"The witness," Dr. Orne said, "is now also convinced about an aspect of her story (being hit over the head and knocked out) which is an obvious falsehood. Not only does the prosecution psychiatrist acknowledge that she was probably not hit over the head, independent of my own evaluation, but we also have the record of a physical examination conducted within forty-eight hours of the event where a physician failed to report any evidence of trauma."[11]

Dr. Orne warns that there is no way in which the process that has taken place during hypnosis (the altering of a witness' memory) can be reliably reversed. "The defense simply does not have the opportunity to cross-examine the witness who existed prior to hypnosis."

The plain fact is, contends Dr. Orne, that hypnosis can lead either to increased recall or to increased confabulation, and highly trained medical scientists cannot tell the difference with certainty. Policemen, he implies, cannot be expected to do better.

Hypnotize an individual and suggest age progression by telling him it is the year 2000. Ask him to describe the world around him, says Dr. Orne, and such a suggestion given to a deeply hypnotized individual will lead to a vivid and compelling description of new, as yet unseen, scientific marvels, depending upon the individual's scientific knowledge, reading, intelligence, and imagination.

The same process of confabulation can be involved when an individual is urged to recall what happened six months ago, especially if he lacks the memory traces relating to the events. Dr. Orne calls these fantasies pseudomemories and includes among them such bizarre "memories" as when people "recall" their previous lives or encounters with flying saucers and become convinced that these events really took place.

"Unfortunately," the Pennsylvania psychiatrist says, "if such pseudomemories relate to events that occurred six months ago and that are eminently plausible, there is no way for the hypnotist or the subject or the finder of fact to distinguish between them and actual recall of what happened."[12]

Dr. Orne's misgivings about investigative hypnosis are echoed by his fellow hypnosis experts. One of these is Harry Kozol, M.D., who was a prosecution witness against Patricia Hearst (Dr. Orne testified for the defense).

"Law enforcement use of hypnosis," says Dr. Kozol, "is often little but a specious gimmick. It is the showmanship of the procedure that elicits information, not clinically controlled hypnosis."[13]

Harvard psychiatrist Fred Fankel, M.D., president-elect of the International Society of Hypnosis, stressed that in therapeutic settings "hypnosis is but an adjunct to proper treatment. Magic has always been expected of hypnosis. People who think this way are bound to be disappointed today as they were 200 years ago.

"This is not a closed-shop attitude. We in medicine do not yet completely understand hypnosis, and I feel very uneasy that anyone not trained in medicine or clinical psychology would use hypnosis.

"The medical experts point out that Dr. Reiser's findings 'do not appear in scientific press where they can be analyzed by scientific colleagues.' Show me the scientific journal where Dr. Reiser's research is published."[14]

Dr. Reiser, one of the pioneers in the field of investigative hypnosis, does not agree. He labels objections by medical people strictly proprietary; by civil libertarians, pointless. "In 80-90 percent of our cases we are able to get subsequent corroboration of such things as a composite drawing of suspects, license numbers, and vehicle descriptions. We use hypnosis only on volunteer witnesses; never on the accused. Any evidence based on hypnosis that is admitted into court is subject to cross-examination."

In discussing the mysticism surrounding hypnosis, Dr. Reiser said, "hypnosis is an everday phenomenon. It's nothing more than a state of altered consciousness. We all do it everyday.

"When you read a good book or sit through a three-hour movie or go into a reverie on a summer day at the beach, or daydream, or drive for miles staring at the stripes on a highway, you're in a state of altered consciousness that is not unlike being under hypnosis.

"Hell, when you're in love, it's a little like being under hypnosis."[15]

Well, maybe, but Dr. Orne is not about to have "some policeman from Alaska without training in medicine or psychology hearing about hypnosis for two weeks and then going back to practice it. Such a man is to be considered a competent hypnotist? Poppycock!

"The fact is that the human mind is not a television set, and having hypnosis in the hands of partisan investigators, police or otherwise, is a menace."

Dr. Orne cites his favorite case, one dating back to the 1950s, when a witness to a major Brinks armored-car robbery was hypnotized and came up with some license plate numbers of the supposed getaway car.

"It turned out that they tracked down the license number to a specific vehicle and a specific individual: the president of a local college, who, I assure you, had nothing to do with the crime."[16]

Dr. Reiser is undeterred by these arguments. He points out that hypnosis has been used sporadically over the years as an investigative tool in criminal cases. In recent years, there has been an upsurge of interest in applying hypnosis techniques in investigations of major crimes. Police departments in several major cities, including Los Angeles, San Francisco, New York, and Chicago, have resorted to this technique.

In countering the objections of the medical experts, Dr. Reiser claims that there are many instances in which hypnosis has been used as an adjunct in criminal cases involving homicide, kidnapping, and rape, with an approximate 60 percent increment of success over traditional interrogation techniques.

In addition to the December 17, 1973, murder investigation discussed earlier, the following cases will serve to support Dr. Reiser's claims:

A. Responding to a burglary suspect call, an officer and his partner were assaulted by the suspect. One of the officers was shot several times in the abdomen with his own weapon, and the suspect got away. During the subsequent investigation, the composite pictures by the police artist based on descriptions supplied by the wounded officer and his partner differed considerably. In order to increase the accuracy of his verbal description and because of his strong motivation to aid in capturing his assailant, the critically wounded, hospitalized officer volunteered for hypnosis. His eagerness, combined with extreme pain, enabled him to go into a deep hypnotic state very rapidly and to provide additional descriptors to the police artist. After all of the revisions had been made, it was suggested that the officer, remaining in hypnosis, open his eyes, examine the completed composite drawing and indicate its accuracy, compared to the revivified mental picture of the suspect. With a startled reaction, he looked at the completed drawing and said in an excited voice, "That's him. That's the guy who shot me!" Several months later the suspect was found and was still carrying the officer's .38 caliber weapon. The investigator reported that the suspect was indeed a dead ringer for the composite drawing made under hypnosis.

B. This case involved the kidnapping of an infant from her mother by a woman asked to hold the baby momentarily in the waiting room of a county hospital. The hypnosis session in this case was complicated by the fact that the woman spoke only Spanish and (Dr. Reiser's) use of that language was very rusty. After a brief search, a physician was located who was not only fluent in Spanish but also an accomplished hypnotist. With their joint collaboration and assistance, the subject was able to recall under hypnosis significant information which allowed the case investigators to go back to the hospital records and zero in on the woman who had walked off with the baby. Fortunately, the baby was recovered unharmed several days later.

In a wide variety of rape, kidnap, and homicide cases (which are usually traumatic for the witness and/or victim who agrees to participate in the hypnosis session in order to help solve the crime) significant details are often uncovered. This may include vehicle information such as make, color, stickers, dent, model, interior, and, in some instances, the actual license plate number. In addition to physical descriptions of suspects, the subject may also recall verbalizations during the transaction, such as names or places mentioned, as well as vocabulary and speech patterns used. Of course, any information elicited under hypnosis is subject to corroboration by the case investigators.

Because the perceptual apparatus works in cybernetic fashion much like a giant computerized videotape recorder, the plethora of information perceived by the sensory system is recorded and stored in the brain at a subconscious level. Much of this data, momentarily nonrelevant or repressed because of emotional trauma, is difficult to recall; the problem: one of amnesia. However, hypnosis may provide the key in a significant number of cases by encouraging hyperamnesia, relaxing the censorship and permitting suppressed or repressed material to return to conscious awareness.[17]

Dr. Herbert Spiegel, a clinical psychiatrist at Columbia University, is a strong advocate for the use of hypnosis as an investigative tool.

According to Timothy Bay, Dr. Spiegel probably has done more than anyone else to bring hypnosis out of the midway and into the realm of serious medical and psychiatric use. In addition to his university post, Dr. Spiegel is an attending psychiatrist at Columbia-Presbyterian Medical Center in New York City and also maintains a private practice. Soft spoken and highly articulate, he is a persuasive voice for hypnosis, whether among colleagues, to students, or in his appearance on radio and television.

Dr. Spiegel talked recently about his work with hypnosis in both private practice and the laboratory. Some of his work has taken him far outside the office. Not long ago, for example, he was called in to help unravel a mysterious series of deaths at the VA hospital in Ann Arbor, Michigan.

"In a short time, eleven patients had died unexpectedly of respiratory arrest. Investigators suspected that someone on the staff had injected them with Pavulon®, a variant of lethal curare. Dr. Spiegel hypnotized the remaining patients in the ward, as well as the physicians and nurses. One male patient suffered partial amnesia but, put under a hypnotic trance by Dr. Spiegel, he was able to recall a forgotten incident and to identify a nurse who was later picked up by the FBI as one of the two suspects.

"He observes that hypnosis has become accepted increasingly as a tool in crime detection: 'The Los Angeles Police Department, for example, has its own hypnosis unit in its detective squad. There is nothing mysterious about it. Hypnosis happens to be an excellent technique for having people recall information that they might have forgotten or buried in their mind.' "[18] The Los Angeles Police Department also conducted a hypnosis survey of 370 sessions between the years of 1975 and 1978. The data they obtained from this study is given next. Also, the types of crimes related to the study may be seen in Table 10-I.

1. To what degree was any additional information elicited when the witness was in a state of hypnosis?
   A. None at all 72 (20.7%)
   B. Some additional information 121 (34.8%)
   C. Moderate amount of information 103 (29.6%)
   D. A great deal of information 52 (14.9%)
      No answer (9)
      Pending (1)
2. If any information was obtained as a result of hypnosis, either during, immediately after, or at some later date, how valuable do you feel that information was to the case investigator?
   43 Extremely valuable (12.5%)
   74 Very valuable (21.4%)
   112 Of some value (32.5%)
   41 Of little value (11.9%)
   27 Of no value (7.8%)
   48 No new information was obtained (13.9%)
      No answer (12)
      Pending (1)
3. If any new information was obtained through hypnosis, how accurate was that information found to be?

35 Extremely accurate (23.2%)
62 Very accurate (41.1%)
39 Somewhat accurate (25.8%)
 4 Not very accurate (2.6%)
11 Inaccurate (7.3%)
144 Accuracy unable to be determined (48.8%)
295 Total
    No answer (62)
    Pending (1)
4. Was the case solved?
    Yes 113 (31.9%)
    No 241 (68.1%)
    No answer (3)
    Pending (1)
5. If the case was solved how much value do you give to the information obtained through the use of hypnosis.
    8 The case probably wouldn't have been solved without it (7.1%)
  18 Extremely valuable (15.9%)
  25 Very valuable (22.1%)
  23 Of some value (20.4%)
  12 Of little value (10.6%)
  13 Of no value (11.5%)
  14 No new information was obtained (12.4%)

TABLE 10-I

TYPES OF CRIMES IN HYPNOSIS PROGRAM

Crimes	1975		1976		1977		1978		4 Years	
Homicides	(18)	60.0	(61)	64.9	(91)	65.5	(50)	48.1	(220)	59.9
Robberies	(1)	3.3	(15)	16.0	(12)	8.6	(15)	14.4	(43)	11.7
Rapes	(4)	13.4	(7)	7.4	(20)	14.4	(18)	17.3	(49)	13.6
Burglaries	(1)	3.3	(2)	2.1	(3)	2.2	(7)	6.7	(13)	3.5
Others	(6)	20.0	(9)	9.6	(13)	9.3	(14)	13.5	(42)	11.5
Totals	(30)	100.0	(94)	100.0	(139)	100.0	(104)	100.0	(367)	100.0

SOURCE: Bunco-Forgery Division, Los Angeles Police Department, March 14, 1979.

NOTE: Decimal fraction = fraction of total; number in parentheses = absolute number.

Another pioneer in the field of investigative hypnosis, Harry Arons, director of the Ethical Hypnosis Center, Irvington, New Jersey, considers hypnosis to be an everyday phenomenon.

According to Dr. Arons, hypnosis is merely a subjective state which can be observed in various activities of everyday life. For example, when a person is in an abstracted state or when he drives along an unbroken stretch of highway he may enter a trance-like state because of some repetitive, monotonous action such as the constant drone of the engine or staring at equally spaced roadside fence posts.[19]

Dr. Arons has labeled this trance-like state, *Highway Hypnosis*. Returning to conscious awareness from this state, a person may be surprised upon observing a signpost that he had passed through one or two towns without realizing it. Actually, he can drive quite safely in this subconscious state, up to a certain point: If he does not return to conscious awareness soon enough, the continued monotony may eventually cause his trance to merge into natural sleep. That's when he may go off the road or run into another car. Highway hypnosis is only hypnosis to the point where he falls asleep. He is safe enough in hypnosis; the danger consists of falling asleep.[20]

Dr. Arons also believes that ". . . the use of hypnosis . . . in specific areas of application — in medicine, for example — should be regulated. But its application in nonmedical (nontherapeutic) areas like education, arts, sports, business, advertising and law enforcement should remain free from the monopolistic designs of any professional group that seeks exclusive ownership of this "universally phenomenon of everyday life."[21]

To Dr. Arons and other experts, therefore, there is nothing mysterious about hypnosis. It is a phenomenon that is not new to the human experience and one that can be understood by the average person. It is something more. It is a tool that has the potential to change the nature of present criminal investigative practices.

The Use of Hypnosis on Elderly Victims of Crime

Although Sergeant Byrnes received training in investigative hypnosis and is a certified hypnotechnician, the senior citizen robbery unit has not had the opportunity to use this technique in its investigations.

In discussing the reasons why this investigative tool has not been used, Sergeant Byrnes said:

> There is no question in my mind that hypnosis can be of value to us in solving crimes. We have had to let a number of suspects go free because the victims could not identify them. This can be very frustrating to us, but we don't put any pressure on the victims.
>
> Usually, I'll talk to her for a few minutes. I'll ask her to describe the suspect for me. When she begins to have difficulty, I'll suggest that I could help her to remember through the use of hypnotism. I make certain that she understands that she will not be put to sleep, and that it is not a harmful method. If she agrees, I'll ask her for the name of her doctor, explaining that I need his permission to hypnotize her. He must be present during the session. If she does not agree, I drop the subject. A few women have agreed to be hypnotized, but their doctors refused to grant the permission.
>
> I hope that some day we will be able to convince people that hypnosis is not harmful, and that we really need their cooperation if we are ever going to reduce the crime in this city.[22]

In responding to the author's question regarding the use of hypnotism on elderly victims, Dr. Martin Reiser, director of the Law Enforcement Hypnosis Institute said: "Hypnosis has been used with elderly subjects, age 65 and older, with mixed success. Although hypnotic ability tends to decrease with advancing age, motivation and concentration ability appear primary. It seems that rather than chronological age as such, the person's state of mind and functioning ability are important."[23]

The author agrees with Sergeant Byrnes and Dr. Reiser in their opinions of the value of hypnosis in dealing with elderly victims. During the summer of 1979, approximately 90 percent of the victims interviewed by SCRU investigators were alert and able to recall many details of the crimes. It is not unreasonable to assume, therefore, that these victims under hypnosis would have been able to supply additional information to assist the police in solving some cases. Specifically, it could have led to an earlier identification of Alvin Boland, the Silk Stocking suspect.

NOTES

1. Ruff, Robert and Scheerer, Martin, Memory and Hypnotic Age Regression (New York: International Universities Press Inc., 1970), p. 3.
2. *Ibid.*
3. Marcuse, Frederick L., Hypnosis, Fact and Fiction (Baltimore: Penguin Books, 1974), p. 17.

4. Marcuse, p. 17.
5. Chertok, L., M.D., Hypnosis (New York: Pergamon Press, 1966), pp. 12-13.
6. Gauch, David A. and Fross, Garland, H., D.D.S., What Every Subject Should Know About Hypnosis and Self-Hypnosis (New Jersey: Powers Publishers, Inc.), 1976, pp. 1-4.
7. Dellinger, R. W., "Investigative Hypnosis: Tapping our Cerebral Memory Banks," Human Behavior, April, 1978, pp. 36-37.
8. Breo, Dennis L., "Hypnosis in the Courtroom," American Medical News, November, 1978.
9. *Ibid.*, p. 380.
10. *Ibid.*, p. 381.
11. *Ibid.*, p. 382.
12. *Ibid.*, p. 383.
13. *Ibid.*, p. 384.
14. *Ibid.*, p. 385.
15. *Ibid.*, p. 386.
16. *Ibid.*, p. 384.
17. Reiser, Martin, Ph.D., "Hypnosis as a Tool in Criminal Investigation," The Police Chief, November, 1976, pp. 38-40.
18. Bay, Timothy, "Threshold of Consciousness," Science Digest, June, 1977, Vol. 81, #6, p. 45.
19. Arons, Harry, Hypnosis in Criminal Investigation (Springfield: Charles C Thomas, Publisher, 1967), p. 18.
20. Arons, p. 18.
21. Arons, p. 19.
22. Author tapes. Interview with Sergeant Byrnes, July 31, 1979.
23. Reiser, Martin, Ph.D., Director, Law Enforcement Hypnosis Institute, Inc. Letter dated June 15, 1981, Los Angeles.

CHAPTER 11

EPILOGUE

THE establishment of the senior citizen robbery unit in four of the city's five boroughs and the implementation of extraordinary procedures have enabled the police to reduce the number of crimes committed against the elderly. Their continuing efforts to effect a further reduction in such crimes, however, have been hindered by a number of social and political factors.

One of the more important of these factors is the changing role of the family in our society. This change is reflected in the reluctance of many family members to accept the responsibility for the physical well-being of an elderly parent. For example, while many children will contribute to the financial support of a parent, few will want the parent to live with them. Thus, most parents will remain in the "old neighborhood," while their children will move to better neighborhoods or to other cities. Some of these people will tell social workers and the police that they prefer to live alone, but the truth of the matter is that few were given a choice. The neglected parent is not an uncommon phenomenon in our society. The problem has taken on an added dimension in recent years, however, because of the vulnerability of the elderly person to acts of violence. This vulnerability is reflected in the number of crimes that continue to be committed against elderly persons by youthful offenders.

It follows, therefore, that the families of elderly persons should provide for their physical well-being by removing them from the hostile environment of the inner city. It is not suggested that this will solve the problem of crimes against the elderly, but it is not inconceivable that a further and more significant reduction in crimes against the elderly will occur.

A second factor is the quality of the criminal justice system. In the United States the quality of the system normally reflects the current political and moral climates in each of the fifty state jurisdictions. For example, in some states possession of or the use of marijuana is punishable by a small fine or a short term in jail; in other states the offender may receive a ten-year prison term.

308

In New York City the quality of the criminal justice system reflects an overlenient judicial policy that has been and continues to be influenced by racial and ethnic problems.

Most of the policemen and court officials who were interviewed by the author (judges were not interviewed) expressed a general dissatisfaction with the system. Their dissatisfaction focused on three major areas. First, the most complained that the system returns the criminal to the streets too soon. The police voiced the most concern here, because they feel that their efforts to control crime are being undermined by an ineffective criminal justice system. The second complaint was against the discretionary power of the prosecutor. Police and court officials argue that this power is subject to abuse by ambitious or unscrupulous prosecutors and should be controlled by administrative authorities or by legislation. Finally, police and court officials alike favor incapacitation to rehabilitation or restitution as the most efficient method of controlling crime.

In discussing the role of the courts in the criminal justice system, the police complained that most judges were too lenient when dealing with juveniles and youthful offenders. The judges, they say, return these criminals to the streets too soon by dismissing a case on a technicality, by placing the prisoner on probation, or by handing down a light sentence. Both the police and court officials agree that it is this lenient judicial policy that has contributed to the problem of crime control in the inner city. As one officer said, "It doesn't make much sense to expend the time, effort, and money to catch a criminal when you know beforehand that some liberal judge is going to send him back on the street in a matter of weeks or even days. Sending him back out there just makes our job more difficult." They believe, therefore, that a successful crime control program will require a coordinated effort between the courts, the prosecutors, and the police. This cannot be accomplished without a change in the present attitude of the judiciary.

When the police make an arrest they are primarily concerned with removing the criminal from society to prevent him from committing additional crimes. They are not at all concerned with crowded court calendars, or with heavy case loads, or with the fate of the individual after he is sent to prison.

The prosecutor, on the other hand, will view the same situation in a very different way. In each instance he/she must decide on whether to prosecute the defendant, or to accept a guilty plea, or to dismiss the defendant because of lack of sufficient evidence. Some of the factors that the prosecutor must take into consideration are: the size of the criminal case load; the burden of a trial on the inadequate resources of the court system; the nature of the crime and the severity of the punishment; the age and the criminal record of the defendant; and whether the evidence is sufficient to obtain a conviction. After considering these and other factors, the prosecutor will usually grant the defendant a concession in return for a guilty plea. It is this tremendous power of prosecutorial discretion that concerns law enforcement authorities, legal scholars, lawyers, and jurists alike.

To the police authorities, acceptance of a guilty plea may mean that the defendant will be back on the street in a matter of months or, perhaps, weeks. The decision not to prosecute means that he will be back on the street in a matter of days after his arrest. This power, they argue, is no different than the power of a judge and serves no purpose other than to impede the work of the police in the area of crime control.

To the jurist, to the lawyer, and to the legal scholar, the guilty plea and the decision not to prosecute raise a number of constitutional questions. First, in accepting the prosecutor's concession of a lesser charge, the defendant waives his right to a jury trial. No one can say for certain how a jury will decide a case. It is quite possible that the defendant might have been acquitted.

Another important point in waiving a jury trial is that in some cases the prosecutor will agree to charge the defendant on only one count, let us say, in a five-count indictment. To the defendant, one out of five is a good exchange. If one is familiar with the sentencing policies of most judges, however, then the exchange is less than favorable to the defendant. For example, if the defendant decides to accept the one-count indictment, the judge, after accepting the guilty plea, will sentence him to a five-year prison term. On the other hand, if the defendant decides on a jury trial and is found guilty on all five counts, it is possible that he will receive a five-year prison sentence (provided that the maximum penalty on each count is five years), because most judges will impose concurrent sentences, except in extraordinary cases. It is also possible that the jury will acquit the defendant.

Second, in agreeing to the guilty plea, the defendant forgoes the opportunity to appeal his conviction. Before sentencing the defendant the judge will ask him if his plea is voluntary. He will also ask the defendant if it was the result of an agreement between himself or his lawyer and the prosecutor. After denying that an agreement had been made, it is not likely that the defendant will admit to the court that he lied under oath.

Finally, the guilty plea denies to the court the opportunity to exercise the power of judicial review over the decision of the prosecutor. There is no way for the court to review an agreement that was made in secret and on which there are no records.

The use of the negative discretionary power by the prosecutor — that is, the decision not to prosecute the defendant — also denies to the court the opportunity to exercise its power of judicial review. Although most legal scholars, jurists, and lawyers recognize the need for reforms in the guilty plea, only Professor Kenneth Culp Davis and a few other scholars have addressed themselves to the problem of developing adequate guidelines for this purpose.

Of the various policies and theories proposed and used for the control of deviant behavior in the past thirty years, most police and court officials prefer incapacitation. They argue that the criminal must be removed from society to deprive him of the opportunity to commit crime. Although they do not suggest that incapacitation is the entire answer to the problem of controlling crime, they feel that it is the only policy that will produce a reduction in crime. In reply to the suggestion that the costs of incapacitation are high, the advocates of this policy say that part of the required funds could be obtained from the savings that will be realized by the elimination of the rehabilitation policy.

The proponents of rehabilitation do not agree. They claim that the crime rate can be reduced by altering the personality of the criminal. This change can be effected by the use of rehabilitation programs that may include testing, counseling, medical treatment, psychotherapy, education, and job training. After a number of sessions, which may require the application of several of these elements, they claim that the criminal's propensity toward crime will be diminished to the point where he will no longer be considered a danger to society.

Critics of the policy argue that after more than ten years of study and experiments, the rehabilitation program has not produced any measureable data to substantiate the claims of its advocates. They say that it is difficult to measure the success of rehabilitation, because no one can tell for certain whether or not the criminal has been reformed, and because there are no universal standards to measure recidivism. Who can tell what goes on in a person's mind? The rapist may be able to convince the rehabilitation officer that he is cured, but there is no guarantee that he will not go back to a life of crime after he is returned to society.

If he does return to the street, it is quite possible that he may not be caught for a year or more. It is also possible that he may be arrested and convicted for committing a crime entirely different from the one for which he underwent rehabilitation treatment. For example, if a man convicted of burglary who underwent rehabilitation were to be found guilty later of larceny, it is not certain that he would be considered a recidivist in all jurisdictions. The success of a rehabilitation program, therefore, depends on the standard used to measure recidivism. If the standard is not clear, the success of the program will be questionable.

The restitution concept requires the offender to compensate the person whom he has injured. The defendant may be required to compensate the victim through his own earnings, or he may be required to provide a service directly to the victim. For example, he may help the victim paint his porch or repair damage to his property. If the crime is of a public nature the offender may be required to perform a community service.

Although restitution has not enjoyed widespread acceptance, it is a concept that is being used in a number of states in cases of minor crimes involving juveniles. Those who support the restitution policy believe that by offering the juvenile offender the opportunity to avoid a criminal record he will change his behavior, and the change in his behavior will result in a reduction of the recidivism rate. It should be observed, however, that in measuring the success or failure of a restitution program in a given jurisdiction much depends upon the standards that it uses to measure recidivism.

Since the 1960s the New York City Police Department has been reduced from a high of more than 30,000 officers and administrators to its present strength of approximately 23,000 personnel. This reduction and the increase in crimes during the same period have combined to form a third factor in the diminished ability of the police to cope with the problem of crime control in the inner city. In an effort to reverse this trend, police administrators requested and have received approval to add 2,500 officers to the force in the next two years. From this total approximately 1,000 positions will be used to fill vacancies created by retirements and resignations. The remaining positions will be assigned to the various borough commands. A number of officers from this latter group will be assigned to foot patrol duty. The return of the "cop on the beat" to augment the uniformed police patrols and the street anti-crime units, it is hoped, will significantly increase the ability of the police to reduce crime in the inner city.

A fourth factor is the apparent reluctance of many members of the community to cooperate with the police in their efforts to reduce crime. The New York City Police Department has been a pioneer among the nation's police departments in establishing programs to develop citizens awareness of crimes.

The department publishes a number of pamphlets on techniques of crime prevention and on programs for the assistance of victims, and the pamphlets are distributed to the elderly through citizen community groups. In addition, senior citizen robbery unit investigators visit community centers regularly to instruct the elderly on how to avoid being victims of crime.

The department has encouraged members of the community to participate in programs of collective action, such as the block-watchers, the Elderly Citizen Escort Service, and the Auxiliary patrols. The record indicates, however, that few citizens have participated in these programs. There are a number of reasons that may be offered for this lack of cooperation. Those that have been repeated most often are the desire not to become involved, fear of reprisal, and a general dislike for the police.

It follows that there is no single policy that can be applied to solve the problem of juvenile crimes against the elderly. The best hope for the success of a crime control program in the inner city, therefore, rests in a cooperative effort between the law enforcement authorities, the families of the victims, and an aroused and concerned citizenry.

BIBLIOGRAPHY

Harry Arons, Hypnosis in Criminal Investigation, Springfield, Charles C Thomas, 1967.

Timothy Bay, "Threshold of Consciousness," *Science Digest*, June, 1977.

Harold J. Berman, Justice in the U.S.S.R.: An Interpretation of Soviet Law, Cambridge, Harvard University Press, 1963.

Dennis L. Breo, "Hypnosis in the Courtroom," *American Medical News*, November, 1978.

Robert M. Carter and Malcolm W. Klein, Back on the Street, Englewood Cliffs, Prentice-Hall, 1976.

L. Chertok, Hypnosis, New York, Pergamon Press, 1966.

Howard Daudistel, William Sanders, and David Luckenbill, Criminal Justice, New York, Holt, Reinehart and Winston, 1979.

R. W. Dellinger, "Investigative Hypnosis: Tapping our Cerebral Memory Banks," *Human Behavior*, April, 1978, p. 36-37.

David A. Gauch, M.D., and Garland H. Fross, D.D.S., What Every Subject Should Know About Hypnosis and Self-Hypnosis, South Orange, Powers Publishers, Inc., 1976, p. 1-4.

Andrew Halper and Richard Ku, An Exemplary — Project New York City Police Department — Street Crime Unit, Washington, D.C., U.S. Government Printing Office, 1975.

Alan Kalmanoff, Criminal Justice: Enforcement and Administration, Boston, Little, Brown and Company, 1976.

Hazel B. Kerper, Introduction to the Criminal Justice System, as revised by Jerold H. Israel, St. Paul, West Publishing Company, 1979.

Peter W. Lewis and Kenneth D. Peoples, The Supreme Court and the Criminal Process, Philadelphia, W. B. Saunders Company, 1978.

Frederick L. Marcuse, Hypnosis: Fact and Fiction, Baltimore, Penguin Books, 1974 .

————, New York City Police Department, Precinct Anti-Crime Tactical Training Manual, New York, Police Academy, 1976.

Robert Reiff and Martin Scheerer, Memory and Hypnotic Age Regression, New York, International Univerisites Press Inc., 1973.

Martin Reiser, "Hypnosis as a Tool in Criminal Justice," *Police Chief*, November, 1976, p. 38-40.

Joseph J. Senna and Larry J. Siegel, Introduction to Criminal Justice, St. Paul, West Publishing Company, 1978.

Jerome Skolnick, Justice Without Trial: Law Enforcement in Democratic Society, New York, John Wiley, 1966.

315

RECOMMENDED READINGS

R. N. Butler, Victimization of the Elderly. *In* his *Why Survive — Being Old in America*, New York, Harper and Row, 1975.

I. Drapkin and EiViano, Victimology, Lexington, D. C. Heath and Company, 1974.

Erika Fromm and Ronald E. Shor, Hypnosis: Research Developments and Perspectives, Chicago, Aldine Publishing Company, 1972.

J. Goldsmith, Criminal Victimization of Older Persons: Problems and Programs, West Hartford, University of Connecticut Law School, 1977.

J. Goldsmith and S. S. Goldsmith, Eds. Crime and the Elderly: Challenge and Response, Lexington, D. C. Heath and Company, 1976.

P. H. Hahn, Crime Against the Aging, Santa Cruz, Davis Publishing Company, undated.

P. A. Kerschner, Law, Justice, and Public Policy. In RiFai, M. A., Ed., *Justice and Older Americans*, Lexington, D. C. Heath and Company, 1977.

B. D. Lebowitz, "Age and Fearfulness: Personal and Situational Factors," *Journal of Gerontology*, V. 30, N. 6:696-700, 1975.

A. A. Malinchak and D. Wright, "Older Americans and Crime: The Scope of Elderly Victimization," *Aging*, N. 282-282: 10-16, March-April, 1978.

Mary A. Mendelson, Tender Loving Greed, New York, Vintage Books, 1975.

S. E. Newman, A. Nelson and D. Van Buren, Crimes Against the Elderly in Public Housing: Police Alternatives, Albany, State University of New York, 1975.

A. H. Patterson, "Territorial Behaviour and Fear of Crime in the Elderly," *Environmental Psychology and Non Verbal Behavior*, V. 2, N. 3:131-144, Spring, 1978.

C. E. Pope and W. Feyerhern, "Review of Recent Trends: Effects of Crime on the Elderly," *Police Chief*, V. 43, N. 2:48-51, February, 1976.

R. A. Sundeen, Fear of Crime and Urban Elderly, *In* RiFai, M. A., Ed., *Justice and Older Americans*, Lexington, D. C. Heath and Company, 1977.

Texas Criminal Justice Division, Criminal Victimization of the Aged in Texas. By C. A. Martin and A. S. Raban, Austin, University Center for Community Services, 1976.

U.S. Department of Health, Education, and Welfare, Administration on Aging. Crimes Against the Aging: Patterns and Prevention. By R. Parks and C. Unger, Washington, Midwest Research Institute, 1977.

NAME INDEX

A

Ackerman, Thomas, 209
Alper, Jules, 10, 14, 15, 175, 176, 178, 179, 180, 181, 185, 188, 189, 194, 195, 197, 200, 201, 208
Alwill, Ellen, 14, 15, 76, 77, 144, 172, 174, 178, 179, 197, 235, 236, 237, 239
Arons, Harry, 305

B

Bader, Clara, 8, 9
Bailey, Mary, 235, 236, 238, 246, 252
Baker, Dolly, 236, 246
Baker, Esther, 230
Bay, Timothy, 302
Beckel, Julia, 19, 97-110, 204, 209
Beltram, Paul, 242, 243
Bernstein, Rose, 247
Bickel, I., 124
Bisset, Ernest, 259-262
Blackner, Ruby, 184, 230
Boland, Alvin, 242, 243, 244, 245, 246, 250, 251, 252, 253, 306
Breo, Dennis, L., 297
Breslin, John, 228, 229, 232
Bromberg, Irene, 184, 230
Brown, Fred, 94
Buonineontri, F., 218, 219, 236
Byrnes, Timothy P., 15, 26, 35, 38, 39, 40, 55, 169, 170, 171, 172, 175, 176-177, 178, 179, 189, 192, 197, 200, 204, 218, 220, 221, 222, 224, 225, 226, 228, 233, 235, 236, 237, 238, 239, 240, 241, 242, 305-306

C

Campbell, Ranzano "Monsie," 209, 210
Carbonaro, Rosemary, 9, 10, 26, 47, 55, 56, 57, 113, 121, 122, 123, 124, 129, 201, 202, 212, 213
Carley, Esther, 122, 124, 129, 130, 131
Carley, James, Vincenzo, 121-131
Carson, Romuald, 248
Carter, Robert, 4
Chacon, Ramon, 266-268
Chapman, Gary, 280-282
Chertok, L., 292, 293
Chisolm, Leroy, 282-284
Clifford, Anthony, 219, 227
Clinard, Marshall, 113
Coles, Raymond, 26, 33, 34, 35, 38, 39, 40, 55, 72, 90, 167, 168, 178, 179, 187-188, 189, 197, 204, 233, 236, 237, 238, 239, 240, 241
Conry, Carol, 76, 80, 82, 175, 176, 178, 179, 181, 185, 188, 189, 192, 193, 194, 197, 198, 199, 236, 237, 238
Cumberbatch, Bettina, 247, 248

D

Dailey, Joe, 10, 69-74, 76, 174, 175, 176, 177, 182, 183, 185, 186, 187, 192, 194, 195, 197, 200
Dattolico, Frank, 35, 174, 198, 199
Daudistel, Howard, 60
Davids, Judson, 125
Davis, Kenneth Culp, 311
Davis, Laverne, 268-269
Davis, Mark, 125
DeAngelo, Philip, 95-96, 133-134, 139-144, 189, 201, 203
Dellinger, R. W., 295
DeMarco, Jerry, 170, 171, 174, 175
Dexter, James, 262-263
DiCostanzo, Joe, 94, 170, 209, 212, 213, 220, 221, 226, 227, 228, 233, 234, 235, 236, 241, 242, 243, 244, 245, 246, 251, 252

SUBJECT INDEX

323

T

U

V